GW00871536

THE ENGLISH IN THE WEST INDIES OR, THE BOW OF ULYSSES

James Anthony Froude

www.GeneralBooksClub.com

Publication Data:
Title: The English in the West Indies Or, the Bow of Ulysses;
Author: Froude, James Anthony, 1818-1894
Reprinted: 2010, General Books LLC, Memphis, Tennessee, USA
Contact the publisher: http://generalbooksclub.com/contactus.cfm
Limit of Liability/Disclaimer of Warranty: The publisher makes no representations or warranties with respect to the accuracy or completeness of the book. The information in the book may not be suitable for your situation. You should consult with a professional where appropriate. The publisher is not liable for any damages resulting from the book.

THE ENGLISH IN THE WEST INDIES OR, THE BOW OF ULYSSES

MOUNTAIN CRATER, DOMINICA.
MOUNTAIN CRATER, DOMINICA.
THE ENGLISH
INTHE WEST INDIES
ORTHE BOW OF ULYSSES
BYJAMES ANTHONY FROUDE
WITH ILLUSTRATIONS ENGRAVED ON WOOD BY G. PEARSON AFTER
DRAWINGS BY THE AUTHOR
NEW EDITIONLONDON
LONGMANS, GREEN, AND CO.
1888
All rights reserved
Fürsten prägen so oft auf kaum versilbertes Kupfer
Ihr bedeutendes Bild: lange betrügt sich das Volk
Schwärmer prägen den Stempel des Geist's auf Lügen und Unsinn:
Wem der Probirstein fehlt, hält sie für redliches Gold.
Goethe.
PREFACE TO FIRST EDITION.

My purpose in writing this book is so fully explained in the book itself that a Preface is unnecessary. I visited the West India Islands in order to increase my acquaintance with the condition of the British Colonies. I have related what I saw and what I heard, with the general impressions which I was led to form.

In a few instances, when opinions were conveyed to me which were important in themselves, but which it might be undesirable to assign to the persons from whom I heard them, I have altered initials and disguised localities and circumstances.

The illustrations are from sketches of my own, which, except so far as they are tolerably like the scenes which they represent, are without value. They have been made producible by the skill and care of the engraver, Mr. Pearson, to whom my warmest thanks are due.

J.A.F.

Onslow Gardens

: November 15, 1887.

View larger image

ILLUSTRATIONS.

THE ENGLISH IN THE WEST INDIES.

CHAPTER I.

Colonial policy—Union or separation—Self-government—Varieties of condition—The Pacific colonies—The West Indies—Proposals for a West Indian federation—Nature of the population—American union and British plantations—Original conquest of the West Indies.

The Colonial Exhibition has come and gone. Delegates from our great self-governed dependencies have met and consulted together, and have determined upon a common course of action for Imperial defence. The British race dispersed over the world have celebrated the Jubilee of the Queen with an enthusiasm evidently intended to bear a special and peculiar meaning. The people of these islands and their sons and brothers and friends and kinsfolk in Canada, in Australia, and in New Zealand have declared with a general voice, scarcely disturbed by a discord, that they are fellow-subjects of a single sovereign, that they are united in feeling, united in loyalty, united in interest, and that they wish and mean to preserve unbroken the integrity of the British Empire. This is the answer which the democracy has given to the advocates of the doctrine of separation. The desire for union while it lasts is its own realisation. As long as we have no wish to part we shall not part, and the wish can never rise if when there is occasion we can meet and deliberate together with the same regard for each other's welfare which has been shown in the late conference in London.

Events mock at human foresight, and nothing is certain but the unforeseen. Constitutional government and an independent executive were conferred upon our larger colonies, with the express and scarcely veiled intention that at the earliest moment they were to relieve the mother country of responsibility for them. They were regarded as fledgelings who are fed only by the parent birds till their feathers are grown, and are then expected to shift for themselves. They were provided with the full plumage of parliamentary institutions on the home pattern and model, and the expectation of experienced politicians was that they would each at the earliest moment go off on their separate accounts, and would bid us a friendly farewell. The irony of fate has turned to folly the wisdom of the wise. The wise themselves, the same political party which were most anxious twenty years ago to see the colonies independent, and contrived constitutions for them which they conceived must inevitably lead to separation, appeal now to the effect of those very constitutions in drawing the Empire closer together, as a reason why a similar method should be immediately adopted to heal the differences between Great Britain and Ireland. New converts to any belief, political or theological, are proverbially zealous, and perhaps in this instance they are over-hasty. It does not follow that because people of the same race and character are drawn together by equality and liberty, people of different races and different characters, who have quarrelled for centuries, will be similarly attracted to one another. Yet so far as our own colonies are concerned it is clear that the abandonment by the mother country of all pretence to interfere in their internal management has removed the only cause which could possibly have created a desire for independence. We cannot, even if we wish it ourselves, shake off connections who cost us nothing and themselves refuse to be divided. Politicians may quarrel; the democracies have refused to quarrel; and the result of the wide extension of the suffrage throughout the Empire has been to show that being one the British people everywhere intend to remain one. With the same blood, the same language, the same habits, the same traditions, they do not mean to be shattered into dishonoured fragments. All of us, wherever we are, can best manage our own affairs within our own limits; yet local spheres of self-management can revolve round a common centre while there is a centripetal power sufficient to hold them; and so long as England 'to herself is true' and continues worthy of her ancient reputation, there are no causes working visibly above the political horizon which are likely to induce our self-governed colonies to take wing and leave us. The strain will come with the next great war. During peace these colonies have only experienced the advantage of union with us. They will then have to share our dangers, and may ask why they are to be involved in quarrels which are not of their own making. How they will act then only experience can tell; and that there is any doubt about it is a sufficient answer to those rapid statesmen who would rush at once into the application of the same principle to countries whose continuance with us is vital to our own safety, whom we cannot part with though they were to demand it at the cannon's mouth.

But the result of the experiment is an encouragement as far as it has gone to those who would extend self-government through the whole of our colonial system.

It seems to lead as a direct road into the 'Imperial Federation' which has fascinated the general imagination. It removes friction. We relieve ourselves of responsibilities. If federation is to come about at all as a definite and effective organisation, the spontaneous action of the different members of the Empire in a position in which they are free to stay with us or to leave us as they please, appears the readiest and perhaps the only means by which it can be brought to pass. So plausible is the theory, so obviously right would it be were the problem as simple and the population of all our colonies as homogeneous as in Australia, that one cannot wonder at the ambition of politicians to win themselves a name and achieve a great result by the immediate adoption of it. Great results generally imply effort and sacrifice. Here effort is unnecessary and sacrifice is not demanded. Everybody is to have what he wishes, and the effect is to come about of itself. When we think of India, when we think of Ireland, prudence tells us to hesitate. Steps once taken in this direction cannot be undone, even if found to lead to the wrong place. But undoubtedly, wherever it is possible, the principle of self-government ought to be applied in our colonies and will be applied, and the danger now is that it will be tried in haste in countries either as yet unripe for it or from the nature of things unfit for it. The liberties which we grant freely to those whom we trust and who do not require to be restrained, we bring into disrepute if we concede them as readily to perversity or disaffection or to those who, like most Asiatics, do not desire liberty, and prosper best when they are led and guided.

In this complex empire of ours the problem presents itself in many shapes, and each must be studied and dealt with according to its character. There is the broad distinction between colonies and conquered countries. Colonists are part of ourselves. Foreigners attached by force to our dominions may submit to be ruled by us, but will not always consent to rule themselves in accordance with our views or interests, or remain attached to us if we enable them to leave us when they please. The Crown, therefore, as in India, rules directly by the police and the army. And there are colonies which are neither one nor the other, where our own people have been settled and have been granted the land in possession with the control of an insubordinate population, themselves claiming political privileges which had to be refused to the rest. This was the position of Ireland, and the result of meddling theoretically with it ought to have taught us caution. Again, there are colonies like the West Indies, either occupied originally by ourselves, as Barbadoes, or taken by force from France or Spain, where the mass of the population were slaves who have been since made free, but where the extent to which the coloured people can be admitted to share in the administration is still an unsettled question. To throw countries so variously circumstanced under an identical system would be a wild experiment. Whether we ought to try such an experiment at all, or even wish to try it and prepare the way for it, depends perhaps on whether we have determined that under all circumstances the retention of them under our own flag is indispensable to our safety.

I had visited our great Pacific colonies. Circumstances led me afterwards to attend more particularly to the West ladies. They were the earliest, and once the most prized, of all our distant possessions. They had been won by the most desperate struggles, and had been the scene of our greatest naval glories. In the recent discussion on the possibility of an organised colonial federation, various schemes came under my notice, in every one of which the union of the West Indian Islands under a free parliamentary constitution was regarded as a necessary preliminary. I was reminded of a conversation which I had held seventeen years ago with a high colonial official specially connected with the West Indian department, in which the federation of the islands under such a constitution was spoken of as a measure already determined on, though with a view to an end exactly the opposite of that which was now desired. The colonies universally were then regarded in such quarters as a burden upon our resources, of which we were to relieve ourselves at the earliest moment. They were no longer of special value to us; the whole world had become our market; and whether they were nominally attached to the Empire, or were independent, or joined themselves to some other power, was of no commercial moment to us. It was felt, however, that as long as any tie remained, we should be obliged to defend them in time of war; while they, in consequence of their connection, would be liable to attack. The sooner, therefore, the connection was ended, the better for them and for us.

By the constitutions which had been conferred upon them, Australia and Canada, New Zealand and the Cape, were assumed to be practically gone. The same measures were to be taken with the West Indies. They were not prosperous. They formed no outlet for British emigration; the white population was diminishing; they were dissatisfied; they lay close to the great American republic, to which geographically they more properly belonged. Representative assemblies under the Crown had failed to produce the content expected from them or to give an impulse to industry. The free negroes could not long be excluded from the franchise. The black and white races had not amalgamated and were not inclining to amalgamate. The then recent Gordon riots had been followed by the suicide of the old Jamaican constitution. The government of Jamaica had been flung back upon the Crown, and the Crown was impatient of the addition to its obligations. The official of whom I speak informed me that a decision had been irrevocably taken. The troops were to be withdrawn from the islands, and Jamaica, Trinidad, and the English Antilles were to be masters of their own destiny, either to form into free communities like the Spanish American republics, or to join the United States, or to do what they pleased, with the sole understanding that we were to have no more responsibilities.

I do not know how far the scheme was matured. To an outside spectator it seemed too hazardous to have been seriously meditated. Yet I was told that it had not been meditated only but positively determined upon, and that further discussion of a settled question would be fruitless and needlessly irritating.

Politicians with a favourite scheme are naturally sanguine. It seemed to me that in a West Indian Federation the black race would necessarily be admitted to their full rights as citizens. Their numbers enormously preponderated, and the late scenes in Jamaica were signs that the two colours would not blend into one, that there might be, and even inevitably would be, collisions between them which would lead to actions which we could not tolerate. The white residents and the negroes had not been drawn together by the abolition of slavery, but were further apart than ever. The whites, if by superior intelligence they could gain the upper hand, would not be allowed to keep it. As little would they submit to be ruled by a race whom they despised; and I thought it quite certain that something would happen which would compel the British Government to interfere again, whether we liked it or not. Liberty in Hayti had been followed by a massacre of the French inhabitants, and the French settlers had done no worse than we had done to deserve the ill will of their slaves. Fortunately opinion changed in England before the experiment could be tried. The colonial policy of the doctrinaire statesmen was no sooner understood than it was universally condemned, and they could not press proposals on the West Indies which the West Indians showed so little readiness to meet.

So things drifted on, remaining to appearance as they were. The troops were not recalled. A minor confederation was formed in the Leeward Antilles. The Windward group was placed under Barbadoes, and islands which before had governors of their own passed under subordinate administrators. Local councils continued under various conditions, the popular element being cautiously and silently introduced. The blacks settled into a condition of easy-going peasant proprietors. But so far as the white or English interest was concerned, two causes which undermined West Indian prosperity continued to operate. So long as sugar maintained its price the planters with the help of coolie labour were able to struggle on; but the beetroot bounties came to cut from under them the industry in which they had placed their main dependence; the reports were continually darker of distress and rapidly approaching ruin; petitions for protection were not or could not be granted. They were losing heart—the worst loss of all; while the Home Government, no longer with a view to separation, but with the hope that it might produce the same effect which it produced elsewhere, were still looking to their old remedy of the extension of the principle of self-government. One serious step was taken very recently towards the re-establishment of a constitution in Jamaica. It was assumed that it had failed before because the blacks were not properly represented. The council was again made partially elective, and the black vote was admitted on the widest basis. A power was retained by the Crown of increasing in case of necessity the nominated official members to a number which would counterbalance the elected members; but the power had not been acted on and was not perhaps designed to continue, and a restless hope was said to have revived among the negroes that the day was not far off when Jamaica would be as Hayti and they would have the island to themselves.

To a person like myself, to whom the preservation of the British Empire appeared to be the only public cause in which just now it was possible to feel concern, the problem was extremely interesting. I had no prejudice against self-government. I had seen the Australian colonies growing under it in health and strength with a rapidity which rivalled the progress of the American Union itself. I had observed in South Africa that the confusions and perplexities there diminished exactly in proportion as the Home Government ceased to interfere. I could not hope that as an outsider I could see my way through difficulties where practised eyes were at a loss. But it was clear that the West Indies were suffering, be the cause what it might. I learnt that a party had risen there at last which was actually in favour of a union with America, and I wished to find an answer to a question which I had long asked myself to no purpose. My old friend Mr. Motley was once speaking to me of the probable accession of

Canada to the American republic. I asked him if he was sure that Canada would like it. 'Like it?' he replied. 'Would I like the house of Baring to take me into partnership?' To be a partner in the British Empire appeared to me to be at least as great a thing as to be a State under the stars and stripes. What was it that Canada, what was it that any other colony, would gain by exchanging British citizenship for American citizenship? What did America offer to those who joined her which we refused to give or neglected to give? Was it that Great Britain did not take her colonies into partnership at all? was it that while in the United States the blood circulated freely from the heart to the extremities, so that 'if one member suffered all the body suffered with it,' our colonies were simply (as they used to be called) 'plantations,' offshoots from the old stock set down as circumstances had dictated in various parts of the globe, but vitally detached and left to grow or to wither according to their own inherent strength?

At one time the West Indian colonies had been more to us than such casual seedlings. They had been precious regarded as jewels, which hundreds of thousands of English lives had been sacrificed to tear from France and Spain. The Caribbean Sea was the cradle of the Naval Empire of Great Britain. There Drake and Hawkins intercepted the golden stream which flowed from Panama into the exchequer at Madrid, and furnished Philip with the means to carry on his war with the Reformation. The Pope had claimed to be lord of the new world as well as of the old, and had declared that Spaniards, and only Spaniards, should own territory or carry on trade there within the tropics. The seamen of England took up the challenge and replied with cannon shot. It was not the Crown, it was not the Government, which fought that battle: it was the people of England who fought it with their own hands and their own resources. Adventurers, buccaneers, corsairs, privateers, call them by what name we will, stand as extraordinary, but characteristic figures on the stage of history, disowned or acknowledged by their sovereign as suited diplomatic convenience. The outlawed pirate of one year was promoted the next to be a governor and his country's representative. In those waters, the men were formed and trained who drove the Armada through the Channel into wreck and ruin. In those waters, in the centuries which followed, France and England fought for the ocean empire, and England won it—won it on the day when her own politicians' hearts had failed them, and all the powers of the world had combined to humiliate her, and Rodney shattered the French fleet, saved Gibraltar, and avenged York Town. If ever the naval exploits of this country are done into an epic poem—and since the Iliad there has been no subject better fitted for such treatment or better deserving it—the West Indies will be the scene of the most brilliant cantos. For England to allow them to drift away from her because they have no immediate marketable value would be a sign that she had lost the feelings with which great nations always treasure the heroic traditions of their fathers. When those traditions come to be regarded as something which concerns them no longer, their greatness is already on the wane.

CHAPTER II.

In the train for Southampton—Morning papers—The new 'Locksley Hall'—Past and present—The 'Moselle'—Heavy weather—The petrel—The Azores.

The last week in December, when the year 1886 was waning to its close, I left Waterloo station to join a West Indian mail steamer at Southampton. The air was frosty; the fog lay thick over city and river; the Houses of Parliament themselves were scarcely visible as I drove across Westminster Bridge in the heavy London vapour—a symbol of the cloud which was hanging over the immediate political future. The morning papers were occupied with Lord Tennyson's new 'Locksley Hall' and Mr. Gladstone's remarks upon it. I had read neither; but from the criticisms it appeared that Lord Tennyson fancied himself to have seen a change pass over England since his boyhood, and a change which was not to his mind. The fruit of the new ideas which were then rising from the ground had ripened, and the taste was disagreeable to him. The day which had followed that 'august sunrise' had not been 'august' at all; and 'the beautiful bold brow of Freedom' had proved to have something of brass upon it. The 'use and wont' England, the England out of which had risen the men who had won her great position for her, was losing its old characteristics. Things which in his eager youth Lord Tennyson had despised he saw now that he had been mistaken in despising; and the new notions which were to remake the world were not remaking it in a shape that pleased him. Like Goethe, perhaps he felt that he was stumbling over the roots of the tree which he had helped to plant.

The contrast in Mr. Gladstone's article was certainly remarkable. Lord Tennyson saw in institutions which were passing away the decay of what in its time had been great and noble, and he saw little rising in the place of them which humanly could be called improvement. To Mr. Gladstone these revolutionary years had been years of the sweeping off of long intolerable abuses, and of awaking to higher and truer perceptions of duty. Never, according to him, in any period of her history had England made more glorious progress, never had stood higher than at the present moment in material power and moral excellence. How could it be otherwise when they were the years of his own ascendency?

Metaphysicians tell us that we do not know anything as it really is. What we call outward objects are but impressions generated upon our sense by forces of the actual nature of which we are totally ignorant. We imagine that we hear a sound, and that the sound is something real which is outside us; but the sound is in the ear and is made by the ear, and the thing outside is but a vibration of air. If no animal existed with organs of hearing, the vibrations might be as before, but there would be no such thing as sound; and all our opinions on all subjects whatsoever are equally subjective. Lord Tennyson's opinions and Mr. Gladstone's opinions reveal to us only the nature and texture of their own minds, which have been affected in this way or that way. The scale has not been made in which we can weigh the periods in a nation's life, or measure them one against the other. The past is gone, and nothing but the bones of it can be recalled. We but half understand the present, for each age is a chrysalis, and we are ignorant into what it may develop. We do not even try to understand it honestly, for we shut our eyes against what we do not wish to see. I will not despond with Lord Tennyson. To take a gloomy view of things will not mend them, and modern enlightenment may have excellent gifts in store for us which will come by-and-by. But I will not say that they have come as yet. I will not say that public life is improved when party spirit has degenerated into an organised civil war, and a civil war which can never end, for it renews its life like the giant of fable at every fresh election. I will not say that men are more honest and more law-abiding when debts are repudiated and law is defied in half the country, and Mr. Gladstone himself applauds or refuses to condemn acts of open dishonesty. We are to congratulate ourselves that duelling has ceased, but I do not know that men act more honourably because they can be called less sharply to account. 'Smuggling,' we are told, has disappeared also, but the wrecker scuttles his ship or runs it ashore to cheat the insurance office. The Church may perhaps be improved in the arrangement of the services and in the professional demonstrativeness of the clergy, but I am not sure that the clergy have more influence over the minds of men than they had fifty years ago, or that the doctrines which the Church teaches are more powerful over public opinion. One would not gather that our morality was so superior from the reports which we see in the newspapers, and girls now talk over novels which the ladies' maids of their grandmothers might have read in secret but would have blushed while reading. Each age would do better if it studied its own faults and endeavoured to mend them, instead of comparing itself with others to its own advantage.

This only was clear to me in thinking over what Mr. Gladstone was reported to have said, and in thinking of his own achievements and career, that there are two classes of men who have played and still play a prominent part in the world—those who accomplish great things, and those who talk and make speeches about them. The doers of things are for the most part silent. Those who build up empires or discover secrets of science, those who paint great pictures or write great poems, are not often to be found spouting upon platforms. The silent men do the work. The talking men cry out at what is done because it is not done as they would have had it, and afterwards take possession of it as if it was their own property. Warren Hastings wins India for us; the eloquent Burke desires and passionately tries to hang him for it. At the supreme crisis in our history when America had revolted and Ireland was defiant, when the great powers of Europe had coalesced to crush us, and we were staggering under the disaster at York Town, Rodney struck a blow in the West Indies which sounded over the world and saved for Britain her ocean sceptre. Just in time, for the popular leaders had persuaded the House of Commons that Rodney ought to be recalled and peace made on any terms. Even in politics the names of oratorical statesmen are rarely associated with the organic growth of enduring institutions. The most distinguished of them have been conspicuous only as instruments of destruction. Institutions are the slow growths of centuries. The orator cuts them down in a day. The tree falls, and the hand that wields the axe is admired and applauded. The speeches of Demosthenes and Cicero pass into literature, and are studied as models of language. But Demosthenes and Cicero did not understand the facts of their time; their language might be beautiful, and their sentiments noble, but with their fine words and sentiments they only misled their countrymen. The periods where the orator is supreme are marked always by confusion and disintegration. Goethe could say of Luther that he had thrown back for centuries the spiritual cultivation of mankind, by calling the passions of the multitude to judge of matters which should have been left to the thinkers. We ourselves are just now in one of those uneasy periods, and we have decided that orators are the fittest people to rule over us. The constituencies choose their members according to the fluency of their tongues. Can he make a speech? is the one test of competency for a legislator, and the most persuasive of the whole we make prime minister. We admire the man for his gifts, and we accept what he says for the manner in which it is uttered. He may contradict to-day what he asserted yesterday. No matter. He can persuade others wherever he is persuaded himself. And such is the nature of him that he can convince himself of anything which it is his interest to believe. These are the persons who are now regarded as our wisest. It was not always so. It is not so now with nations who are in a sound state of health. The Americans, when they choose a President or a Secretary of State or any functionary from whom they require wise action, do not select these famous speech-makers. Such periods do not last, for the condition which they bring about becomes always intolerable. I do not believe in the degeneracy of our race. I believe the present generation of Englishmen to be capable of all that their fathers were and possibly of more; but we are just now in a moulting state, and are sick while the process is going on. Or to take another metaphor. The bow of Ulysses is unstrung. The worms have not eaten into the horn or the moths injured the string, but the owner of the house is away and the suitors of Penelope Britannia consume her substance, rivals one of another, each caring only for himself, but with a common heart in evil. They cannot string the bow. Only the true lord and master can string it, and in due time he comes, and the cord is stretched once more upon the notch, singing to the touch of the finger with the sharp note of the swallow; and the arrows fly to their mark in the breasts of the pretenders, while Pallas Athene looks on approving from her coign of vantage.

Random meditations of this kind were sent flying through me by the newspaper articles on Tennyson and Mr. Gladstone. The air cleared, and my mind also, as we ran beyond the smoke. The fields were covered deep with snow; a white vapour clung along the ground, the winter sky shining through it soft and blue. The ponds and canals were hard frozen, and men were skating and boys were sliding, and all was brilliant and beautiful. The ladies of the forest, the birch trees beside the line about Farnborough, were hung with jewels of ice, and glittered like a fretwork of purple and silver. It was like escaping out of a nightmare into happy healthy England once more. In the carriage with me were several gentlemen; officers going out to join their regiments; planters who had been at home on business; young sportsmen with rifles and cartridge cases who were hoping to shoot alligators, c., all bound like myself for the West Indian mail steamer. The elders talked of sugar and of bounties, and of the financial ruin of the islands. I had heard of this before I started, and I learnt little from them which I had not known already; but I had misgivings whether I was not wandering off after all on a fool's errand. I did not want to shoot alligators, I did not understand cane growing or want to understand it, nor was I likely to find a remedy for encumbered and bankrupt landowners. I was at an age too when men grow unfit for roaming, and are expected to stay quietly at home. Plato says that to travel to any profit one should go between fifty and sixty; not sooner because one has one's duties to attend to as a citizen; not after because the mind becomes hebetated. The chief object of going abroad, in Plato's opinion, is to converse with θειοι ἄνδρες

inspired men, whom Providence scatters about the globe, and from whom alone wisdom can be learnt. And I, alas! was long past the limit, and θειοι ἄνδρες are not to be met with in these times. But if not with inspired men, I might fall in at any rate with sensible men who would talk on things which I wanted to know. Winter and spring in a warm climate were pleasanter than a winter and spring at home; and as there is compensation in all things, old people can see some objects more clearly than young people can see them. They have no interest of their own to mislead their perception. They have lived too long to believe in any formulas or theories. 'Old age,' the Greek poet says, 'is not wholly a misfortune. Experience teaches things which the young know not.'[1] Old men at any rate like to think so.

The 'Moselle,' in which I had taken my passage, was a large steamer of 4,000 tons, one of the best where all are good—on the West Indian mail line. Her long straight sides and rounded bottom promised that she would roll, and I may say that the promise was faithfully kept; but except to the stomachs of the inexperienced rolling is no disadvantage. A vessel takes less water on board in a beam sea when she yields to the wave than when she stands up stiff and straight against it. The deck when I went on board was slippery with ice. There was the usual crowd and confusion before departure, those who were going out being undistinguishable, till the bell rang to clear the ship, from the friends who had accompanied them to take leave. I discovered, however, to my satisfaction that our party in the cabin would not be a large one. The West Indians who had come over for the Colonial Exhibition were most of them already gone. They, along with the rest, had taken back with them a consciousness that their visit had not been wholly in vain, and that the interest of the old country in her distant possessions seemed quickening into life once more. The commissioners from all our dependencies had been fêted in the great towns, and the people had come to Kensington in millions to admire the productions which bore witness to the boundless resources of British territory. Had it been only a passing emotion of wonder and pride, or was it a prelude to a more energetic policy and active resolution? Anyway it was something to be glad of. Receptions and public dinners and loyal speeches will not solve political problems, but they create the feeling of good will which underlies the useful consideration of them. The Exhibition had served the purpose which it was intended for. The conference of delegates grew out of it which has discussed in the happiest temper the elements of our future relations.

But the Exhibition doors were now closed, and the multitude of admirers or contributors were dispersed or dispersing to their homes. In the 'Moselle' we had only the latest lingerers or the ordinary passengers who went to and fro on business or pleasure. I observed them with the curiosity with which one studies persons with whom one is to be shut up for weeks in involuntary intimacy. One young Demerara planter attracted my notice, as he had with him a newly married and beautiful wife whose fresh complexion would so soon fade, as it always does in those lands where nature is brilliant with colour and English cheeks grow pale. I found also to my surprise and pleasure a daughter of one of my oldest and dearest friends, who was going out to join her husband in Trinidad. This was a happy accident to start with. An announcement printed in Spanish in large letters in a conspicuous position intimated that I must be prepared for habits in some of our companions of a less agreeable kind.

'Se suplica á los señores pasajeros de no escupir sobre la cubierta de popa.'

I may as well leave the words untranslated, but the 'supplication' is not unnecessary. The Spanish colonists, like their countrymen at home, smoke everywhere with the usual consequences. The captain of one of our mail boats found it necessary to read one of them who disregarded it a lesson which he would remember. He sent for the quartermaster with a bucket and a mop, and ordered him to stay by this gentleman and clean up till he had done.

The wind when we started was light and keen from the north. The afternoon sky was clear and frosty. Southampton Water was still as oil, and the sun went down crimson behind the brown woods of the New Forest. Of the 'Moselle's' speed we had instant evidence, for a fast Government launch raced us for a mile or two, and off Netley gave up the chase. We went leisurely along, doing thirteen knots without effort, swept by Calshot into the Solent, and had cleared the Needles before the last daylight had left us. In a few days the ice would be gone, and we should lie in the soft air of perennial summer.

Singula de nobis anni prædantur euntes:

Eripuere jocos, Venerem, convivia, ludum—

But the flying years had not stolen from me the delight of finding myself once more upon the sea; the sea which is eternally young, and gives one back one's own youth and buoyancy.

Down the Channel the north wind still blew, and the water was still smooth. We set our canvas at the Needles, and flew on for three days straight upon our course with a steady breeze. We crossed 'the Bay' without the fiddles on the dinner table; we were congratulating ourselves that, mid-winter as it was, we should reach the tropics and never need them. I meanwhile made acquaintances among my West Indian fellow-passengers, and listened to their tale of grievances. The Exhibition had been well enough in its way, but Exhibitions would not fill an empty exchequer or restore ruined plantations. The mother country I found was still regarded as a stepmother, and from more than one quarter I heard a more than muttered wish that they could be 'taken into partnership' by the Americans. They were wasting away under Free Trade and the sugar bounties. The mother country gave them fine words, but words were all. If they belonged to the United States they would have the benefit of a close market in a country where there were 60,000,000 sugar drinkers. Energetic Americans would come among them and establish new industries, and would control the unmanageable negroes. From the most loyal I heard the despairing cry of the Britons, 'the barbarians drive us into the sea and the sea drives us back upon the barbarians.' They could bear Free Trade which was fair all round, but not Free Trade which was made into a mockery by bounties. And it seemed that their masters in Downing Street answered them as the Romans answered our forefathers. 'We have many colonies, and we shall not miss Britain. Britain is far off, and must take care of herself. She brings us responsibility, and she brings us no revenue; we cannot tax Italy for the sake of Britons. We have given them our arms and our civilisation. We have done enough. Let them do now what they can or please.' Virtually this is what England says to the West Indians, or would say if despair made them actively troublesome, notwithstanding Exhibitions and expansive sentiments. The answer from Rome we can now see was the voice of dying greatness, which was no longer worthy of the place in the world which it had made for itself in the days of its strength; but it doubtless seemed reasonable enough at the time, and indeed was the only answer which the Rome of Honorius could give.

A change in the weather cut short our conversations, and drove half the company to their berths. On the fourth morning the wind chopped back to the north-west. A beam sea set in, and the 'Moselle' justified my conjectures about her. She rolled gunwale under, rolled at least forty degrees each way, and unshipped a boat out of her davits to windward. The waves were not as high as I have known the Atlantic produce when in the humour for it, but they were short, steep, and curling. Tons of water poured over the deck. The few of us who ventured below to dinner were hit by the dumb waiters which swung over our heads; and the living waiters staggered about with the dishes and upset the soup into our laps. Everybody was grumbling and miserable. Driven to my cabin I was dozing on a sofa when I was jerked off and dropped upon the floor. The noise down below on these occasions is considerable. The steering chains clank, unfastened doors slam to and fro, plates and dishes and glass fall crashing at some lurch which is heavier than usual, with the roar of the sea underneath as a constant accompaniment.

When a wave strikes the ship full on the quarter and she staggers from stem to stern, one wonders how any construction of wood and iron can endure such blows without being shattered to fragments. And it would be shattered, as I heard an engineer once say, if the sea was not such a gentle creature after all. I crept up to the deck house to watch through the lee door the wild magnificence of the storm. Down came a great green wave, rushed in a flood over everything, and swept me drenched to the skin down the stairs into the cabin. I crawled to bed to escape cold, and slid up and down my berth like a shuttle at every roll of the ship till I fell into the unconsciousness which is a substitute for sleep, slept at last really, and woke at seven in the morning to find the sun shining, and the surface of the ocean still undulating but glassy calm. The only signs left of the tempest were the swallow-like petrels skimming to and fro in our wake, picking up the scraps of food and the plate washings which the cook's mate had thrown overboard; smallest and beautifullest of all the gull tribe, called petrel by our ancestors, who went to their Bibles more often than we do for their images, in memory of St. Peter, because they seem for a moment to stand upon the water when they stoop upon any floating object.[2] In the afternoon we passed the Azores, rising blue and fairy-like out of the ocean; unconscious they of the bloody battles which once went on under their shadows. There it was that Grenville, in the 'Revenge,' fought through a long summer day alone against a host of enemies, and died there and won immortal honour. The Azores themselves are Grenville's monument, and in the memory of Englishmen are associated for ever with his glorious story. Behind these islands, too, lay Grenville's comrades, the English privateers, year after year waiting for Philip's plate fleet. Behind these islands lay French squadrons waiting for the English sugar ships. They are calm and silent now, and are never likely to echo any more to battle thunder. Men come and go and play out their little dramas, epic or tragic, and it matters nothing to nature. Their wild pranks leave no scars, and the decks are swept clean for the next comers.

FOOTNOTES:

[1]
ὦ τέκνον, οὐχ ἅπαντα τῷ γήρᾳ κακά;
   ἡ 'εμπειρία
ἔχει τι λέξαι τῶν νέων σοφώτερον.
[2]
This is the explanation of the name which is given by Dampier.

CHAPTER III.

The tropics—Passengers on board—Account of the Darien Canal—Planters' complaints—West Indian history—The Spanish conquest—Drake and Hawkins—The buccaneers—The pirates—French and English—Rodney—Battle of April 12—Peace with honour—Doers and talkers.

Another two days and we were in the tropics. The north-east trade blew behind us, and our own speed being taken off from the speed of the wind there was scarcely air enough to fill our sails. The waves went down and the ports were opened, and we had passed suddenly from winter into perpetual summer, as Jean Paul says it will be with us in death. Sleep came back soft and sweet, and the water was warm in our morning bath, and the worries and annoyances of life vanished in these sweet surroundings like nightmares when we wake. How well the Greeks understood the spiritual beauty of the sea! θάλασσα κλύξει πάντα τὰνθρώπων κακά

, says Euripides. 'The sea washes off all the woes of men.' The passengers lay about the decks in their chairs reading story books. The young ones played Bull. The officers flirted mildly with the pretty young ladies. For a brief interval care and anxiety had spread their wings and flown away, and existence itself became delightful.

There was a young scientific man on board who interested me much. He had been sent out from Kew to take charge of the Botanical Gardens in Jamaica—was quiet, modest, and unaffected, understood his own subjects well, and could make others understand them; with him I had much agreeable conversation. And there was another singular person who attracted me even more. I took him at first for an American. He was a Dane I found, an engineer by profession, and was on his way to some South American republic. He was a long lean man with grey eyes, red hair, and a laugh as if he so enjoyed the thing that amused him that he wished to keep it all to himself, laughing inwardly till he choked and shook with it. His chief amusement seemed to have lain in watching the performances of Liberal politicians in various parts of the world. He told me of an opposition leader in some parliament whom his rival in office had disposed of by shutting him up in the caboose. 'In the caboose,' he repeated, screaming with enjoyment at the thought of it, and evidently wishing that all the parliamentary orators on the globe were in the same place. In his wanderings he had been lately at the Darien Canal, and gave me a wonderful account of the condition of things there. The original estimate of the probable cost had been twenty-six millions of our (English) money. All these millions had been spent already, and only a fifth of the whole had as yet been executed. The entire cost would not be less, under the existing management, than one hundred millions, and he evidently doubted whether the canal would ever be completed at all, though professionally he would not confess to such an opinion. The waste and plunder had been incalculable. The works and the gold that were set moving by them made a feast for unclean harpies of both sexes from every nation in the four continents. I liked everything about Mr. ——. Tom Cringle's Obed might have been something like him, had not Obed's evil genius driven him into more dangerous ways.

There was a small black boy among us, evidently of pure blood, for his hair was wool and his colour black as ink. His parents must have been well-to-do, for the boy had been in Europe to be educated. The officers on board and some of the ladies played with him as they would play with a monkey. He had little more sense than a monkey, perhaps less, and the gestures of him grinning behind gratings and pushing out his long thin arms between the bars were curiously suggestive of the original from whom we are told now that all of us came. The worst of it was that, being lifted above his own people, he had been taught to despise them. He was spoilt as a black and could not be made into a white, and this I found afterwards was the invariable and dangerous consequence whenever a superior negro contrived to raise himself. He might do well enough himself, but his family feel their blood as a degradation. His children will not marry among their own people, and not only will no white girl marry a negro, but hardly any dowry can be large enough to tempt a West Indian white to make a wife of a black lady. This is one of the most sinister features in the present state of social life there.

Small personalities cropped up now and then. We had representatives of all professions among us except the Church of England clergy. Of them we had not one. The captain, as usual, read us the service on Sundays on a cushion for a desk, with the union jack spread over it. On board ship the captain, like a sovereign, is supreme, and in spiritual matters as in secular. Drake was the first commander who carried the theory into practice when he excommunicated his chaplain. It is the law now, and the tradition has gone on unbroken. In default of clergy we had a missionary, who for the most part kept his lips closed. He did open them once, and at my expense. Apropos of nothing he said to me, 'I wonder, sir, whether you ever read the remarks upon you in the newspapers. If all the attacks upon your writings which I have seen were collected together they would make an interesting volume.' This was all. He had delivered his soul and relapsed into silence.

From a Puerto Rico merchant I learnt that, if the English colonies were in a bad way, the Spanish colonies were in a worse. His own island, he said, was a nest of squalor, misery, vice, and disease. Blacks and whites were equally immoral; and so far as habits went, the whites were the filthier of the two. The complaints of the English West Indians were less sweeping, and, as to immorality between whites and blacks, neither from my companions in the 'Moselle' nor anywhere afterward did I hear or see a sign of it. The profligacy of planter life passed away with slavery, and the changed condition of the two races makes impossible any return to the old habits. But they had wrongs of their own, and were eloquent in their exposition of them. We had taken the islands from France and Spain at an enormous expense, and we were throwing them aside like a worn-out child's toy. We did nothing for them. We allowed them no advantage as British subjects, and when they tried to do something for themselves, we interposed with an Imperial veto. The United States, seeing the West Indian trade gravitating towards New York, had offered them a commercial treaty, being willing to admit their sugar duty free, in consideration of the islands admitting in return their salt fish and flour and notions. A treaty was in process of negotiation between the United States and the Spanish islands. A similar treaty had been freely offered to them, which might have saved them from ruin, and the Imperial Government had disallowed it. How, under such treatment, could we expect them to be loyal to the British connection?

It was a relief to turn back from these lamentations to the brilliant period of past West Indian history. With the planters of the present it was all sugar—sugar and the lazy blacks who were England's darlings and would not work for them. The hand-books were equally barren. In them I found nothing but modern statistics pointing to dreary conclusions, and in the place of any human interest, long stories of constitutions, suffrages, representative assemblies, powers of elected members, and powers reserved to the Crown. Such things, important as they might be, did not touch my imagination; and to an Englishman, proud of his country, the West Indies had a far higher interest. Strange scenes streamed across my memory, and a shadowy procession of great figures who have printed their names in history. Columbus and Cortez, Vasco Nuñez, and Las Casas; the millions of innocent Indians who, according to Las Casas, were destroyed out of the islands, the Spanish grinding them to death in their gold mines; the black swarms who were poured in to take their place, and the frightful story of the slave trade. Behind it all was the European drama of the sixteenth century—Charles V. and Philip fighting against the genius of the new era, and feeding their armies with the ingots of the new world. The convulsion spread across the Atlantic. The English Protestants and the French Huguenots took to sea like water dogs, and challenged their enemies in their own special domain. To the popes and the Spaniards the new world was the property of the Church and of those who had discovered it. A papal bull bestowed on Spain all the countries which lay within the tropics west of the Atlantic—a form of Monroe doctrine, not unreasonable as long as there was force to maintain it, but the force was indispensable, and the Protestant adventurers tried the question with them at the cannon's mouth. They were of the reformed faith all of them, these sea rovers of the early days, and, like their enemies, they were of a very mixed complexion. The Spaniards, gorged with plunder and wading in blood, were at the same time, and in their own eyes, crusading soldiers of the faith, missionaries of the Holy Church, and defenders of the doctrines which were impiously assailed in Europe. The privateers from Plymouth and Rochelle paid also for the cost of their expeditions with the pillage of ships and towns and the profits of the slave trade; and they too were the unlicensed champions of spiritual freedom in their own estimate of themselves. The gold which was meant for Alva's troops in Flanders found its way into the treasure houses of the London companies. The logs of the voyages of the Elizabethan navigators represent them faithfully as they were, freebooters of the ocean in one aspect of them; in another, the sea warriors of the Reformation—uncommissioned, unrecognised, fighting on their own responsibility, liable to be disowned when they failed, while the Queen herself would privately be a shareholder in the adventure. It was a wild anarchic scene, fit cradle of the spiritual freedom of a new age, when the nations of the earth were breaking the chains in which king and priest had bound them.

To the Spaniards, Drake and his comrades were corsarios, robbers, enemies of the human race, to be treated to a short shrift whenever found and caught. British seamen who fell into their hands were carried before the Inquisition at Lima or Carthagena and burnt at the stake as heretics. Four of Drake's crew were unfortunately taken once at Vera Cruz. Drake sent a message to the governor-general that if a hair of their heads was singed he would hang ten Spaniards for each one of them. (This curious note is at Simancas, where I saw it.) So great an object of terror at Madrid was El Draque that he was looked on as an incarnation of the old serpent, and when he failed in his last enterprise and news came that he was dead, Lope de Vega sang a hymn of triumph in an epic poem which he called the 'Dragontea.'

When Elizabeth died and peace was made with Spain, the adventurers lost something of the indirect countenance which had so far been extended to them; the execution of Raleigh being one among other marks of the change of mind. But they continued under other names, and no active effort was made to suppress them. The Spanish Government did in 1627 agree to leave England in possession of Barbadoes, but the pretensions to an exclusive right to trade continued to be maintained, and the English and French refused to recognise it. The French privateers seized Tortuga, an island off St. Domingo, and they and their English friends swarmed in the Caribbean Sea as buccaneers or flibustiers. They exchanged names, perhaps as a symbol of their alliance. 'Flibustier' was English and a corruption of freebooter. 'Buccaneer' came from the boucan, or dried beef, of the wild cattle which the French hunters shot in Española, and which formed the chief of their sea stores. Boucan became a French verb, and, according to Labat, was itself the Carib name for the cashew nut.

War breaking out again in Cromwell's time, Penn and Venables took Jamaica. The flibustiers from the Tortugas drove the Spaniards out of Hayti, which was annexed to the French crown. The comradeship in religious enthusiasm which had originally drawn the two nations together cooled by degrees, as French Catholics as well as Protestants took to the trade. Port Royal became the headquarters of the English buccaneers—the last and greatest of them being Henry Morgan, who took and plundered Panama, was knighted for his services, and was afterwards made vice-governor of Jamaica. From the time when the Spaniards threw open their trade, and English seamen ceased to be delivered over to the Inquisition, the English buccaneers ceased to be respectable characters and gradually drifted into the pirates of later history, when under their new conditions they produced their more questionable heroes, the Kidds and Blackbeards. The French flibustiers continued long after—far into the eighteenth century—some of them with commissions as privateers, others as forbans or unlicensed rovers, but still connived at in Martinique.

Adventurers, buccaneers, pirates pass across the stage—the curtain falls on them, and rises on a more glorious scene. Jamaica had become the depôt of the trade of England with the western world, and golden streams had poured into Port Royal. Barbadoes was unoccupied when England took possession of it, and never passed out of our hands; but the Antilles—the Anterior Isles—which stand like a string of emeralds round the neck of the Caribbean Sea, had been most of them colonised and occupied by the French, and during the wars of the last century were the objects of a never ceasing conflict between their fleets and ours. The French had planted their language there, they had planted their religion there, and the blacks of these islands generally still speak the French patois and call themselves Catholics; but it was deemed essential to our interests that the Antilles should be not French but English, and Antigua, Martinique, St. Lucia, St. Vincent, and Grenada were taken and retaken and taken again in a struggle perpetually renewed. When the American colonies revolted, the West Indies became involved in the revolutionary hurricane. France, Spain, and Holland—our three ocean rivals—combined in a supreme effort to tear from us our Imperial power. The opportunity was seized by Irish patriots to clamour for Irish nationality, and by the English Radicals to demand liberty and the rights of man. It was the most critical moment in later English history. If we had yielded to peace on the terms which our enemies offered, and the English Liberals wished us to accept, the star of Great Britain would have set for ever.

The West Indies were then under the charge of Rodney, whose brilliant successes had already made his name famous. He had done his country more than yeoman's service. He had torn the Leeward Islands from the French. He had punished the Hollanders for joining the coalition by taking the island of St. Eustachius and three millions' worth of stores and money. The patriot party at home led by Fox and Burke were ill pleased with these victories, for they wished us to be driven into surrender. Burke denounced Rodney as he denounced Warren Hastings, and Rodney was called home to answer for himself. In his absence Demerara, the Leeward Islands, St. Eustachius itself, were captured or recovered by the enemy. The French fleet, now supreme in the western waters, blockaded Lord Cornwallis at York Town and forced him to capitulate. The Spaniards had fitted out a fleet at Havannah, and the Count de Grasse, the French admiral, fresh from the victorious thunder of the American cannon, hastened back to refurnish himself at Martinique, intending to join the Spaniards, tear Jamaica from us, and drive us finally and completely out of the West Indies. One chance remained. Rodney was ordered back to his station, and he went at his best speed, taking all the ships with him which could then be spared. It was mid-winter. He forced his way to Barbadoes in five weeks spite of equinoctial storms. The Whig orators were indignant. They insisted that we were beaten; there had been bloodshed enough, and we must sit down in our humiliation. The Government yielded, and a peremptory order followed on Rodney's track, 'Strike your flag and come home.' Had that fatal command reached him Gibraltar would have fallen and Hastings's Indian Empire would have melted into air. But Rodney knew that his time was short, and he had been prompt to use it. Before the order came, the severest naval battle in English annals had been fought and won. De Grasse was a prisoner, and the French fleet was scattered into wreck and ruin.

De Grasse had refitted in the Martinique dockyards. He himself and every officer in the fleet was confident that England was at last done for, and that nothing was left but to gather the fruits of the victory which was theirs already. Not Xerxes, when he broke through Thermopylae and watched from the shore his thousand galleys streaming down to the Gulf of Salamis, was more assured that his prize was in his hands than De Grasse on the deck of the 'Ville de Paris,' the finest ship then floating on the seas, when he heard that Rodney was at St. Lucia and intended to engage him. He did not even believe that the English after so many reverses would venture to meddle with a fleet superior in force and inspirited with victory. All the Antilles except St. Lucia were his own. Tobago, Grenada, the Grenadines, St. Vincent, Martinique, Dominica, Guadaloupe, Montserrat, Nevis, Antigua, and St. Kitts, he held them all in proud possession, a string of gems, each island large as or larger than the Isle of Man, rising up with high volcanic peaks clothed from base to crest with forest, carved into deep ravines, and fringed with luxuriant plains. In St. Lucia alone, lying between St. Vincent and Dominica, the English flag still flew, and Rodney lay there in the harbour at Castries. On April 8, 1782, the signal came from the north end of the island that the French fleet had sailed. Martinique is in sight of St. Lucia, and the rock is still shown from which Rodney had watched day by day for signs that they were moving. They were out at last, and he instantly weighed and followed. The air was light, and De Grasse was under the high lands of Dominica before Rodney came up with him. Both fleets were becalmed, and the English were scattered and divided by a current which runs between the islands. A breeze at last blew off the land. The French were the first to feel it, and were able to attack at advantage the leading English division. Had De Grasse 'come down as he ought,' Rodney thought that the consequences might have been serious. In careless imagination of superiority they let the chance go by. They kept at a distance, firing long shots, which as it was did considerable damage. The two following days the fleets manœuvred in sight of each other. On the night of the eleventh Rodney made signal for the whole fleet to go south under press of sail. The French thought he was flying. He tacked at two in the morning, and at daybreak found himself where he wished to be, with the, French fleet on his lee quarter. The French looking for nothing but again a distant cannonade, continued leisurely along under the north highlands of Dominica towards the channel which separates that island from Guadaloupe. In number of ships the fleets were equal; in size and complement of crew the French were immensely superior; and besides the ordinary ships' companies they had twenty thousand soldiers on board who were to be used in the conquest of Jamaica. Knowing well that a defeat at that moment would be to England irreparable ruin, they did not dream that Rodney would be allowed, even if he wished it, to risk a close and decisive engagement. The English admiral was aware also that his country's fate was in his hands. It was one of those supreme moments which great men dare to use and small men tremble at. He had the advantage of the wind, and could force a battle or decline it, as he pleased. With clear daylight the signal to engage was flying from the masthead of the 'Formidable,' Rodney's ship. At seven in the morning, April 12, 1782, the whole fleet bore down obliquely on the French line, cutting it directly in two. Rodney led in person. Having passed through and broken up their order he tacked again, still keeping the wind. The French, thrown into confusion, were unable to reform, and the battle resolved itself into a number of separate engagements in which the English had the choice of position.

Rodney in passing through the enemy's lines the first time had exchanged broadsides with the 'Glorieux,' a seventy-four, at close range. He had shot away her masts and bowsprit, and left her a bare hull; her flag, however, still flying, being nailed to a splintered spar. So he left her unable to stir; and after he had gone about came himself yardarm to yardarm with the superb 'Ville de Paris,' the pride of France, the largest ship in the then world, where De Grasse commanded in person. All day long the cannon roared. Rodney had on board a favourite bantam cock, which stood perched upon the poop of the 'Formidable' through the whole action, its shrill voice heard crowing through the thunder of the broadsides. One by one the French ships struck their flags or fought on till they foundered and went down. The carnage on board them was terrible, crowded as they were with the troops for Jamaica. Fourteen thousand were reckoned to have been killed, besides the prisoners. The 'Ville de Paris' surrendered last, fighting desperately after hope was gone till her masts were so shattered that they could not bear a sail, and her decks above and below were littered over with mangled limbs. De Grasse gave up his sword to Rodney on the 'Formidable's' quarter-deck. The gallant 'Glorieux,' unable to fly, and seeing the battle lost, hauled down her flag, but not till the undisabled remnants of her crew were too few to throw the dead into the sea. Other ships took fire and blew up. Half the French fleet were either taken or sunk; the rest crawled away for the time, most of them to be picked up afterwards like crippled birds.

So on that memorable day was the English Empire saved. Peace followed, but it was 'peace with honour.' The American colonies were lost; but England kept her West Indies; her flag still floated over Gibraltar; the hostile strength of Europe all combined had failed to twist Britannia's ocean sceptre from her: she sat down maimed and bleeding, but the wreath had not been torn from her brow, she was still sovereign of the seas.

The bow of Ulysses was strung in those days. The order of recall arrived when the work was done. It was proudly obeyed; and even the great Burke admitted that no honour could be bestowed upon Rodney which he had not deserved at his country's hands. If the British Empire is still to have a prolonged career before it, the men who make empires are the men who can hold them together. Oratorical reformers can overthrow what deserves to be overthrown. Institutions, even the best of them, wear out, and must give place to others, and the fine political speakers are the instruments of their overthrow. But the fine speakers produce nothing of their own, and as constructive statesmen their paths are strewed with failures. The worthies of England are the men who cleared and tilled her fields, formed her laws, built her colleges and cathedrals, founded her colonies, fought her battles, covered the ocean with commerce, and spread our race over the planet to leave a mark upon it which time will not efface. These men are seen in their work, and are not heard of in Parliament. When the account is wound up, where by the side of them will stand our famous orators? What will any one of these have left behind him save the wreck of institutions which had done their work and had ceased to serve a useful purpose? That was their business in this world, and they did it and do it; but it is no very glorious work, not a work over which it is possible to feel any 'fine enthusiasm.' To chop down a tree is easier than to make it grow. When the business of destruction is once completed, they and their fame and glory will disappear together. Our true great ones will again be visible, and thenceforward will be visible alone.

Is there a single instance in our own or any other history of a great political speaker who has added anything to human knowledge or to human worth? Lord Chatham may stand as a lonely exception. But except Chatham who is there? Not one that

I know of. Oratory is the spendthrift sister of the arts, which decks itself like a strumpet with the tags and ornaments which it steals from real superiority. The object of it is not truth, but anything which it can make appear truth; anything which it can persuade people to believe by calling in their passions to obscure their intelligence.

CHAPTER IV.

First sight of Barbadoes—Origin of the name—Père Labat—Bridgetown two hundred years ago—Slavery and Christianity—Economic crisis—Sugar bounties—Aspect of the streets—Government House and its occupants—Duties of a governor of Barbadoes.

England was covered with snow when we left it on December 30. At sunrise on January 12 we were anchored in the roadstead at Bridgetown, and the island of Barbadoes lay before us shining in the haze of a hot summer morning. It is about the size of the Isle of Wight, cultivated so far as eye could see with the completeness of a garden; no mountains in it, scarcely even high hills, but a surface pleasantly undulating, the prevailing colour a vivid green from the cane fields; houses in town and country white from the coral rock of which they are built, but the glare from them relieved by heavy clumps of trees. What the trees were I had yet to discover. You could see at a glance that the island was as thickly peopled as an ant-hill. Not an inch of soil seemed to be allowed to run to waste. Two hundred thousand is, I believe, the present number of Barbadians, of whom nine-tenths are blacks. They refuse to emigrate. They cling to their home with innocent vanity as though it was the finest country in the world, and multiply at a rate so rapid that no one likes to think about it. Labour at any rate is abundant and cheap. In Barbadoes the negro is willing enough to work, for he has no other means of living. Little land is here allowed him to grow his yams upon. Almost the whole of it is still held by the whites in large estates, cultivated by labourers on the old system, and, it is to be admitted, cultivated most admirably. If the West Indies are going to ruin, Barbadoes, at any rate, is being ruined with a smiling face. The roadstead was crowded with shipping—large barques, steamers, and brigs, schooners of all shapes and sorts. The training squadron had come into the bay for a day or two on their way to Trinidad, four fine ships, conspicuous by their white ensigns, a squareness of yards, and generally imposing presence. Boats were flying to and fro under sail or with oars, officials coming off in white calico dress, with awnings over the stern sheets and chattering crews of negroes. Notwithstanding these exotic symptoms, it was all thoroughly English; we were under the guns of our own men-of-war. The language of the Anglo-Barbadians was pure English, the voices without the smallest transatlantic intonation. On no one of our foreign possessions is the print of England's foot more strongly impressed than on Barbadoes. It has been ours for two centuries and three-quarters, and was organised from the first on English traditional lines, with its constitution, its parishes and parish churches and churchwardens, and schools and parsons, all on the old model; which the unprogressive inhabitants have been wise enough to leave undisturbed.

Little is known of the island before we took possession of it—so little that the origin of the name is still uncertain. Barbadoes, if not a corruption of some older word, is Spanish or Portuguese, and means 'bearded.' The local opinion is that the word refers to a banyan or fig tree which is common there, and which sends down from its branches long hairs or fibres supposed to resemble beards. I disbelieve in this derivation. Every Spaniard whom I have consulted confirms my own impression that 'barbados' standing alone could no more refer to trees than 'barbati' standing alone could refer to trees in Latin. The name is a century older than the English occupation, for I have seen it in a Spanish chart of 1525. The question is of some interest, since it perhaps implies that at the first discovery there was a race of bearded Caribs there. However this may be, Barbadoes, after we became masters of the island, enjoyed a period of unbroken prosperity for two hundred years. Before the conquest of Jamaica, it was the principal mart of our West Indian trade; and even after that conquest, when all Europe drew its new luxury of sugar from these islands, the wealth and splendour of the English residents at Bridgetown astonished and stirred the envy of every passing visitor. Absenteeism as yet was not. The owners lived on their estates, governed the island as magistrates unpaid for their services, and equally unpaid, took on themselves the defences of the island. Père Labat, a French missionary, paid a visit to Barbadoes at the beginning of the eighteenth century. He was a clever, sarcastic kind of man, with fine literary skill, and describes what he saw with a jealous appreciation which he intended to act upon his own countrymen. The island, according to him, was running over with wealth, and was very imperfectly fortified. The jewellers' and silversmiths' shops in Bridgetown were brilliant as on the Paris boulevards. The port was full of ships, the wharves and warehouses crammed with merchandise from all parts of the globe. The streets were handsome, and thronged with men of business, who were piling up fortunes. To the Father these sumptuous gentlemen were all most civil. The governor, an English milor, asked him to dinner, and talked such excellent French that Labat forgave him his nationality. The governor, he said, resided in a fine palace. He had a well-furnished library, was dignified, courteous, intelligent, and lived in state like a prince. A review was held for the French priest's special entertainment, of the Bridgetown cavalry. Five hundred gentlemen turned out from this one district admirably mounted and armed. Altogether in the island he says that there were 3,000 horse and 2,000 foot, every one of them of course white and English. The officers struck him particularly. He met one who had been five years a prisoner in the Bastille, and had spent his time there in learning mathematics. The planters opened their houses to him. Dinners then as now were the received form of English hospitality. They lived well, Labat says. They had all the luxuries of the tropics, and they had imported the partridges which they were so fond of from England. They had the costliest and choicest wines, and knew how to enjoy them. They dined at two o'clock, and their dinner lasted four hours. Their mansions were superbly furnished, and gold and silver plate, he observed with an eye to business, was so abundant that the plunder of it would pay the cost of an expedition for the reduction of the island.

There was another side to all this magnificence which also might be turned to account by an enterprising enemy. There were some thousands of wretched Irish, who had been transplanted thither after the last rebellion, and were bound under articles to labour. These might be counted on to rise if an invading force appeared; and there were 60,000 slaves, who would rebel also if they saw a hope of success. They were ill fed and hard driven. On the least symptom of insubordination they were killed without mercy: sometimes they were burnt alive, or were hung up in iron cages to die.[4] In the French and Spanish islands care was taken of the souls of the poor creatures. They were taught their catechism, they were baptised, and attended mass regularly. The Anglican clergy, Labat said with professional malice, neither baptised them nor taught them anything, but regarded them as mere animals. To keep Christians in slavery they held would be wrong and indefensible, and they therefore met the difficulty by not making their slaves into Christians. That baptism made any essential difference, however, he does not insist. By the side of Christianity, in the Catholic islands, devil worship and witchcraft went on among the same persons. No instance had ever come to his knowledge of a converted black who returned to his country who did not throw away his Christianity just as he would throw away his clothes; and as to cruelty and immorality, he admits that the English at Barbadoes were no worse than his own people at Martinique.

In the collapse of West Indian prosperity which followed on emancipation, Barbadoes escaped the misfortunes of the other islands. The black population being so dense, and the place itself being so small, the squatting system could not be tried; there was plenty of labour always, and the planters being relieved of the charge of their workmen when they were sick or worn out, had rather gained than lost by the change. Barbadoes, however, was not to escape for ever, and was now having its share of misfortunes. It is dangerous for any country to commit its fortunes to an exclusive occupation. Sugar was the most immediately lucrative of all the West Indian productions. Barbadoes is exceptionally well suited to sugar-growing. It has no mountains and no forests. The soil is clean and has been carefully attended to for two hundred and fifty years. It had been owned during the present century by gentlemen who for the most part lived in England on the profits of their properties, and left them to be managed by agents and attorneys. The method of management was expensive. Their own habits were expensive. Their incomes, to which they had lived up, had been cut short lately by a series of bad seasons. Money had been borrowed at high interest year after year to keep the estates and their owners going. On the top of this came the beetroot competition backed up by a bounty, and the Barbadian sugar interest, I was told, had gone over a precipice. Even the unencumbered resident proprietors could barely keep their heads above water. The returns on three-quarters of the properties on the island no longer sufficed to pay the expenses of cultivation and the interest of the loans which had been raised upon them. There was impending a general bankruptcy which might break up entirely the present system and leave the negroes for a time without the wages which were the sole dependence.

A very dark picture had thus been drawn to me of the prospects of the poor little island which had been once so brilliant. Nothing could be less like it than the bright sunny landscape which we saw from the deck of our vessel. The town, the shipping, the pretty villas, the woods, and the wide green sea of waving cane had no suggestion of ruin about them. If the ruin was coming, clearly enough it had not yet come. After breakfast we went on shore in a boat with a white awning over it, rowed by a crew of black boatmen, large, fleshy, shining on the skin with ample feeding and shining in the face with innocent happiness. They rowed well. They were amusing. There was a fixed tariff, and they were not extortionate. The temperature seemed to rise ten degrees when we landed. The roads were blinding white from the coral dust, the houses were white, the sun scorching. The streets were not the streets described by Labat; no splendid magazines or jewellers' shops like those in Paris or London; but there were lighters at the quays loading or unloading, carts dashing along with mule teams and making walking dangerous; signs in plenty of life and business; few white faces, but blacks and mulattoes swarming. The houses were substantial, though in want of paint. The public buildings, law courts, hall of assembly c. were solid and handsome, nowhere out of repair, though with something to be desired in point of smartness. The market square would have been well enough but for a statue of Lord Nelson which stands there, very like, but small and insignificant, and for some extraordinary reason they have painted it a bright pea-green.

We crept along in the shade of trees and warehouses till we reached the principal street. Here my friends brought me to the Icehouse, a sort of club, with reading rooms and dining rooms, and sleeping accommodation for members from a distance who do not like colonial hotels. Before anything else could be thought of I was introduced to cocktail, with which I had to make closer acquaintance afterwards, cocktail being the established corrective of West Indian languor, without which life is impossible. It is a compound of rum, sugar, lime juice, Angostura bitters, and what else I know not, frisked into effervescence by a stick, highly agreeable to the taste and effective for its immediate purpose. Cocktail over, and walking in the heat being a thing not to be thought of, I sat for two hours in a balcony watching the people, who were thick as bees in swarming time. Nine-tenths of them were pure black; you rarely saw a white face, but still less would you see a discontented one, imperturbable good humour and self-satisfaction being written on the features of every one. The women struck me especially. They were smartly dressed in white calico, scrupulously clean, and tricked out with ribands and feathers; but their figures were so good, and they carried themselves so well and gracefully, that, although they might make themselves absurd, they could not look vulgar. Like the old Greek and Etruscan women, they are trained from childhood to carry heavy weights on their heads. They are thus perfectly upright, and plant their feet firmly and naturally on the ground. They might serve for sculptors' models, and are well aware of it. There were no signs of poverty. Old and young seemed well-fed. Some had brought in baskets of fruit, bananas, oranges, pine apples, and sticks of sugar cane; others had yams and sweet potatoes from their bits of garden in the country. The men were active enough driving carts, wheeling barrows, or selling flying fish, which are caught off the island in shoals and are cheaper than herrings in Yarmouth. They chattered like a flock of jackdaws, but there was no quarrelling; not a drunken man was to be seen, and all was merriment and good humour. My poor downtrodden black brothers and sisters, so far as I could judge from this first introduction, looked to me a very fortunate class of fellow-creatures.

Government House, where we went to luncheon, is a large airy building shaded by heavy trees with a garden at the back of it. West Indian houses, I found afterwards, are all constructed on the same pattern, the object being to keep the sun out and let in the wind. Long verandahs or galleries run round them protected by green Venetian blinds which can be opened or closed at pleasure; the rooms within with polished floors, little or no carpet, and contrivances of all kinds to keep the air in continual circulation. In the subdued green light, human figures lose their solidity and look as if they were creatures of air also.

Sir Charles Lees and his lady were all that was polite and hospitable. They invited me to make their house my home during my stay, and more charming host and hostess it would have been impossible to find or wish for. There was not the state which Labat described, but there was the perfection of courtesy, a courtesy which must have belonged to their natures, or it would have been overstrained long since by the demands made upon it. Those who have looked on at a skating ring will have observed an orange or some such object in the centre round which the evolutions are described, the ice artist sweeping out from it in long curves to the extreme circumference, returning on interior arcs till he gains the orange again, and then off once more on a fresh departure. Barbadoes to the West Indian steam navigation is like the skater's orange. All mails, all passengers from Europe, arrive at Barbadoes first. There the subsidiary steamers catch them up, bear them north or south to the Windward or Leeward Isles, and on their return bring them back to Carlisle Bay. Every vessel brings some person or persons to whom the Governor is called on to show hospitality. He must give dinners to the officials and gentry of the island, he must give balls and concerts for their ladies, he must entertain the officers of the garrison. When the West Indian squadron or the training squadron drop into the roadstead, admirals, commodores, captains must all be invited. Foreign ships of war go and come continually, Americans, French, Spaniards, or Portuguese. Presidents of South American republics, engineers from Darien, all sorts and conditions of men who go to Europe in the English mail vessels, take their departure from Carlisle Bay, and if they are neglected regard it as a national affront. Cataracts of champagne must flow if the British name is not to be discredited. The expense is unavoidable and is enormous, while the Governor's very moderate salary is found too large by economic politicians, and there is a cry for reduction of it.

I was of course most grateful for Sir Charles's invitation to myself. From him, better perhaps than from anyone, I could learn how far the passionate complaints which I had heard about the state of the islands were to be listened to as accounts of actual fact. I found, however, that I must postpone both this particular pleasure and my stay in Barbadoes itself till a later opportunity. My purpose had been to remain there till I had given it all the time which I could spare, thence to go on to Jamaica, and from Jamaica to return at leisure round the Antilles. But it had been ascertained that in Jamaica there was small-pox. I suppose that there generally is small-pox there, or typhus fever, or other infectious disorder. But spasms of anxiety assail periodically the souls of local authorities. Vessels coming from Jamaica had been quarantined in all the islands, and I found that if I proceeded thither as I proposed, I should be refused permission to land afterwards in any one of the other colonies. In my perplexity my Trinidad friends invited me to accompany them at once to Port of Spain. Trinidad was the most thriving, or was at all events the least dissatisfied, of all the British possessions. I could have a glance at the Windward Islands on the way. I could afterwards return to Barbadoes, where Sir Charles assured me that I should still find a room waiting for me. The steamer to Trinidad sailed the same afternoon. I had to decide in haste, and I decided to go. Our luncheon over, we had time to look over the pretty gardens at Government House. There were great cabbage palms, cannon-ball trees, mahogany trees, almond trees, and many more which were wholly new acquaintances. There was a grotto made by climbing plants and creepers, with a fountain playing in the middle of it, where orchids hanging on wires threw out their clusters of flowers for the moths to fertilize, ferns waved their long fronds in the dripping showers, humming birds cooled their wings in the spray, and flashed in and out like rubies and emeralds. Gladly would I have lingered there, at least for a cigar, but it could not be; we had to call on the Commander of the Forces, Sir C. Pearson, the hero of Ekowe in the Zulu war. Him, too, I was to see again, and hear interesting stories from about our tragic enterprise in the Transvaal. For the moment my mind was filled sufficiently with new impressions. One reads books about places, but the images which they create are always unlike the real object. All that I had seen was absolutely new and unexpected. I was glad of an opportunity to readjust the information which I had brought with me. We joined our new vessel before sunset, and we steamed away into the twilight.

FOOTNOTES:

[4]

Labat seems to say that they were hung up alive in these cages, and left to die there. He says elsewhere, and it may be hoped that the explanation is the truer one, that the recently imported negroes often destroyed themselves, in the belief that when dead they would return to their own country. In the French islands as well as the English, the bodies of suicides were exposed in these cages, from which they could not be stolen, to convince the poor people of their mistake by their own eyes. He says that the contrivance was successful, and that after this the slaves did not destroy themselves any more.

CHAPTER V.

West Indian politeness—Negro morals and felicity—Island of St. Vincent—Grenada—The harbour—Disappearance of the whites—An island of black freeholders—Tobago—Dramatic art—A promising incident.

West Indian civilisation is old-fashioned, and has none of the pushing manners which belong to younger and perhaps more thriving communities. The West Indians themselves, though they may be deficient in energy, are uniformly ladies and gentlemen, and all their arrangements take their complexion from the general tone of society. There is a refinement visible at once in the subsidiary vessels of the mail service which ply among the islands. They are almost as large as those which cross the Atlantic, and never on any line in the world have I met with officers so courteous and cultivated. The cabins were spacious and as cool as a temperature of 80°, gradually rising as we went south, would permit. Punkahs waved over us at dinner. In our berths a single sheet was all that was provided for us, and this was one more than we needed. A sea was running when we cleared out from under the land. Among the cabin passengers was a coloured family in good circumstances moving about with nurses and children. The little things, who had never been at sea before, sat on the floor, staring out of their large helpless black eyes, not knowing what was the matter with them. Forward there were perhaps two or three hundred coloured people going from one island to another, singing, dancing, and chattering all night long, as radiant and happy as carelessness and content could make them. Sick or not sick made no difference. Nothing could disturb the imperturbable good humour and good spirits.

It was too hot to sleep; we sat several of us smoking on deck, and I learnt the first authentic particulars of the present manner of life of these much misunderstood people. Evidently they belonged to a race far inferior to the Zulus and Caffres, whom I had known in South Africa. They were more coarsely formed in limb and feature. They would have been slaves in their own country if they had not been brought to ours, and at the worst had lost nothing by the change. They were good-natured, innocent, harmless, lazy perhaps, but not more lazy than is perfectly natural when even Europeans must be roused to activity by cocktail.

In the Antilles generally, Barbadoes being the only exception, negro families have each their cabin, their garden ground, their grazing for a cow. They live surrounded by most of the fruits which grew in Adam's paradise—oranges and plantains, bread-fruit, and cocoa-nuts, though not apples. Their yams and cassava grow without effort, for the soil is easily worked and inexhaustibly fertile. The curse is taken off from nature, and like Adam again they are under the covenant of innocence. Morals in the technical sense they have none, but they cannot be said to sin, because they have no knowledge of a law, and therefore they can commit no breach of the law. They are naked and not ashamed. They are married as they call it, but not parsoned. The woman prefers a looser tie that she may be able to leave a man if he treats her unkindly. Yet they are not licentious. I never saw an immodest look in one their faces, and never heard of any venal profligacy. The system is strange, but it answers. A missionary told me that a connection rarely turns out well which begins with a legal marriage. The children scramble up anyhow, and shift for themselves like chickens as soon as they are able to peck. Many die in this way by eating unwholesome food, but also many live, and those who do live grow up exactly like their parents. It is a very peculiar state of things, not to be understood, as priest and missionary agree, without long acquaintance. There is immorality, but an immorality which is not demoralising. There is sin, but it is the sin of animals, without shame, because there is no sense of doing wrong. They eat the forbidden fruit, but it brings with it no knowledge of the difference between good and evil. They steal, but as a tradition of the time when they were themselves chattels, and the laws of property did not apply to them. They are honest about money, more honest perhaps than a good many whites. But food or articles of use they take freely, as they were allowed to do when slaves, in pure innocence of heart. In fact these poor children of darkness have escaped the consequences of the Fall, and must come of another stock after all.

Meanwhile they are perfectly happy. In no part of the globe is there any peasantry whose every want is so completely satisfied as her Majesty's black subjects in these West Indian islands. They have no aspirations to make them restless. They have no guilt upon their consciences. They have food for the picking up. Clothes they need not, and lodging in such a climate need not be elaborate. They have perfect liberty, and are safe from dangers, to which if left to themselves they would be exposed, for the English rule prevents the strong from oppressing the weak. In their own country they would have remained slaves to more warlike races. In the West Indies their fathers underwent a bondage of a century or two, lighter at its worst than the easiest form of it in Africa; their descendants in return have nothing now to do save to laugh and sing and enjoy existence. Their quarrels, if they have any, begin and end in words. If happiness is the be all and end all of life, and those who have most of it have most completely attained the object of their being, the 'nigger' who now basks among the ruins of the West Indian plantations is the supremest specimen of present humanity.

We retired to our berths at last. At waking we were at anchor off St. Vincent, an island of volcanic mountains robed in forest from shore to crest. Till late in the last century it was the headquarters of the Caribs, who kept up a savage independence there, recruited by runaway slaves from Barbadoes or elsewhere. Brandy and Sir Ralph Abercrombie reduced them to obedience in 1796, and St. Vincent throve tolerably down to the days of free trade. Even now when I saw it, Kingston, the principal town, looked pretty and well to do, reminding me, strange to say, of towns in Norway, the houses stretching along the shore painted in the same tints of blue or yellow or pink, with the same red-tiled roofs, the trees coming down the hill sides to the water's edge, villas of modest pretensions shining through the foliage, with the patches of cane fields, the equivalent in the landscape of the brilliant Norwegian grass. The prosperity has for the last forty years waned and waned. There are now two thousand white people there, and forty thousand coloured people, and proportions alter annually to our disadvantage. The usual remedies have been tried. The constitution has been altered a dozen times. Just now I believe the Crown is trying to do without one, having found the results of the elective principle not encouraging, but we shall perhaps revert to it before long; any way, the tables show that each year the trade of the island decreases, and will continue to decrease while the expenditure increases and will increase.

I did not land, for the time was short, and as a beautiful picture the island was best seen from the deck. The characteristics of the people are the same in all the Antilles, and could be studied elsewhere. The bustle and confusion in the ship, the crowd of boats round the ladder, the clamour of negro men's tongues, and the blaze of colours from the negro women's dresses, made up together a scene sufficiently entertaining for the hour which we remained. In the middle of it the Governor, Mr. S——, came on board with another official. They were going on in the steamer to Tobago, which formed part of his dominions.

Leaving St. Vincent, we were all the forenoon passing the Grenadines, a string of small islands fitting into their proper place in the Antilles semicircle, but as if Nature had forgotten to put them together or else had broken some large island to pieces and scattered them along the line. Some were large enough to have once carried sugar plantations, and are now made over wholly to the blacks; others were fishing stations, droves of whales during certain months frequenting these waters; others were mere rocks, amidst which the white-sailed American coasting schooners were beating up against the north-east trade. There was a stiff breeze, and the sea was white with short curling waves, but we were running before it and the wind kept the deck fresh. At Grenada, the next island, we were to go on shore.

Grenada was, like St. Vincent, the home for centuries of man-eating Caribs, French for a century and a half, and finally, after many desperate struggles for it, was ceded to England at the peace of Versailles. It is larger than St. Vincent, though in its main features it has the same character. There are lakes in the hills, and a volcanic crater not wholly quiescent; but the especial value of Grenada, which made us fight so hardly to win it, is the deep and landlocked harbour, the finest in all the Antilles.

Père Labat, to whose countrymen it belonged at the time of his own visit there, says that 'if Barbadoes had such a harbour as Grenada it would be an island without a rival in the world. If Grenada belonged to the English, who knew how to turn to profit natural advantages, it would be a rich and powerful colony. In itself it was all that man could desire. To live there was to live in paradise.' Labat found the island occupied by countrymen of his own, 'paisans aisez', he calls them, growing their tobacco, their indigo and scarlet rocou, their pigs and their poultry, and contented to be without sugar, without slaves, and without trade. The change of hands from which he expected so much had actually come about. Grenada did belong to the English, and had belonged to us ever since Rodney's peace. I was anxious to see how far Labat's prophecy had been fulfilled.

St. George's, the 'capital,' stands on the neck of a peninsula a mile in length, which forms one side of the harbour. Of the houses, some look out to sea, some inwards upon the carenage, as the harbour is called. At the point there was a fort, apparently of some strength, on which the British flag was flying. We signalled that we had the Governor on board, and the fort replied with a puff of smoke. Sound there was none or next to none, but we presumed that it had come from a gun of some kind. We anchored outside. Mr. S—— landed in an official boat with two flags, a missionary in another, which had only one. The crews of a dozen other boats then clambered up the gangway to dispute possession of the rest of us, shouting, swearing, lying, tearing us this way and that way as if we were carcases and they wild beasts wanting to dine upon us. We engaged a boat for ourselves as we supposed; we had no sooner entered it than the scandalous boatman proceeded to take in as many more passengers as it would hold. Remonstrance being vain, we settled the matter by stepping into the boat next adjoining, and amidst howls and execrations we were borne triumphantly off and were pulled in to the land.

Labat had not exaggerated the beauty of the landlocked basin into which we entered on rounding the point. On three sides wooded hills rose high till they passed into mountains; on the fourth was the castle with its slopes and batteries, the church and town beyond it, and everywhere luxuriant tropical forest trees overhanging the violet-coloured water. I could well understand the Frenchman's delight when he saw it, and also the satisfaction with which he would now acknowledge that he had been a shortsighted prophet. The English had obtained Grenada, and this is what they had made of it. The forts which had been erected by his countrymen had been deserted and dismantled; the castle on which we had seen our flag flying was a ruin; the walls were crumbling and in many places had fallen down. One solitary gun was left, but that was honeycombed and could be fired only with half a charge to salute with. It was true that the forts had ceased to be of use, but that was because there was nothing left to defend. The harbour is, as I said, the best in the West Indies. There was not a vessel in it, nor so much as a boat-yard that I could see where a spar could be replaced or a broken rivet mended. Once there had been a line of wharves, but the piles had been eaten by worms and the platforms had fallen through. Round us when we landed were unroofed warehouses, weed-choked courtyards, doors gone, and window frames fallen in or out. Such a scene of desolation and desertion I never saw in my life save once, a few weeks later at Jamaica. An English lady with her children had come to the landing place to meet my friends. They, too, were more like wandering ghosts than human beings with warm blood in them. All their thoughts were on going home—home out of so miserable an exile.[5]

Nature and the dark race had been simply allowed by us to resume possession of the island. Here, where the cannon had roared, and ships and armies had fought, and the enterprising English had entered into occupancy, under whom, as we are proud to fancy, the waste places of the earth grow green, and industry and civilisation follow as an inevitable fruit, all was now silence. And this was an English Crown colony, as rich in resources as any area of soil of equal size in the world. England had demanded and seized the responsibility of managing it—this was the result.

A gentleman who for some purpose was a passing resident in the island, had asked us to dine with him. His house was three or four miles inland. A good road remained as a legacy from other times, and a pair of horses and a phaeton carried us swiftly to his door. The town of St. George's had once been populous, and even now there seemed no want of people, if mere numbers sufficed. We passed for half a mile through a straggling street, where the houses were evidently occupied though unconscious for many a year of paint or repair. They were squalid and dilapidated, but the luxuriant bananas and orange trees in the gardens relieved the ugliness of their appearance. The road when we left the town was overshadowed with gigantic mangoes planted long ago, with almond trees and cedar trees, no relations of our almonds or our cedars, but the most splendid ornaments of the West Indian forest. The valley up which we drove was beautiful, and the house, when we reached it, showed taste and culture. Mr. —— had rare trees, rare flowers, and was taking advantage of his temporary residence in the tropics to make experiments in horticulture. He had been brought there, I believe, by some necessities of business. He told us that Grenada was now the ideal country of modern social reformers. It had become an island of pure peasant proprietors. The settlers, who had once been a thriving and wealthy community, had almost melted away. Some thirty English estates remained which could still be cultivated, and were being cultivated with remarkable success. But the rest had sold their estates for anything which they could get. The free blacks had bought them, and about 8,000 negro families, say 40,000 black souls in all, now shared three-fourths of the soil between them. Each family lived independently, growing coffee and cocoa and oranges, and all were doing very well. The possession of property had brought a sense of its rights with it. They were as litigious as Irish peasants; everyone was at law with his neighbour, and the island was a gold mine to the Attorney-General; otherwise they were quiet harmless fellows, and if the politicians would only let them alone, they would be perfectly contented, and might eventually, if wisely managed, come to some good. To set up a constitution in such a place was a ridiculous mockery, and would only be another name for swindling and jobbery. Black the island was, and black it would remain. The conditions were never likely to arise which would bring back a European population; but a governor who was a sensible man, who would reside and use his natural influence, could manage it with perfect ease. The island belonged to England; we were responsible for what we made of it, and for the blacks' own sakes we ought not to try experiments upon them. They knew their own deficiencies and would infinitely prefer a wise English ruler to any constitution which could be offered them. If left entirely to themselves, they would in a generation or two relapse into savages; there were but two alternatives before not Grenada only, but all the English West Indies—either an English administration pure and simple, like the East Indian, or a falling eventually into a state like that of Hayti, where they eat the babies, and no white man can own a yard of land.

It was dark night when we drove back to the port. The houses along the road, which had looked so miserable on the outside, were now lighted with paraffin lamps. I could see into them, and was astonished to observe signs of comfort and even signs of taste—arm-chairs, sofas, sideboards with cut glass upon them, engravings and coloured prints upon the walls. The old state of things is gone, but a new state of things is rising which may have a worth of its own. The plant of civilisation as yet has taken but feeble root, and is only beginning to grow. It may thrive yet if those who have troubled all the earth will consent for another century to take their industry elsewhere.

The ship's galley was waiting at the wharf when we reached it. The captain also had been dining with a friend on shore, and we had to wait for him. The off-shore night breeze had not yet risen. The harbour was smooth as a looking glass, and the stars shone double in the sky and on the water. The silence was only broken by the whistle of the lizards or the cry of some far-off marsh frog. The air was warmer than we ever feel it in the depth of an English summer, yet pure and delicious and charged with the perfume of a thousand flowers. One felt it strange that with so beautiful a possession lying at our doors, we should have allowed it to slide out of our hands. I could say for myself, like Père Labat, the island was all that man could desire. 'En un mot, la vie y est délicieuse.'

The anchor was got up immediately that we were on board. In the morning we were to find ourselves at Port of Spain. Mr. S——, the Windward Island governor, who had joined us at St. Vincent, was, as I said, going to Tobago. De Foe took the human part of his Robinson Crusoe from the story of Juan Fernandez. The locality is supposed to have been Tobago, and Trinidad the island from which the cannibal savages came. We are continually shuffling the cards, in a hope that a better game may be played with them. Tobago is now-annexed to Trinidad. Last year it was a part of Mr. S——'s dominions which he periodically visited. I fell in with him again on his return, and he told us an incident which befell him there, illustrating the unexpected shapes in which the schoolmaster is appearing among the blacks. An intimation was brought to him on his arrival that, as the Athenian journeymen had played Pyramus and Thisbe at the nuptials of Theseus and Hippolyta, so a party of villagers from the interior of Tobago would like to act before his Excellency. Of course he consented. They came, and went through their performance. To Mr. S——'s, and probably to the reader's astonishment, the play which they had selected was the 'Merchant of Venice.' Of the rest of it he perhaps thought, like the queen of the Amazons, that it was 'sorry stuff;' but Shylock's representative, he said, showed real appreciation. With freedom and a peasant proprietary, the money lender is a necessary phenomenon, and the actor's imagination may have been assisted by personal recollections.

FOOTNOTES:

[5]

I have been told that this picture is overdrawn, that Grenada is the most prosperous of the Antilles, that its exports are increasing, that English owners are making large profits again, that the blacks are thriving beyond example, that there are twenty guns in the Fort, that the wharves and Quay are in perfect condition, that there are no roofless warehouses, that in my description of St. George's I must have been asleep or dreaming. I can only repeat and insist upon what I myself saw. I know very well that in parts of the island a few energetic English gentlemen are cultivating their land with remarkable success. Any enterprising Englishman with capital and intelligence might do the same. I know also that in no part of the West Indies are the blacks happier or better off. But notwithstanding the English interest in the Island has sunk to relatively nothing. Once Englishmen owned the whole of it. Now there are only thirty English estates. There are five thousand peasant freeholds, owned almost entirely by coloured men, and the effect of the change is written upon the features of the harbour. Not a vessel of any kind was to be seen in it. The great wooden jetty where cargoes used to be landed, or taken on board, was a wreck, the piles eaten through, the platform broken. On the Quay there was no sign of life, or of business, the houses along the side mean and insignificant, while several large and once important buildings, warehouses, custom houses, dwelling houses, or whatever they had been, were lying in ruins, tropical trees growing in the courtyards, and tropical creepers climbing over the masonry showing how long the decay had been going on. These buildings had once belonged to English merchants, and were evidence of English energy and enterprise, which once had been and now had ceased to be. As to the guns in the fort, I cannot say how much old iron may be left there. But I was informed that only one gun could be fired and that with but half a charge.

This is of little consequence or none, but unless the English population can be reinforced, Grenada in another generation will cease to be English at all, while the prosperity, the progress, even the continued civilisation of the blacks depends on the maintenance there of English influence and authority.

CHAPTER VI.

Charles Kingsley at Trinidad—'Lay of the Last Buccaneer'—A French for-ban—Adventure at Aves—Mass on board a pirate ship—Port of Spain—A house in the tropics—A political meeting—Government House—The Botanical Gardens'—Kingsley's rooms—Sugar estates and coolies.

I might spare myself a description of Trinidad, for the natural features of the place, its forests and gardens, its exquisite flora, the loveliness of its birds and insects, have been described already, with a grace of touch and a fullness of knowledge which I could not rival if I tried, by my dear friend Charles Kingsley. He was a naturalist by instinct, and the West Indies and all belonging to them had been the passion of his life. He had followed the logs and journals of the Elizabethan adventurers till he had made their genius part of himself. In Amyas Leigh, the hero of 'Westward Ho,' he produced a figure more completely representative of that extraordinary set of men than any other novelist, except Sir Walter, has ever done for an age remote from his own. He followed them down into their latest developments, and sang their swan song in his 'Lay of the Last Buccaneer.' So characteristic is this poem of the transformation of the West Indies of romance and adventure into the West Indies of sugar and legitimate trade, that I steal it to ornament my own prosaic pages.

THE LAY OF THE LAST BUCCANEER.

Oh! England is a pleasant place for them that's rich and high,
But England is a cruel place for such poor folks as I;
And such a port for mariners I'll never see again
As the pleasant Isle of Aves beside the Spanish main.

There were forty craft in Aves that were both swift and stout,
All furnished well with small arms and cannon all about;
And a thousand men in Aves made laws so fair and free
To choose their valiant captains and obey them loyally.

Then we sailed against the Spaniard with his hoards of plate and gold,
Which he wrung with cruel tortures from Indian folks of old;
Likewise the merchant captains, with hearts as hard as stone,
Who flog men and keelhaul them and starve them to the bone.

Oh! palms grew high in Aves, and fruits that shone like gold,
And the colibris and parrots they were gorgeous to behold,
And the negro maids to Aves from bondage fast did flee
To welcome gallant sailors a sweeping in from sea.

Oh! sweet it was in Aves to hear the landward breeze,
A swing with good tobacco in a net between the trees,
With a negro lass to fan you while you listened to the roar
Of the breakers on the reef outside which never touched the shore.

But Scripture saith an ending to all fine things must be,
So the king's ships sailed on Aves and quite put down were we.
All day we fought like bull dogs, but they burnt the booms at night,
And I fled in a piragua sore wounded from the fight.

Nine days I floated starving, and a negro lass beside,
Till for all I tried to cheer her the poor young thing she died.
But as I lay a gasping a Bristol sail came by,
And brought me home to England here to beg until I die.

And now I'm old and going: I'm sure I can't tell where.
One comfort is, this world's so hard I can't be worse off there.
If I might but be a sea dove, I'd fly across the main
To the pleasant Isle of Aves to look at it once again.

By the side of this imaginative picture of a poor English sea rover, let me place another, an authentic one, of a French forban or pirate in the same seas. Kingsley's

Aves, or Isle of Birds, is down on the American coast. There is another island of the same name, which was occasionally frequented by the same gentry, about a hundred miles south of Dominica. Père Labat going once from Martinique to Guadaloupe had taken a berth with Captain Daniel, one of the most noted of the French corsairs of the day, for better security. People were not scrupulous in those times, and Labat and Daniel had been long good friends. They were caught in a gale off Dominica, blown away, and carried to Aves, where they found an English merchant ship lying a wreck. Two English ladies from Barbadoes and a dozen other people had escaped on shore. They had sent for help, and a large vessel came for them the day after Daniel's arrival. Of course he made a prize of it. Labat said prayers on board for him before the engagement, and the vessel surrendered after the first shot. The good humour of the party was not disturbed by this incident. The pirates, their prisoners, and the ladies stayed together for a fortnight at Aves, catching turtles and boucanning them, picnicking, and enjoying themselves. Daniel treated the ladies with the utmost politeness, carried them afterwards to St. Thomas's, dismissed them unransomed, sold his prizes, and wound up the whole affair to the satisfaction of every one. Labat relates all this with wonderful humour, and tells, among other things, the following story of Daniel. On some expedition, when he was not so fortunate as to have a priest on board, he was in want of provisions. Being an outlaw he could not furnish himself in an open port. One night he put into the harbour of a small island, called Los Santos, not far from Dominica, where only a few families resided. He sent a boat on shore in the darkness, took the priest and two or three of the chief inhabitants out of their beds, and carried them on board, where he held them as hostages, and then under pretence of compulsion requisitioned the island to send him what he wanted. The priest and his companions were treated meanwhile as guests of distinction. No violence was necessary, for all parties understood one another. While the stores were being collected, Daniel suggested that there was a good opportunity for his crew to hear mass. The priest of Los Santos agreed to say it for them. The sacred vessels c. were sent for from the church on shore. An awning was rigged over the forecastle, and an altar set up under it. The men chanted the prayers. The cannon answered the purpose of music. Broadsides were fired at the first sentence, at the Exaudiat, at the Elevation, at the Benediction, and a fifth at the prayer for the king. The service was wound up by a Vive le Roi! A single small accident only had disturbed the ceremony. One of the pirates, at the Elevation, being of a profane mind, made an indecent gesture. Daniel rebuked him, and, as the offence was repeated, drew a pistol and blew the man's brains out, saying he would do the same to any one who was disrespectful to the Holy Sacrament. The priest being a little startled, Daniel begged him not to be alarmed; he was only chastising a rascal to teach him his duty. At any rate, as Labat observed, he had effectually prevented the rascal from doing anything of the same kind again. Mass being over, the body was thrown overboard, and priest and congregation went their several ways.

Kingsley's 'At Last' gave Trinidad an additional interest to me, but even he had not prepared me completely for the place which I was to see. It is only when one has seen any object with one's own eyes, that the accounts given by others become recognisable and instructive.

Trinidad is the largest, after Jamaica, of the British West Indian Islands, and the hottest absolutely after none of them. It is square-shaped, and, I suppose, was once a part of South America. The Orinoco river and the ocean currents between them have cut a channel between it and the mainland, which has expanded into a vast shallow lake known as the Gulf of Paria. The two entrances by which the gulf is approached are narrow and are called bocas or mouths—one the Dragon's Mouth, the other the Serpent's. When the Orinoco is in flood, the water is brackish, and the brilliant violet blue of the Caribbean Sea is changed to a dirty yellow; but the harbour which is so formed would hold all the commercial navies of the world, and seems formed by nature to be the depôt one day of an enormous trade.

Trinidad has had its period of romance. Columbus was the first discoverer of it. Raleigh was there afterwards on his expedition in search of his gold mine, and tarred his vessels with pitch out of the famous lake. The island was alternately Spanish and French till Picton took it in 1797, since which time it has remained English. The Carib part of the population has long vanished. The rest of it is a medley of English, French, Spaniards, negroes, and coolies. The English, chiefly migratory, go there to make money and go home with it. The old colonial families have few representatives left, but the island prospers, trade increases, coolies increase, cocoa and coffee plantations and indigo plantations increase. Port of Spain, the capital, grows annually; and even sugar holds its own in spite of low prices, for there is money at the back of it, and a set of people who, being speculative and commercial, are better on a level with the times than the old-fashioned planter aristocracy of the other islands. The soil is of extreme fertility, about a fourth of it under cultivation, the rest natural forest and unappropriated Crown land.

We passed the 'Dragon's Jaws' before daylight. The sun had just risen when we anchored off Port of Spain. We saw before us the usual long line of green hills with mountains behind them; between the hills and the sea was a low, broad, alluvial plain, deposited by an arm of the Orinoco and by the other rivers which run into the gulf. The cocoa-nut palms thrive best on the water's edge. They stretched for miles on either side of us as a fringe to the shore. Where the water was shoal, there were vast swamps of mangrove, the lower branches covered with oysters.

However depressed sugar might be, business could not be stagnant. Ships of all nations lay round us taking in or discharging cargo. I myself formed for the time being part of the cargo of my friend and host Mr. G——, who had brought me to Trinidad, the accomplished son of a brilliant mother, himself a distinguished lawyer and member of the executive council of the island, a charming companion, an invaluable public servant, but with the temperament of a man of genius, half humorous, half melancholy, which does not find itself entirely at home in West Indian surroundings.

On landing we found ourselves in a large foreign-looking town, 'Port of Spain' having been built by French and Spaniards according to their national tendencies, and especially with a view to the temperature, which is that of a forcing house and rarely falls below 80°. The streets are broad and are planted with trees for shade, each house where room permits having a garden of its own, with palms and mangoes and coffee plants and creepers. Of sanitary arrangements there seemed to be none.

There is abundance of rain, and the gutters which run down by the footway are flushed almost every day. But they are all open. Dirt of every kind lies about freely, to be washed into them or left to putrefy as fate shall direct. The smell would not be pleasant without the help of that natural scavenger the Johnny crow, a black vulture who roosts on the trees and feeds in the middle of the streets. We passed a dozen of these unclean but useful birds in a fashionable thoroughfare gobbling up chicken entrails and refusing to be disturbed. When gorged they perch in rows upon the roofs. On the ground they are the nastiest to look at of all winged creatures; yet on windy days they presume to soar like their kindred, and when far up might be taken for eagles.

The town has between thirty and forty thousand people living in it, and the rain and Johnny crows between them keep off pestilence. Outside is a large savannah or park, where the villas are of the successful men of business. One of these belonged to my host, a cool airy habitation with open doors and windows, overhanging portico, and rooms into which all the winds might enter, but not the sun. A garden in front was shut off from the savannah by a fence of bananas. At the gate stood as sentinel a cabbage palm a hundred feet high; on the lawn mangoes, oranges, papaws, and bread-fruit trees, strange to look at, but luxuriantly shady. Before the door was a tree of good dimensions, whose name I have forgotten, the stem and branches of which were hung with orchids which G—— had collected in the woods. The borders were blazing with varieties of the single hibiscus, crimson, pink, and fawn colour, the largest that I had ever seen. The average diameter of each single flower was from seven to eight inches. Wind streamed freely through the long sitting room, loaded with the perfume of orange trees; on table and in bookcase the hand and mind visible of a gifted and cultivated man. The particular room assigned to myself would have been equally delightful but that my possession of it was disputed even in daylight by mosquitoes, who for bloodthirsty ferocity had a bad pre-eminence over the worst that I had ever met with elsewhere. I killed one who was at work upon me, and examined him through a glass. Bewick, with the inspiration of genius, had drawn his exact likeness as the devil—a long black stroke for a body, nick for neck, horns on the head, and a beak for a mouth, spindle arms, and longer spindle legs, two pointed wings, and a tail. Line for line there the figure was before me which in the unforgetable tailpiece is driving the thief under the gallows, and I had a melancholy satisfaction in identifying him. I had been warned to be on the look-out for scorpions, centipedes, jiggers, and land crabs, who would bite me if I walked slipperless over the floor in the dark. Of these I met with none, either there or anywhere, but the mosquito of Trinidad is enough by himself. For malice, mockery, and venom of tooth and trumpet, he is without a match in the world.

From mosquitoes, however, one could seek safety in tobacco smoke, or hide behind the lace curtains with which every bed is provided. Otherwise I found every provision to make life pass deliciously. To walk is difficult in a damp steamy temperature hotter during daylight than the hottest forcing house in Kew. I was warned not to exert myself and to take cocktail freely. In the evening I might venture out with the bats and take a drive if I wished in the twilight. Languidly charming as it all was, I could not help asking myself of what use such a possession could be either to England or the English nation. We could not colonise it, could not cultivate it, could not draw a revenue from it. If it prospered commercially the prosperity would be of French and Spaniards, mulattoes and blacks, but scarcely, if at all, of my own countrymen. For here too, as elsewhere, they were growing fewer daily, and those who remained were looking forward to the day when they could be released. If it were not for the honour of the thing, as the Irishman said after being carried in a sedan chair which had no bottom, we might have spared ourselves so unnecessary a conquest.

Beautiful, however, it was beyond dispute. Before sunset a carriage took us round the savannah. Tropical human beings, like tropical birds, are fond of fine colours, especially black human beings, and the park was as brilliant as Kensington Gardens on a Sunday. At nightfall the scene became yet more wonderful; air, grass, and trees being alight with fireflies, each as brilliant as an English glowworm. The palm tree at our own gate stood like a ghostly sentinel clear against the starry sky, a single long dead frond hanging from below the coronet of leaves and clashing against the stem as it was blown to and fro by the night wind, while long-winged bats swept and whistled over our heads.

The commonplace intrudes upon the imaginative. At moments one can fancy that the world is an enchanted place after all, but then comes generally an absurd awakening. On the first night of my arrival, before we went to bed there came an invitation to me to attend a political meeting which was to be held in a few days on the savannah. Trinidad is a purely Crown colony, and has escaped hitherto the introduction of the election virus. The newspapers and certain busy gentlemen in 'Port of Spain' had discovered that they were living under 'a degrading tyranny,' and they demanded a 'constitution.' They did not complain that their affairs had been ill managed. On the contrary, they insisted that they were the most prosperous of the West Indian colonies, and alone had a surplus in their treasury. If this was so, it seemed to me that they had better let well alone. The population, all told, was but 170,000, less by thirty thousand than that of Barbadoes. They were a mixed and motley assemblage of all races and colours, busy each with their own affairs, and never hitherto troubling themselves about politics. But it had pleased the Home Government to set up the beginning of a constitution again in Jamaica, no one knew why, but so it was, and Trinidad did not choose to be behindhand. The official appointments were valuable, and had been hitherto given away by the Crown. The local popularities very naturally wished to have them for themselves. This was the reality in the thing so far as there was a reality. It was dressed up in the phrases borrowed from the great English masters of the art, about privileges of manhood, moral dignity, the elevating influence of the suffrage, c., intended for home consumption among the believers in the orthodox Radical faith.

For myself I could but reply to the gentlemen who had sent the invitation, that I was greatly obliged by the compliment, but that I knew too little of their affairs to make my presence of any value to them. As they were doing so well, I did not see myself why they wanted an alteration. Political changes were generally little more than turns of a kaleidoscope; you got a new pattern, but it was made of the same pieces, and things went on much as before. If they wanted political liberty I did not doubt that they would get it if they were loud and persistent enough. Only they must understand that at home we were now a democracy. Any constitution which was granted them would be on the widest basis. The blacks and coolies outnumbered the Europeans by four to one, and perhaps when they had what they asked for they might be less pleased than they expected.

You rise early in the tropics. The first two hours of daylight are the best of the day. My friend drove me round the town in his buggy the next morning. My second duty was to pay my respects to the Governor, Sir William Robinson, who had kindly offered me hospitality, and for which I must present myself to thank him. In Sir William I found one of those happy men whose constitution is superior to climate, who can do a long day's work in his office, play cricket or lawn tennis in the afternoon, and entertain his miscellaneous subjects in the evening with sumptuous hospitality—a vigorous, effective, perhaps ambitious gentleman, with a clear eye to the views of his employers at home on whom his promotion depends—certain to make himself agreeable to them, likely to leave his mark to useful purpose on the colonies over which he presides or may preside hereafter. Here in Trinidad he was learning Spanish in addition to his other linguistic accomplishments, that he might show proper courtesies to Spanish residents and to visitors from South America.

The 'Residence' stands in a fine situation, in large grounds of its own at the foot of the mountains. It has been lately built regardless of expense, for the colony is rich, and likes to do things handsomely. On the lawn, under the windows, stood a tree which was entirely new to me, an enormous ceiba or silk cotton tree, umbrella shaped, fifty yards in diameter, the huge and buttressed trunk throwing out branches so massive that one wondered how any woody fibre could bear the strain of their weight, the boughs twisting in and out till they made a roof over one's head, which was hung with every fantastic variety of parasites.

Vast as the ceibas were which I saw afterwards in other parts of the West Indies, this was the largest. The ceiba is the sacred tree of the negro, the temple of Jumbi the proper home of Obeah. To cut one down is impious. No black in his right mind would wound even the bark. A Jamaica police officer told me that if a ceiba had to be removed, the men who used the axe were well dosed with rum to give them courage to defy the devil.

From Government House we strolled into the adjoining Botanical Gardens. I had long heard of the wonders of these. The reality went beyond description. Plants with which I was familiar as shrubs in English conservatories were here expanded into forest giants, with hundreds of others of which we cannot raise even Lilliputian imitations. Let man be what he will, nature in the tropics is always grand. Palms were growing in the greatest luxuriance, of every known species, from the cabbage towering up into the sky to the fan palm of the desert whose fronds are reservoirs of water. Of exogenous trees, the majority were leguminous in some shape or other, forming flowers like a pea or vetch and hanging their seed in pods; yet in shape and foliage they distanced far the most splendid ornaments of an English park. They had Old World names with characters wholly different: cedars which were not conifers, almonds which were no relations to peaches, and gum trees as unlike eucalypti as one tree can be unlike another. Again, you saw forms which you seemed to recognise till some unexpected anomaly startled you out of your mistake. A gigantic Portugal laurel, or what I took for such, was throwing out a flower direct from the stem like a cactus. Grandest among them all, and happily in full bloom, was the sacred tree of Burmah, the Amherstia nobilis, at a distance like a splendid horse-chestnut, with crimson blossoms in pendant bunches, each separate flower in the convolution of its parts exactly counterfeiting a large orchid, with which it has not the faintest affinity, the Amherstia being leguminous like the rest.

Underneath, and dispersed among the imperial beauties, were spice trees, orange trees, coffee plants and cocoa, or again, shrubs with special virtues or vices. We had to be careful what we were about, for fruits of fairest appearance were tempting us all round. My companion was preparing to eat something to encourage me to do the same. A gardener stopped him in time. It was nux vomica. I was straying along a less frequented path, conscious of a heavy vaporous odour, in which I might have fainted had I remained exposed to it. I was close to a manchineel tree.

Prettiest and freshest were the nutmegs, which had a glen all to themselves and perfumed the surrounding air. In Trinidad and in Grenada I believe the nutmegs are the largest that are known, being from thirty to forty feet high; leaves brilliant green, something like the leaves of an orange, but extremely delicate and thin, folded one over the other, the lowest branches sweeping to the ground till the whole tree forms a natural bower, which is proof against a tropical shower. The fragrance attracts moths and flies; not mosquitoes, who prefer a ranker atmosphere. I saw a pair of butterflies the match of which I do not remember even in any museum, dark blue shot with green like a peacock's neck, and the size of English bats. I asked a black boy to catch me one. 'That sort no let catchee, massa,' he said; and I was penitently glad to hear it.

Among the wonders of the gardens are the vines as they call them, that is, the creepers of various kinds that climb about the other trees. Standing in an open space there was what once had been a mighty 'cedar.' It was now dead, only the trunk and dead branches remaining, and had been murdered by a 'fig' vine which had started from the root, twined itself like a python round the stem, strangled out the natural life, and spreading out in all directions had covered boughs and twigs with a foliage not their own. So far the 'vine' had done no worse than ivy does at home, but there was one feature about it which puzzled me altogether. The lowest of the original branches of the cedar were about twenty feet above our heads. From these in four or five places the parasite had let fall shoots, perhaps an inch in diameter, which descended to within a foot of the ground and then suddenly, without touching that or anything, formed a bight like a rope, went straight up again, caught hold of the branch from which they started, and so hung suspended exactly as an ordinary swing. In three distinctly perfect instances the 'vine' had executed this singular evolution, while at the extremity of one of the longest and tallest branches high up in the air it had made a clean leap of fifteen feet without visible help and had caught hold of another tree adjoining on the same level. These performances were so inexplicable that I conceived that they must have been a freak of the gardener's. I was mistaken. He said that at particular times in the year the fig vine threw out fine tendrils which hung downwards like strings. The strongest among them would lay hold of two or three others and climb up upon them, the rest would die and drop off, while the successful one, having found support for itself above, would remain swinging in the air and thicken and prosper. The leap he explained by the wind. I retained a suspicion that the wind had been assisted by some aspiring energy in the plant itself, so bold it was and so ambitious.

But the wonders of the garden were thrown into the shade by the cottage at the extreme angle of it (the old Government House before the present fabric had been erected), where Kingsley had been the guest of Sir Arthur Gordon. It is a long straggling wooden building with deep verandahs lying in a hollow overshadowed by trees, with views opening out into the savannah through arches formed by clumps of tall bamboos, the canes growing thick in circular masses and shooting up a hundred feet into the air, where they meet and form frames for the landscape, peculiar and even picturesque when there are not too many of them. These bamboos were Kingsley's special delight, as he had never seen the like of them elsewhere. The room in which he wrote is still shown, and the gallery where he walked up and down with his long pipe. His memory is cherished in the island as of some singular and beautiful presence which still hovers about the scenes which so delighted him in the closing evening of his own life.

It was the dry season, mid-winter, yet raining every day for two or three hours, and when it rains in these countries it means business. When the sky cleared the sun was intolerably hot, and distant expeditions under such conditions suited neither my age nor my health. With cocktail I might have ventured, but to cocktail I could never heartily reconcile myself. Trinidad has one wonder in it, a lake of bitumen some ninety acres in extent, which all travellers are expected to visit, and which few residents care to visit. A black lake is not so beautiful as an ordinary lake. I had no doubt that it existed, for the testimony was unimpeachable. Indeed I was shown an actual specimen of the crystallised pitch itself. I could believe without seeing and without undertaking a tedious journey. I rather sympathised with a noble lord who came to Port of Spain in his yacht, and like myself had the lake impressed upon him. As a middle course between going thither and appearing to slight his friends' recommendations, he said that he would send his steward.

In Trinidad, as everywhere else, my own chief desire was to see the human inhabitants, to learn what they were doing, how they were living, and what they were thinking about, and this could best be done by drives about the town and neighbourhood. The cultivated land is a mere fringe round the edges of the forest. Three-fourths of the soil are untouched. The rivers running out of the mountains have carved out the usual long deep valleys, and spread the bottoms with rich alluvial soil. Here among the wooded slopes are the country houses of the merchants. Here are the cabins of the black peasantry with their cocoa and coffee and orange plantations, which as in Grenada they hold largely as freeholds, reproducing as near as possible the life in Paradise of our first parents, without the consciousness of a want which they are unable to gratify, not compelled to work, for the earth of her own self bears for them all that they need, and ignorant that there is any difference between moral good and evil.

Large sugar estates, of course, there still are, and as the owners have not succeeded in bringing the negroes to work regularly for them,[6] they have introduced a few thousand Coolies under indentures for five years. These Asiatic importations are very happy in Trinidad; they save money, and many of them do not return home when their time is out, but stay where they are, buy land, or go into trade. They are proud, however, and will not intermarry with the Africans. Few bring their families with them; and women being scanty among them, there arise inconveniences and sometimes serious crimes.

It were to be wished that there was more prospect of the Coolie race becoming permanent than I fear there is. They work excellently. They are picturesque additions to the landscape, as they keep to the bright colours and graceful drapery of India. The grave dignity of their faces contrasts remarkably with the broad, good-humoured, but common features of the African. The black women look with envy at the straight hair of Asia, and twist their unhappy wool into knots and ropes in the vain hope of being mistaken for the purer race; but this is all. The African and the Asiatic will not mix, and the African being the stronger will and must prevail in Trinidad as elsewhere in the West Indies. Out of a total population of 170,000, there are 25,000 whites and mulattoes, 10,000 coolies, the rest negroes. The English part of the Europeans shows no tendency to increase. The English come as birds of passage, and depart when they have made their fortunes. The French and Spaniards may hold on to Trinidad as a home. Our people do not make homes there, and must be looked on as a transient element.

FOOTNOTES:

[6]

The negroes in the interior are beginning to cultivate sugar cane in small patches, with common mills to break it up. If the experiment succeeds it may extend.

CHAPTER VII.

A Coolie village—Negro freeholds—Waterworks—Pythons—Slavery—Evidence of Lord Rodney—Future of the negroes—Necessity of English rule—The Blue Basin—Black boy and cray fish.

The second morning after my arrival, my host took me to a Coolie village three miles beyond the town. The drive was between spreading cane fields, beneath the shade of bamboos, or under rows of cocoa-nut palms, between the stems of which the sea was gleaming.

Human dwelling places are rarely interesting in the tropics. A roof which will keep the rain out is all that is needed. The more free the passage given to the air under the floor and through the side, the more healthy the habitation; and the houses, when we came among them, seemed merely enlarged packing cases loosely nailed together and raised on stones a foot or two from the ground. The rest of the scene was picturesque enough. The Indian jewellers were sitting cross-legged before their charcoal pans, making silver bracelets and earrings. Brilliant garments, crimson and blue and orange, were hanging to dry on clothes lines. Men were going out to their work, women cooking, children (not many) playing or munching sugar cane, while great mango trees and ceibas spread a cool green roof over all. Like Rachel, the Coolies had brought their gods to their new home. In the centre of the village was a

Hindoo temple, made up rudely out of boards with a verandah running round it. The doors were locked. An old man who had charge told us we could not enter; a crowd, suspicious and sullen, gathered about us as we tried to prevail upon him; so we had to content ourselves with the outside, which was gaudily and not unskilfully painted in Indian fashion. There were gods and goddesses in various attitudes; Vishnu fighting with the monkey god, Vishnu with cutlass and shield, the monkey with his tail round one tree while he brandished two others, one in each hand, as clubs. I suppose that we smiled, for our curiosity was resented, and we found it prudent to withdraw.

The Coolies are useful creatures. Without them sugar cultivation in Trinidad and Demerara would cease altogether. They are useful and they are singularly ornamental. Unfortunately they have not the best character with the police. There is little crime among the negroes, who quarrel furiously with their tongues only. The Coolies have the fiercer passions of their Eastern blood. Their women being few are tempted occasionally into infidelities, and would be tempted more often but that a lapse in virtue is so fearfully avenged. A Coolie regards his wife as his property, and if she is unfaithful to him he kills her without the least hesitation. One of the judges told me that he had tried a case of this kind, and could not make the man understand that he had done anything wrong. It is a pity that a closer intermixture between them and the negroes seems so hopeless, for it would solve many difficulties. There is no jealousy. The negro does not regard the Coolie as a competitor and interloper who has come to lower his wages. The Coolie comes to work. The negro does not want to work, and both are satisfied. But if there is no jealousy there is no friendship. The two races are more absolutely apart than the white and the black. The Asiatic insists the more on his superiority in the fear perhaps that if he did not the white might forget it.

Among the sights in the neighbourhood of Port of Spain are the waterworks, extensive basins and reservoirs a few miles off in the hills. We chose a cool afternoon, when the temperature in the shade was not above 86°, and went to look at them. It was my first sight of the interior of the island, and my first distinct acquaintance with the change which had come over the West Indies. Trinidad is not one of our oldest possessions, but we had held it long enough for the old planter civilisation to take root and grow, and our road led us through jungles of flowering shrubs which were running wild over what had been once cultivated estates. Stranger still (for one associates colonial life instinctively with what is new and modern), we came at one place on an avenue of vast trees, at the end of which stood the ruins of a mansion of some great man of the departed order. Great man he must have been, for there was a gateway half crumbled away on which were his crest and shield in stone, with supporters on either side, like the Baron of Bradwardine's Bears; fallen now like them, but unlike them never, I fear, to be set up again. The Anglo-West Indians, like the English gentry in Ireland, were a fine race of men in their day, and perhaps the improving them off the earth has been a less beneficial process in either case than we are in the habit of supposing.

Entering among the hills we came on their successors. In Trinidad there are 18,000 freeholders, most of them negroes and representatives of the old slaves. Their cabins are spread along the road on either side, overhung with bread-fruit trees, tamarinds, calabash trees, out of which they make their cups and water jugs. The luscious granadilla climbs among the branches; plantains throw their cool shade over the doors; oranges and limes and citrons perfume the air, and droop their boughs under the weight of their golden burdens. There were yams in the gardens and cows in the paddocks, and cocoa bushes loaded with purple or yellow pods. Children played about in swarms, in happy idleness and abundance, with schools, too, at intervals, and an occasional Catholic chapel, for the old religion prevails in Trinidad, never having been disturbed. What form could human life assume more charming than that which we were now looking on? Once more, the earth does not contain any peasantry so well off, so well cared for, so happy, so sleek and contented as the sons and daughters of the emancipated slaves in the English West Indian Islands. Sugar may fail the planter, but cocoa, which each peasant can grow with small effort for himself, does not fail and will not. He may 'better his condition,' if he has any such ambition, without stirring beyond his own ground, and so far, perhaps, his ambition may extend, if it is not turned off upon politics. Even the necessary evils of the tropics are not many or serious. His skin is proof against mosquitoes. There are snakes in Trinidad as there were snakes in Eden. 'Plenty snakes,' said one of them who was at work in his garden, 'plenty snakes, but no bitee.' As to costume, he would prefer the costume of innocence if he was allowed. Clothes in such a climate are superfluous for warmth, and to the minds of the negroes, unconscious as they are of shame, superfluous for decency. European prejudice, however, still passes for something; the women have a love for finery, which would prevent a complete return to African simplicity; and in the islands which are still French, and in those like Trinidad, which the French originally colonised, they dress themselves with real taste. They hide their wool in red or yellow handkerchiefs, gracefully twisted; or perhaps it is not only to conceal the wool. Columbus found the Carib women of the island dressing their hair in the same fashion.[7]

The waterworks, when we reached them, were even more beautiful than we had been taught to expect. A dam has been driven across a perfectly limpid mountain stream; a wide open area has been cleared, levelled, strengthened with masonry, and divided into deep basins and reservoirs, through which the current continually flows. Hedges of hibiscus shine with crimson blossoms. Innumerable humming birds glance to and fro among the trees and shrubs, and gardens and ponds are overhung by magnificent bamboos, which so astonished me by their size that I inquired if their height had been measured. One of them, I was told, had lately fallen, and was found to be 130 feet long. A single drawback only there was to this enchanting spot, and it was again the snakes. There are huge pythons in Trinidad which are supposed to have crossed the straits from the continent. The cool water pools attract them, and they are seen occasionally coiled among the branches of the bamboos. Some washerwomen at work in the stream had been disturbed a few days before our visit by one of these monsters, who had come down to see what they were about. They are harmless, but trying to the nerves. One of the men about the place shot this one, and he told me that he had shot another a short time before asleep in a tree. The keeper of the works was a retired soldier, an Irish-Scot from Limerick, hale, vigorous, and happy as the blacks themselves. He had married one of them—a remarkable exception to an almost universal rule. He did not introduce us, but the dark lady passed by us in gorgeous costume, just noticing our presence with a sweep which would have done credit to a duchess.

We made several similar small expeditions into the settled parts of the neighbourhood, seeing always (whatever else we saw) the boundless happiness of the black race. Under the rule of England in these islands the two million of these poor brothers-in-law of ours are the most perfectly contented specimens of the human race to be found upon the planet. Even Schopenhauer, could he have known them, would have admitted that there were some of us who were not hopelessly wretched. If happiness be the satisfaction of every conscious desire, theirs is a condition which admits of no improvement: were they independent, they might quarrel among themselves, and the weaker become the bondmen of the stronger; under the beneficent despotism of the English Government, which knows no difference of colour and permits no oppression, they can sleep, lounge, and laugh away their lives as they please, fearing no danger. If they want money, work and wages are waiting for them. No one can say what may be before them hereafter. The powers which envy human beings too perfect felicity may find ways one day of disturbing the West Indian negro; but so long as the English rule continues, he may be assured of the same tranquil existence.

As life goes he has been a lucky mortal. He was taken away from Dahomey and Ashantee—to be a slave indeed, but a slave to a less cruel master than he would have found at home. He had a bad time of it occasionally, and the plantation whip and the branding irons are not all dreams, yet his owner cared for him at least as much as he cared for his cows and his horses. Kind usage to animals is more economical than barbarity, and Englishmen in the West Indies were rarely inhuman. Lord Rodney says:

'I have been often in all the West India Islands, and I have often made my observations on the treatment of the negro slaves, and can aver that I never knew the least cruelty inflicted on them, but that in general they lived better than the honest day-labouring man in England, without doing a fourth part of his work in a day, and I am fully convinced that the negroes in our islands are better provided for and live better than when in Guinea.'

Rodney, it is true, was a man of facts and was defective in sentiment. Let us suppose him wrong, let us believe the worst horrors of the slave trade or slave usage as fluent tongue of missionary or demagogue has described them, yet nevertheless, when we consider what the lot of common humanity has been and is, we shall be dishonest if we deny that the balance has been more than redressed; and the negroes who were taken away out of Africa, as compared with those who were left at home, were as the 'elect to salvation,' who after a brief purgatory are secured an eternity of blessedness. The one condition is the maintenance of the authority of the English crown. The whites of the islands cannot equitably rule them. They have not shaken off the old traditions. If, for the sake of theory or to shirk responsibility, we force them to govern themselves, the state of Hayti stands as a ghastly example of the condition into which they will then inevitably fall. If we persist, we shall be sinning against light—the clearest light that was ever given in such affairs. The most hardened believers in the regenerating effects of political liberty cannot be completely blind to the ruin which the infliction of it would necessarily bring upon the race for whose interests they pretend particularly to care.

The Pitch Lake I resisted all exhortations to visit, but the days in the forest were delightful—pre-eminently a day which we spent at the 'Blue Basin,' a pool scooped out in the course of ages by a river falling through a mountain gorge; blue, not from any colour in the water, which is purely transparent, but from a peculiar effect of sky reflection through an opening in the overhanging trees. As it was far off, we had to start early and encounter the noonday heat. We had to close the curtains of the carriage to escape the sun, and in losing the sun we shut out the wind. All was well, however, when we turned into the hills. Thenceforward the road followed the bottom of a densely wooded ravine; impenetrable foliage spreading over our heads, and a limpid river flashing along in which our horses cooled their feet and lips as we crossed it again and again. There were the usual cabins and gardens on either side of us, sometimes single, sometimes clustering into villages, and high above them the rocks stood out, broken into precipices or jutting out into projecting crags, with huge trees starting from the crevices, dead trunks with branching arms clothed scantily with creepers, or living giants with blue or orange-coloured flowers. Mangoes scented the valley with their blossom. Bananas waved their long broad leaves—some flat and unbroken as we know them in conservatories, some split into palm-like fronds which quivered in the breeze. The cocoa pods were ripe or ripening, those which had been gathered being left on the ground in heaps as we see apples in autumn in an English orchard.

We passed a lady on the way who was making sketches and daring the mosquitoes, that were feeding at leisure upon her face and arms. The road failed us at last. We alighted with our waterproofs and luncheon basket. A couple of half-naked boys sprang forward to act as guides and porters—nice little fellows, speaking a French patois for their natural language, but with English enough to earn shillings and amuse the British tourist. With their help we scrambled along a steep slippery path, the river roaring below, till we came to a spot where, the rock being soft, a waterfall had cut out in the course of ages a natural hollow, of which the trees formed the roof, and of which the floor was the pool we had come in search of. The fall itself was perpendicular, and fifty or sixty feet high, the water issuing at the top out of a dark green tunnel among overhanging branches. The sides of the basin were draped with the fronds of gigantic ferns and wild plantains, all in wild luxuriance and dripping with the spray. In clefts above the rocks, large cedars or gum trees had struck their roots and flung out their gnarled and twisted branches, which were hung with ferns; while at the lower end of the pool, where the river left it again, there grew out from among the rocks near the water's edge tall and exquisitely grouped acacias with crimson flowers for leaves.

BLUE BASIN, TRINIDAD.
BLUE BASIN, TRINIDAD.

The place broke on us suddenly as we scrambled round a corner from below. Three young blacks were bathing in the pool, and as we had a lady with us, they were induced, though sullenly and with some difficulty, to return into their scanty garments and depart. Never certainly was there a more inviting spot to swim in, the more so from exciting possibilities of adventure. An English gentleman went to bathe there shortly before our coming. He was on a rock, swaying his body for a plunge, when something caught his eye among the shadows at the bottom. It proved to be a large dead python.

We had not the luck ourselves of falling in with so interesting a beast. Great butterflies and perhaps a humming bird or two were flitting among the leaves as we came up; other signs of life there were none, unless we call life the motion of the plantain leaves, waving in the draughts of air which were eddying round the waterfall. We sat down on stones, or on the trunk of a fallen tree, the mosquitoes mercifully sparing us. We sketched a little, talked a little, ate our sandwiches, and the male part of us lighted our cigars. G—— then, to my surprise, produced a fly rod. In the streams in the Antilles, which run out of the mountains, there is a fish in great abundance which they call mullet, an inferior trout, but a good substitute where the real thing is not. He runs sometimes to five pounds weight, will take the fly, and is much sought after by those who try to preserve in the tropics the amusements and habits of home. G—— had caught many of them in Dominica. If in Dominica, why not in Trinidad?

He put his tackle together, tied up a cast of trout flies, and commenced work. He tried the still water at the lower end of the basin. He crept round the rock and dropped his line into the foam at the foot of the fall. No mullet rose, nor fish of any kind. One of our small boys had looked on with evident impatience. He cried out at last, 'No mullet, but plenty crayfish,' pointing down into the water; and there, following the direction of his finger, we beheld strange grey creatures like cuttle-fish, moving about on the points of their toes, the size of small lobsters. The flies were dismounted, a bare hook was fitted on a fine gut trace, with a split shot or two to sink the line, all trim and excellent. A fresh-water shrimp was caught under a stone for a bait. G—— went to work, and the strange things took hold and let themselves be lifted halfway to the surface. But then, somehow, they let go and disappeared.

Our small boy said nothing; but I saw a scornful smite upon his lips. He picked up a thin dry cane, found some twine in the luncheon basket which had tied up our sandwiches, found a pin there also, and bent it, and put a shrimp on it. With a pebble stone for a sinker he started in competition, and in a minute he had brought out upon the rock the strangest thing in the shape of a fish which I had ever seen in fresh water or salt. It was a true 'crayfish,' écrevisse, eight inches long, formed regularly with the thick powerful tail, the sharp serrated snout, the long antennæ, and the spider-like legs of the lobster tribe. As in a crayfish, the claws were represented by the correctly shaped but diminutive substitutes.

When we had done wondering at the prize, we could admire the smile of conscious superiority in the face of the captor. The fine tackle had been beaten, as usual, by the proverbial string and crooked pin, backed by knowledge in the head of a small nigger boy.

FOOTNOTES:

[7]

Traen las cabezas atadas con unos panuelos labrados hermosos que parecen de lejos de seda y almazarrones.

CHAPTER VIII.

Home Rule in Trinidad—Political aspirations—Nature of the problem—Crown administration—Colonial governors—A Russian apologue—Dinner at Government House—'The Three Fishers'—Charles Warner—Alternative futures of the colony.

The political demonstration to which I had been invited came off the next day on the savannah. The scene was pretty enough. Black coats and white trousers, bright-coloured dresses and pink parasols, look the same at a distance whether the wearer has a black face or a white one, and the broad meadow was covered over with sparkling groups. Several thousand persons must have attended, not all to hear the oratory, for the occasion had been taken when the Governor was to play close by in a cricket match, and half the crowd had probably collected to see His Excellency at the wicket. Placards had been posted about the town, setting out the purpose of the meeting. Trinidad, as I said, is at present a Crown colony, the executive council and the legislature being equally nominated by the authorities. The popular orators, the newspaper writers, and some of the leading merchants in Port of Spain had discovered, as I said, that they were living under what they called 'a degrading tyranny.' They had no grievances, or none that they alleged, beyond the general one that they had no control over the finance. They very naturally desired that the lucrative Government appointments for which the colony paid should be distributed among themselves. The elective principle had been reintroduced in Jamaica, evidently as a step towards the restoration of the full constitution which had been surrendered and suppressed after the Gordon riots. Trinidad was almost as large as Jamaica, in proportion to the population wealthier and more prosperous, and the people were invited to come together in overwhelming numbers to insist that the 'tyranny' should end. The Home Government in their action about Jamaica had shown a spontaneous readiness to transfer responsibility from themselves to the inhabitants. The promoters of the meeting at Port of Spain may have thought that a little pressure on their part might not be unwelcome as an excuse for further concessions of the same kind. Whether this was so I do not know. At any rate they showed that they were as yet novices in the art of agitation. The language of the placard of invitation was so violent that, in the opinion of the legal authorities, the printer might have been indicted for high treason. The speakers did their best to imitate the fine phrases of the apostles of liberty in Europe, but they succeeded only in caricaturing their absurdities. The proceedings were described at length in the rival newspapers. One gentleman's speech was said to have been so brilliant that every sentence was a 'gem of oratory,' the gem of gems being when he told his hearers that, 'if they went into the thing at all, they should go the entire animal.' All went off good-humouredly. In the Liberal journal the event of the day was spoken of as the most magnificent demonstration in favour of human freedom which had ever been seen in the West Indian Islands. In the Conservative journal it was called a ridiculous fiasco, and the people were said to have come together only to admire the Governor's batting, and to laugh at the nonsense which was coming from the platform. Finally, the same journal assured us that, beyond a handful of people who were interested in getting hold of the anticipated spoils of office, no one in the island cared about the matter.

The result, I believe, was some petition or other which would go home and pass as evidence, to minds eager to believe, that Trinidad was rapidly ripening for responsible government, promising relief to an overburdened Secretary for the Colonies, who has more to do than he can attend to, and is pleased with opportunities of gratifying popular sentiment, or of showing off in Parliament the development of colonial institutions. He knows nothing, can know nothing, of the special conditions of our hundred dependencies. He accepts what his representatives in the several colonies choose to tell him; and his representatives, being birds of passage responsible only to their employers at home, and depending for their promotion on making themselves agreeable, are under irresistible temptations to report what it will please the Secretary of State to hear.

For the Secretary of State, too, is a bird of passage as they are, passing through the Colonial Office on his way to other departments, or holding the seals as part of an administration whose tenure of office grows every year more precarious, which exists only upon popular sentiment, and cannot, and does not try to look forward beyond at furthest the next session of Parliament.

But why, it may be asked, should not Trinidad govern itself as well as Tasmania or New Zealand? Why not Jamaica, why not all the West Indian Islands? I will answer by another question. Do we wish these islands to remain as part of the British Empire? Are they of any use to us, or have we responsibilities connected with them of which we are not entitled to divest ourselves? A government elected by the majority of the people (and no one would think of setting up constitutions on any other basis) reflects from the nature of things the character of the electors. All these islands tend to become partitioned into black peasant proprietaries. In Grenada the process is almost complete. In Trinidad it is rapidly advancing. No one can stop it. No one ought to wish to stop it. But the ownership of freeholds is one thing, and political power is another. The blacks depend for the progress which they may be capable of making on the presence of a white community among them; and although it is undesirable or impossible for the blacks to be ruled by the minority of the white residents, it is equally undesirable and equally impossible that the whites should be ruled by them. The relative numbers of the two races being what they are, responsible government in Trinidad means government by a black parliament and a black ministry. The negro voters might elect, to begin with, their half-caste attorneys or such whites (the most disreputable of their colour) as would court their suffrages. But the black does not love the mulatto, and despises the white man who consents to be his servant. He has no grievances. He is not naturally a politician, and if left alone with his own patch of land, will never trouble himself to look further. But he knows what has happened in St. Domingo. He has heard that his race is already in full possession of the finest of all the islands. If he has any thought or any hopes about the matter, it is that it may be with the rest of them as it has been with St. Domingo, and if you force the power into his hands, you must expect him to use it. Under the constitution which you would set up, whites and blacks may be nominally equal; but from the enormous preponderance of numbers the equality would be only in name, and such English people, at least, as would be really of any value, would refuse to remain in a false and intolerable position. Already the English population of Trinidad is dwindling away under the uncertainties of their future position. Complete the work, set up a constitution with a black prime minister and a black legislature, and they will withdraw of themselves before they are compelled to go. Spaniards and French might be tempted by advantages of trade to remain in Port of Spain, as a few are still to be found in Hayti. They, it is possible, might in time recover and reassert their supremacy. Englishmen have the world open to them, and will prefer lands where they can live under less degrading conditions. In Hayti the black republic allows no white man to hold land in freehold. The blacks elsewhere with the same opportunities will develop the same aspirations.

Do we, or do we not, intend to retain our West Indian Islands under the sovereignty of the Queen? If we are willing to let them go, the question is settled. But we ought to face the alternative. There is but one form of government under which we can retain these colonies with honour and security to ourselves and with advantage to the negroes whom we have placed there—the mode of government which succeeds with us so admirably that it is the world's wonder in the East Indies, a success so unique and so extraordinary that it seems the last from which we are willing to take example.

In Natal, where the circumstances are analogous, and where report says that efforts are being also made to force on constitutional independence, I remember suggesting a few years ago that the governor should be allowed to form his own council, and that in selecting the members of it he should go round the colony, observe the farms where the land was well inclosed, the fields clean, the farm buildings substantial and in good repair; that he should call on the owners of these to be his advisers and assistants. In all Natal he might find a dozen such. They would be unwilling to leave their own business for so thankless a purpose; but they might be induced by good feeling to grant him a few weeks of their time. Under such an administration I imagine Natal would have a happier future before it than it will experience with the boon which is designed for it.

In the West Indies there is indefinite wealth waiting to be developed by intelligence and capital; and men with such resources, both English and American, might be tempted still to settle there, and lead the blacks along with them into more settled manners and higher forms of civilisation. But the future of the blacks, and our own influence over them for good, depend on their being protected from themselves and from the schemers who would take advantage of them. However little may be the share to which the mass of a population be admitted in the government of their country, they are never found hard to manage where they prosper and are justly dealt with. The children of darkness are even easier of control than the children of light. Under an administration formed on the model of that of our Eastern Empire these islands would be peopled in a generation or two with dusky citizens, as proud as the rest of us of the flag under which they will have thriven, and as willing to defend it against any invading enemy as they are now unquestionably indifferent. Partially elected councils, local elected boards, c., serve only as contrivances to foster discontent and encourage jobbery. They open a rift which time will widen, and which will create for us, on a smaller scale, the conditions which have so troubled us in Ireland, where each concession of popular demands makes the maintenance of the connection more difficult. In the Pacific colonies self-government is a natural right; the colonists are part of ourselves, and have as complete a claim to the management of their own affairs as we have to the management of ours. The less we interfere with them the more heartily they identify themselves with us. But if we choose besides to indulge our ambition with an empire, if we determine to keep attached to our dominion countries which, like the East Indies, have been conquered by the sword, countries, like the West Indies, which, however acquired, are occupied by races enormously outnumbering us, many of whom do not speak our language, are not connected with us by sentiment, and not visibly connected by interest, with whom our own people will not intermarry or hold social intercourse, but keep aloof from, as superior from inferior—to impose on such countries forms of self-government at which we have ourselves but lately arrived, to put it in the power of these overwhelming numbers to shake us off if they please, and to assume that when our real motive has been only to save ourselves trouble they will be warmed into active loyalty by gratitude for the confidence which we pretend to place in them, is to try an experiment which we have not the slightest right to expect to be successful, and which if it fails is fatal.

Once more, if we mean to keep the blacks as British subjects, we are bound to govern them, and to govern them well. If we cannot do it, we had better let them go altogether. And here is the real difficulty. It is not that men competent for such a task cannot be found. Among the public servants of Great Britain there are persons always to be found fit and willing for posts of honour and difficulty if a sincere effort be made to find them. Alas! in times past we have sent persons to rule our Baratarias to whom Sancho Panza was a sage—troublesome members of Parliament, younger brothers of powerful families, impecunious peers; favourites, with backstairs influence, for whom a provision was to be found; colonial clerks, bred in the office, who had been obsequious and useful.

One had hoped that in the new zeal for the colonial connection such appointments would have become impossible for the future, yet a recent incident at the Mauritius has proved that the colonial authorities are still unregenerate. The unfit are still maintained in their places; and then, to prevent the colonies from suffering too severely under their incapacity, we set up the local councils, nominated or elected, to do the work, while the Queen's representative enjoys his salary. Instances of glaring impropriety like that to which I have alluded are of course rare, and among colonial governors there are men of quality so high that we would desire only to see their power equal to it. But so limited is the patronage, on the other hand, which remains to the home administrations, and so heavy the pressure brought to bear upon them, that there are persons also in these situations of whom it may be said that the less they do, and the less they are enabled to do, the better for the colony over which they preside.

The West Indies have been sufferers from another cause. In the absence of other use for them they have been made to serve as places where governors try their 'prentice hand and learn their business before promotion to more important situations. Whether a man has done well or done ill makes, it seems, very little difference unless he has offended prejudices or interests at home: once in the service he acquires a vested right to continue in it. A governor who had been suspended for conduct which is not denied to have been most improper, is replaced with the explanation that if he was not sent back to his old post it would have been necessary to provide a situation for him elsewhere. Why would it? Has a captain of a man-of-war whose ship is taken from him for misconduct an immediate claim to have another? Unfortunate colonies! It is not their interest which is considered under this system. But the subject is so delicate that I must say no more about it. I will recommend only to the attention of the British democracy, who are now the parties that in the last instance are responsible, because they are the real masters of the Empire, the following apologue.

In the time of the Emperor Nicholas the censors of the press seized a volume which had been published by the poet Kriloff, on the ground that it contained treasonable matter. Nicholas sent for Kriloff. The censor produced the incriminated passage, and Kriloff was made to read it aloud. It was a fable. A governor of a Russian province was represented as arriving in the other world, and as being brought up before Rhadamanthus. He was accused, not of any crime, but of having been simply a nonentity—of having received his salary and spent it, and nothing more. Rhadamanthus listened, and when the accusing angel had done sentenced the prisoner into Paradise. 'Into Paradise!' said the angel, 'why, he has done nothing!' 'True,' said Rhadamanthus, 'but how would it have been if he had done anything?'

'Write away, old fellow,' said Nicholas to Kriloff.

Has it never happened that British colonial officials who have similarly done nothing have been sent into the Paradise of promotion because they have kept things smooth and have given no trouble to their employers at home?

In the evening of the day of the political meeting we dined at Government House. There was a large representative party, English, French, Spaniards, Corsicans—ladies and gentlemen each speaking his or her own language. There were the mayors of the two chief towns of Trinidad—Port of Spain and San Fernando—both enthusiastic for a constitution. The latter was my neighbour at dinner, and insisted much on the fine qualities of the leading persons in the island and the splendid things to be expected when responsible government should be conceded. The training squadron had arrived from Barbadoes, and the commodore and two or three officers were present in their uniforms. There was interesting talk about Trinidad's troublesome neighbour, Guzman Blanco, the President of Venezuela. It seems that Sir Walter Raleigh's Eldorado has turned out to be a fact after all. On the higher waters of the Orinoco actual gold mines do exist, and the discovery has quickened into life a long unsettled dispute about boundaries between British Guiana and the republic. Don Guzman had been encroaching, so it was alleged, and in other ways had been offensive and impertinent. Ships were going—had been actually ordered to La Guyra, to pull his nose for him, and to tell him to behave himself. The time is past when we flew our hawks at game birds. The opinion of most of the party was that Don Guzman knew it, and that his nose would not be pulled. He would regard our frigates as picturesque ornaments to his harbour, give the officers in command the politest reception, evade their demands, offer good words in plenty, and nothing else but words, and in the end would have the benefit of our indifference.[8]

In the late evening we had music. Our host sang well, our hostess was an accomplished artist. They had duets together, Italian and English, and the lady then sang 'The Three Fishers,' Kingsley being looked on as the personal property of Trinidad and as one of themselves. She sang it very well, as well as any one could do who had no direct acquaintance with an English sea-coast people. Her voice was beautiful, and she showed genuine feeling. The silence when she ended was more complimentary than the loudest applause. It was broken by a stupid member of council, who said to me, 'Is it not strange that a poet with such a gift of words as Mr. Kingsley should have ended that song with so weak a line? "The sooner it's over the sooner to sleep" is nothing but prose.' He did not see that the fault which he thought he had discovered is no more than the intentional 'dying away' of the emotion created by the story in the common lot of poor humanity. We drove back across the savannah in a blaze of fireflies. It is not till midnight that they put their lights out and go to sleep with the rest of the world.

One duty remained to me before I left the island. The Warners are among the oldest of West Indian families, distinguished through many generations, not the least in their then living chief and representative, Charles Warner, who in the highest ministerial offices had steered Trinidad through the trying times which followed the abolition of slavery. I had myself in early life been brought into relations with other members of his family. He himself was a very old man on the edge of the grave; but hearing that I was in Port of Spain, he had expressed a wish to see me. I found him in his drawing room, shrunk in stature, pale, bent double by weight of years, and but feebly able to lift his head to speak. I thought, and I judged rightly, that he could have but a few weeks, perhaps but a few days, to live.

There is something peculiarly solemn in being brought to speak with a supremely eminent man, who is already struggling with the moment which is to launch him into a new existence. He raised himself in his chair. He gave me his withered hand. His eyes still gleamed with the light of an untouched intelligence. All else of him seemed dead. The soul, untouched by the decay of the frame which had been its earthly tenement, burnt bright as ever on the edge of its release.

When words are scarce they are seldom spent in vain,
And they breathe truth who breathe their words in pain.

He roused himself to talk, and he talked sadly, for all things at home and everywhere were travelling on the road which he well knew could lead to no good end. No statesman had done better practical work than he, or work which had borne better fruit, could it be allowed to ripen. But for him Trinidad would have been a wilderness, savage as when Columbus found the Caribs there. He belonged to the race who make empires, as the orators lose them, who do things and do not talk about them, who build and do not cast down, who reverence ancient habits and institutions as the organic functions of corporate national character; a Tory of the Tories, who nevertheless recognised that Toryism itself was passing away under the universal solvent, and had ceased to be a faith which could be believed in as a guide to conduct.

He no more than any one could tell what it was now wisest or even possible to do. He spoke like some ancient seer, whose eyes looked beyond the present time and the present world, and saw politics and progress and the wild whirlwind of change as the play of atoms dancing to and fro in the sunbeams of eternity. Yet he wished well to our poor earth, and to us who were still struggling upon it. He was sorry for the courses on which he saw mankind to be travelling. Spite of all the newspapers and the blowing of the trumpets, he well understood whither all that was tending. He spoke with horror and even loathing of the sinister leader who was drawing England into the fatal whirlpool. He could still hope, for he knew the power of the race. He knew that the English heart was unaffected, that we were suffering only from delirium of the brain. The day would yet come, he thought, when we should struggle back into sanity again with such wreck of our past greatness as might still be left to us, torn and shattered, but clothed and in our right mind, and cured for centuries of our illusions.

My forebodings of the nearness of the end were too well founded. A month later I heard that Charles Warner was dead. To have seen and spoken with such a man was worth a voyage round the globe.

On the prospects of Trinidad I have a few more words to add. The tendency of the island is to become what Grenada has become already—a community of negro freeholders, each living on his own homestead, and raising or gathering off the ground what his own family will consume. They will multiply, for there is ample room. Three-quarters of the soil are still unoccupied. The 140,000 blacks will rapidly grow into a half-million, and the half-million, as long as we are on the spot to keep the peace, will speedily double itself again. The English inhabitants will and must be crowded out. The geographical advantages of the Gulf of Paria will secure a certain amount of trade. There will be merchants and bankers in the town as floating passage birds, and there will be mulatto lawyers and shopkeepers and newspaper writers. But the blacks hate the mulattoes, and the mulatto breed will not maintain itself, as with the independence of the blacks the intimacy between blacks and whites diminishes and must diminish. The English peasant immigration which enthusiasts have believed in is a dream, a dream which passed through the ivory gate, a dream which will never turn to a waking reality; and unless under the Indian system, which our rulers will never try unless the democracy orders them to adopt it, the English interest will come to an end.

The English have proved in India that they can play a great and useful part as rulers over recognised inferiors. Even in the West Indies the planters were a real something. Like the English in Ireland, they produced a remarkable breed of men: the Codringtons, the Warners, and many illustrious names besides. They governed cheaply on their own resources, and the islands under their rule were so profitable that we fought for them as if our Empire was at stake. All that is gone. The days of ruling races are supposed to be numbered. Trade drifts away to the nearest market—to New York or New Orleans—and in a money point of view the value of such possessions as Trinidad will soon be less than nothing to us.

As long as the present system holds, there will be an appreciable addition to the sum of human (coloured human) happiness. Lighter-hearted creatures do not exist on the globe. But the continuance of it depends on the continuance of the English rule. The peace and order which they benefit by is not of their own creation. In spite of schools and missionaries, the dark connection still maintains itself with Satan's invisible world, and modern education contends in vain with Obeah worship. As it has been in Hayti, so it must be in Trinidad if the English leave the blacks to be their own masters.

Scene after scene passes by on the magic slide. The man-eating Caribs first, then Columbus and his Spaniards, the French conquest, the English occupation, but they have left behind them no self-quickening seed of healthy civilisation, and the prospect darkens once more. It is a pity, for there is no real necessity that it should darken. The West Indian negro is conscious of his own defects, and responds more willingly than most to a guiding hand. He is faithful and affectionate to those who are just and kind to him, and with a century or two of wise administration he might prove that his inferiority is not inherent, and that with the same chances as the white he may rise to the same level. I cannot part with the hope that the English people may yet insist that the chance shall not be denied to him, and that they may yet give their officials to understand that they must not, shall not, shake off their responsibilities for this unfortunate people, by flinging them back upon themselves 'to manage their own affairs,' now that we have no further use for them.

I was told that the keener-witted Trinidad blacks are watching as eagerly as we do the development of the Irish problem. They see the identity of the situation. They see that if the Radical view prevails, and in every country the majority are to rule, Trinidad will be theirs and the government of the English will be at an end. I, for myself, look upon Trinidad and the West Indies generally as an opportunity for the further extension of the influence of the English race in their special capacity of leaders and governors of men. We cannot with honour divest ourselves of our responsibility for the blacks, or after the eloquence we have poured out and the self-laudation which we have allowed ourselves for the suppression of slavery, leave them now to relapse into a state from which slavery itself was the first step of emancipation. Our world-wide dominion will not be of any long endurance if we consider that we have discharged our full duty to our fellow-subjects when we have set them free to follow their own devices. If that is to be all, the sooner it vanishes into history the better for us and for the world.

FOOTNOTES:

[8]

A squadron did go while I was in the West Indies. I have not heard that any advance has been made in consequence towards the settlement of the Border.

CHAPTER IX.

Barbadoes again—Social condition of the island—Political constitution—Effects of the sugar bounties—Dangers of general bankruptcy—The Hall of Assembly—Sir Charles Pearson—Society in Bridgetown—A morning drive—Church of St. John's—Sir Graham Briggs—An old planter's palace—The Chief Justice of Barbadoes.

Again at sea, and on the way back to Barbadoes. The commodore of the training squadron had offered me a berth to St. Vincent, but he intended to work up under sail against the north-east trade, which had risen to half a gale, and I preferred the security and speed of the mail boat. Among the passengers was Miss ——, the lady whom I had seen sketching on the way to the Blue Basin. She showed me her drawings, which were excellent. She showed me in her mosquito-bitten arms what she had endured to make them, and I admired her fortitude. She was English, and was on her way to join her father at Codrington College.

We had a wild night, but those long vessels care little for winds and waves. By morning we had fought our way back to Grenada. In the St. Vincent roadstead, which we reached the same day, the ship was stormed by boatloads of people who were to go on with us; boys on their way to school at Barbadoes, ladies young and old, white, black, and mixed, who were bound I know not where. The night fell dark as pitch, the storm continued, and we were no sooner beyond the shelter of the land than every one save Miss —— and myself was prostrate. The vessel ploughed on upon her way indifferent to us and to them. We were at Bridgetown by breakfast time, and I was now to have an opportunity of studying more at leisure the earliest of our West Indian colonies.

Barbadoes is as unlike in appearance as it is in social condition to Trinidad or the Antilles. There are no mountains in it, no forests, no rivers, and as yet no small freeholders. The blacks, who number nearly 200,000 in an island not larger than the Isle of Wight, are labourers, working for wages on the estates of large proprietors. Land of their own they have none, for there is none for them. Work they must, for they cannot live otherwise. Thus every square yard of soil is cultivated, and turn your eyes where you will you see houses, sugar canes, and sweet potatoes. Two hundred and fifty years of occupation have imprinted strongly an English character; parish churches solid and respectable, the English language, the English police and parochial system. However it may be in the other islands, England in Barbadoes is still a solid fact. The headquarters of the West Indian troops are there. There is a commander-in-chief residing in a 'Queen's House,' so called. There is a savannah where there are English barracks under avenues of almond and mahogany. Red coats are scattered about the grass. Officers canter about playing polo, and naval and military uniforms glitter at the side of carriages, and horsemen and horsewomen take their evening rides, as well mounted and as well dressed as you can see in Rotten Row. Barbadoes is thus in pleasing contrast with the conquered islands which we have not taken the trouble to assimilate. In them remain the wrecks of the French civilisation which we superseded, while we have planted nothing of our own. Barbadoes, the European aspect of it at any rate, is English throughout.

The harbour, when we arrived, was even more brilliant than we had left it a fort-night before. The training squadron had gone, but in the place of it the West Indian fleet was there, and there were also three American frigates, old wooden vessels out merely on a cruise, but heavily sparred, smart and well set up, with the stars and stripes floating carelessly at their sterns, as if in these western seas, be the nominal dominion British, French, or Spanish, the American has a voice also and intends to be heard.

We had no sooner anchored than a well-appointed boat was alongside with an awning and an ensign at the stern. Colonel ——, the chief of the police, to whom it belonged, came on board in search of Miss ——, who was to be his guest in Bridgetown. She introduced me to him. He insisted on my accompanying him home to breakfast, and, as he was a person in authority, I had nothing to do but obey. Colonel ——, to whose politeness then and afterwards I was in many ways indebted, had seen life in various forms. He had been in the navy. He had been in the army. He had been called to the bar. He was now the head of the Barbadoes police, with this anomalous addition to his other duties, that in default of a chaplain he read the Church service on Sundays in the barracks. He had even a license from the bishop to preach sermons, and being a man of fine character and original sense he discharged this last function, I was told, remarkably well. His house was in the heart of the town, but shaded with tropical trees. The rooms were protected by deep outside galleries, which were overrun with Bougainvillier creepers. He was himself the kindest of entertainers, his Irish lady the kindest of hostesses, with the humorous high breeding of the old Sligo aristocracy, to whom she belonged. I found that I had been acquainted with some of her kindred there long ago, in the days when the Anglo-Irish rule had not been discovered to be a upas tree, and cultivated human life was still possible in Connaught. Of the breakfast, which consisted of all the West Indian dainties I had ever heard or read of, I can say nothing, nor of the pleasant talk which followed. I was to see more of Colonel ——, for he offered to drive me some day across the island, a promise which he punctually fulfilled. My stay with him for the present could be but brief, as I was expected at Government House.

I have met with exceptional hospitality from the governors of British colonies in many parts of the world. They are not chosen like the Roman proconsuls from the ranks of trained statesmen who have held high administrative offices at home. They are appointed, as I said just now, from various motives, sometimes with a careful regard to fitness for their post, sometimes with a regard merely to routine or convenience or to personal influence brought to bear in their favour. I have myself seen some for whom I should have thought other employment would have been more suitable; but always and everywhere those that I have fallen in with have been men of honour and integrity above reproach or suspicion, and I have met with one or two gentlemen in these situations whose admirable qualities it is impossible to praise too highly, who in their complicated responsibilities—responsibilities to the colonies and responsibilities to the authorities at home—have considered conscience and duty to be their safest guides, have cared only to do what they believed to be right to the best of their ability, and have left their interests to take care of themselves.

The Governor of Barbadoes is not despotic. He controls the administration, but there is a constitution as old as the Stuarts; an Assembly of thirty-three members, nine of whom the Crown nominates, the rest are elected. The friction is not so violent as when the number of the nominated and elected members is equal, and as long as a property qualification was required for the franchise, the system may have worked tolerably without producing any violent mischief. There have been recent modifications, however, pointing in the same direction as those which have been made in Jamaica. By an ordinance from home the suffrage has been widely extended, obviously as a step to larger intended changes.

Under such conditions and with an uncertain future a governor can do little save lead and influence, entertain visitors, discharge the necessary courtesies to all classes of his subjects, and keep his eyes open. These duties at least Sir Charles Lee discharges to perfection, the entertaining part of them on a scale so liberal that if Père Labat came back he would suppose that the two hundred years which have gone by since his visit was a dream, and that Government House at least was still as he left it. In an establishment which had so many demands upon it, and where so many visitors of all kinds were going and coming, I had no claim to be admitted. I felt that I should be an intruder, and had I been allowed would have taken myself elsewhere, but Sir Charles's peremptory generosity admitted of no refusal. As a subject I was bound to submit to the Queen's representative. I cannot say I was sorry to be compelled. In Government House I should see and hear what I could neither have seen nor heard elsewhere. I should meet people who could tell me what I most wanted to know. I had understood already that owing to the sugar depression the state of the island was critical. Officials were alarmed. Bankers were alarmed. No one could see beyond the next year what was likely to happen. Sir Charles himself would have most to say. He was evidently anxious. Perhaps if he had a fault, he was over anxious; but with the possibility of social confusion before him, with nearly 200,000 peasant subjects, who in a few months might be out of work and so out of food, with the inflammable negro nature, and a suspicious and easily excited public opinion at home, the position of a Governor of Barbadoes is not an enviable one. The Government at home, no doubt with the best intentions, has aggravated any peril which there may be by enlarging the suffrage. The experience of Governor Eyre in Jamaica has taught the danger of being too active, but to be too inactive may be dangerous also. If there is a stir again in any part of these islands, and violence and massacre come of it, as it came in St. Domingo, the responsibility is with the governor, and the account will be strictly exacted of him.

I must describe more particularly the reasons which there are for uneasiness. On the day on which I landed I saw an article in a Bridgetown paper in which my coming there was spoken of as perhaps the last straw which would break the overburdened back. I know not why I should be thought likely to add anything to the load of Barbadian afflictions. I should be a worse friend to the colonies than I have tried to be if I was one of those who would quench the smoking flax of loyalty in any West Indian heart. But loyalty, I very well know, is sorely tried just now. The position is painfully simple. The great prosperity of the island ended with emancipation. Barbadoes suffered less than Jamaica or the Antilles because the population was large and the land limited, and the blacks were obliged to work to keep themselves alive. The abolition of the sugar duties was the next blow. The price of sugar fell, and the estates yielded little more than the expense of cultivation. Owners of properties who were their own managers, and had sense and energy, continued to keep themselves afloat; but absenteeism had become the fashion. The brilliant society which is described by Labat had been melting for more than a century. More and more the old West Indian families removed to England, farmed their lands through agents and overseers, or sold them to speculating capitalists. The personal influence of the white man over the black, which might have been brought about by a friendly intercourse after slavery was abolished, was never so much as attempted. The higher class of gentry found the colony more and more distasteful to them, and they left the arrangement of the labour question to persons to whom the blacks were nothing, emancipated though they might be, except instruments of production. A negro can be attached to his employer at least as easily as a horse or a dog. The horse or dog requires kind treatment, or he becomes indifferent or sullen; so it is with the negro. But the forced equality of the races before the law made more difficult the growth of any kindly feeling. To the overseer on a plantation the black labourer was a machine out of which the problem was to get the maximum of work with the minimum of pay. In the slavery times the horse and dog relation was a real thing. The master and mistress joked and laughed with their dark bondsmen, knew Cæsar from Pompey, knew how many children each had, gave them small presents, cared for them when they were sick, and maintained them when they were old and past work. All this ended with emancipation. Between whites and blacks no relations remained save that of employer and employed. They lived apart. They had no longer, save in exceptional instances, any personal communication with each other. The law refusing to recognise a difference, the social line was drawn the harder, which the law was unable to reach.

In the Antilles the plantations broke up as I had seen in Grenada. The whites went away, and the land was divided among the negroes. In Barbadoes, the estates were kept together. The English character and the English habits were stamped deeper there, and were not so easily obliterated. But the stars in their courses have fought against the old system. Once the West Indies had a monopoly of the sugar trade. Steam and progress have given them a hundred natural competitors; and on the back of these came the unnatural bounty-fed beetroot sugar competition. Meanwhile the expense of living increased in the days of inflated hope and 'unexampled prosperity.' Free trade, whatever its immediate consequences, was to make everyone rich in the end. When the income of an estate fell short one year, it was to rise in the next, and the money was borrowed to make ends meet; when it didn't rise, more money was borrowed; and there is now hardly a property in the island which is not loaded to the sinking point. Tied to sugar-growing, Barbadoes has no second industry to fall back upon. The blacks, who are heedless and light-hearted, increase and multiply. They will not emigrate, they are so much attached to their homes; and the not distant prospect is of a general bankruptcy, which may throw the land for the moment out of cultivation, with a hungry unemployed multitude to feed without means of feeding them, and to control without the personal acquaintance and influence which alone can make control possible.

At home there is a general knowledge that things are not going on well out there. But, true to our own ways of thinking, we regard it as their affair and not as ours. If cheap sugar ruins the planters, it benefits the English workman. The planters had their innings; it is now the consumer's turn. What are the West Indies to us? On the map they appear to belong more to the United States than to us. Let the United States take them and welcome. So thinks, perhaps, the average Englishman; and, analogous to him, the West Indian proprietor reflects that, if admitted into the Union, he would have the benefit of the American market, which would set him on his feet again; and that the Americans, probably finding that they, if not we, could make some profit out of the islands, would be likely to settle the black question for him in a more satisfactory manner.

That such a feeling as this should exist is natural and pardonable; and it would have gone deeper than it has gone if it were not that there are two parties to every bargain, and those in favour of such a union have met hitherto with no encouragement. The Americans are wise in their generation. They looked at Cuba; they looked at St. Domingo. They might have had both on easy terms, but they tell you that their constitution does not allow them to hold dependent states. What they annex they absorb, and they did not wish to absorb another million and a half of blacks and as many Roman Catholics, having enough already of both. Our English islands may be more tempting, but there too the black cloud hangs thick and grows yearly thicker, and through English indulgence is more charged with dangerous elements. Already, they say, they have every advantage which the islands can give them. They exercise a general protectorate, and would probably interfere if France or England were to attempt again to extend their dominions in that quarter; but they prefer to leave to the present owners the responsibility of managing and feeding the cow, while they are to have the milking of it.

Thus the proposal of annexation, which has never gone beyond wishes and talk, has so far been coldly received; but the Americans did make their offer a short time since, at which the drowning Barbadians grasped as at a floating plank. England would give them no hand to save them from the effects of the beetroot bounties. The Americans were willing to relax their own sugar duties to admit West Indian sugar duty free, and give them the benefit of their own high prices. The colonies being unable to make treaties for themselves, the proposal was referred home and was rejected. The Board of Trade had, no doubt, excellent reasons for objecting to an arrangement which would have flung our whole commerce with the West Indies into American hands, and might have formed a prelude to a closer attachment. It would have been a violation also of those free-trade principles which are the English political gospel. Moreover, our attitude towards our colonies has changed in the last twenty years; we now wish to preserve the attachment of communities whom a generation back we should have told to do as they liked, and have bidden them God speed on their way; and this treaty may have been regarded as a step towards separation. But the unfortunate Barbadians found themselves, with the harbour in sight, driven out again into the free-trade hurricane. We would not help them ourselves; we declined to let the Americans help them; and help themselves they could not. They dare not resent our indifference to their interests, which, if they were stronger, would have been more visibly displayed. They must wait now for what the future will bring with as much composure as they can command, but I did hear outcries of impatience to which it was unpleasant to listen. Nay, it was even suggested as a means of inducing the Americans to forego their reluctance to take them into the Union, that we might relinquish such rights as we possessed in Canada if the Americans would relieve us of the West Indies, for which we appeared to care so little.

If Barbadoes is driven into bankruptcy, the estates will have to be sold, and will probably be broken up as they have been in the Antilles. The first difficulty will thus be got over. But the change cannot be carried out in a day. If wages suddenly cease the negroes will starve, and will not take their starvation patiently. At the worst, however, means will probably be found to keep the land from falling out of cultivation. The Barbadians see their condition in the light of their grievances, and make the worst of it. The continental powers may tire of the bounty system, or something else may happen to make sugar rise. The prospect is not a bright one, but what actually happens in this world is generally the unexpected.

As a visit my stay at Government House was made simply delightful to me. I remained there (with interruptions) for a fortnight, and Lady L—— did not only permit, but she insisted that I should be as if in an hotel, and come and go as I liked. The climate of Barbadoes, so far as I can speak of it, is as sparkling and invigorating as champagne. Cocktail may be wanted in Trinidad. In Barbadoes the air is all one asks for, and between night breezes and sea breezes one has plenty of it. Day begins with daylight, as it ought to do. You have slept without knowing anything about it. There are no venomous crawling creatures. Cockroaches are the worst, but they scuttle out of the way so alarmed and ashamed of themselves if you happen to see them, that I never could bring myself to hurt one. You spring out of bed as if the process of getting up were actually pleasant. Well-appointed West Indian houses are generally provided with a fresh-water swimming bath. Though cold by courtesy the water seldom falls below 65°, and you float luxuriously upon it without dread of chill. The early coffee follows the bath, and then the stroll under the big trees, among strange flowers, or in the grotto with the ferns and humming birds. If it were part of one's regular life, I suppose that one would want something to do. Sir Charles was the most active of men, and had been busy in his office for an hour before I had come down to lounge. But for myself I discovered that it was possible, at least for an interval, to be perfectly idle and perfectly happy, surrounded by the daintiest beauties of an English hothouse, with palm trees waving like fans to cool one, and with sensitive plants, which are common as daisies, strewing themselves under one's feet to be trodden upon.

After breakfast the heat would be considerable, but with an umbrella I could walk about the town and see what was to be seen. Alas! here one has something to desire. Where Père Labat saw a display of splendour which reminded him of Paris and London, you now find only stores on the American pattern, for the most part American goods, bad in quality and extravagantly dear. Treaty or no treaty, it is to America that the trade is drifting, and we might as well concede with a good grace what must soon come of itself whether we like it or not. The streets are relieved from ugliness by the trees and by occasional handsome buildings. Often I stood to admire the pea-green Nelson. Once I went into the Assembly where the legislature was discussing more or less unquietly the prospects of the island. The question of the hour was economy. In the opinion of patriot Barbadians, sore at the refusal of the treaty, the readiest way to reduce expenditure was to diminish the salaries of officials from the governor downwards. The officials, knowing that they were very moderately paid already, naturally demurred. The most interesting part of the thing to me was the hall in which the proceedings were going on. It is handsome in itself, and has a series of painted windows representing the English sovereigns from James I. to Queen Victoria. Among them in his proper place stood Oliver Cromwell, the only formal recognition of the great Protector that I know of in any part of the English dominions. Barbadoes had been Cavalier in its general sympathies, but has taken an independent view of things, and here too has had an opinion of its own.

Hospitality was always a West Indian characteristic. There were luncheons and dinners, and distinguished persons to be met and talked to. Among these I had the special good fortune of making acquaintance with Sir Charles Pearson, now commanding-in-chief in those parts. Even in these days, crowded as they are by small incidents made large by newspapers, we have not yet forgotten the defence of a fort in the interior of Zululand where Sir Charles Pearson and his small garrison were cut off from their communications with Natal. For a week or two he was the chief object of interest in every English house. In obedience to orders which it was not his business to question, he had assisted Sir T. Shepstone in the memorable annexation of the Transvaal. He had seen also to what that annexation led, and, being a truth-speaking man, he did not attempt to conceal the completeness of our defeat. Our military establishment in the West Indies is of modest dimensions; but a strong English soldier, who says little and does his duty, and never told a lie in his life or could tell one, is a comforting figure to fall in with. One feels that there will be something to retire upon when parliamentary oratory has finished its work of disintegration.

The pleasantest incident of the day was the evening drive with Lady L——. She would take me out shortly before sunset, and bring me back again when the tropical stars were showing faintly and the fireflies had begun to sparkle about the bushes, and the bats were flitting to and fro after the night moths like spirits of darkness chasing human souls.

The neighbourhood of Bridgetown has little natural beauty; but the roads are excellent, the savannah picturesque with riding parties and polo players and lounging red jackets, every one being eager to pay his or her respect to the gracious lady of the Queen's representative. We called at pretty villas where there would be evening teas and lawn tennis in the cool. The society is not extensive, and here would be collected most of it that was worth meeting. At one of these parties I fell in with the officers of the American squadron, the commodore a very interesting and courteous gentleman whom I should have taken for a fellow-countryman. There are many diamonds, and diamonds of the first water, among the Americans as among ourselves; but the cutting and setting is different. Commodore D—— was cut and set like an Englishman. He introduced me to one of his brother officers who had been in Hayti. Spite of Sir Spenser St. John, spite of all the confirmatory evidence which I had heard, I was still incredulous about the alleged cannibalism there. To my inquiries this gentleman had only the same answer to give. The fact was beyond question. He had himself known instances of it.

The commodore had a grievance against us illustrating West Indian manners. These islands are as nervous about their health as so many old ladies. The yellow flags float on ship after ship in the Bridgetown roadstead, and crews, passengers, and cargoes are sternly interdicted from the land. Jamaica was in ill name from smallpox, and, as Cuba will not drop its intercourse with Jamaica, Cuba falls also under the ban. The commodore had directed a case of cigars from Havana to meet him at Barbadoes. They arrived, but might not be transferred from the steamer which brought them, even on board his own frigate, lest he might bring infection on shore in his pocket. They went on to England, to reach him perhaps eventually in New York.

Colonel ——'s duties, as chief of the police, obliged him to make occasional rounds to visit his stations. He recollected his promise, and he invited me one morning to accompany him. We were to breakfast at his house on our return, so I anticipated an excursion of a few miles at the utmost. He called for me soon after sunrise with a light carriage and a brisk pair of horses. We were rapidly clear of the town. The roads were better than the best I have seen out of England, the only fault in them being the white coral dust which dazzles and blinds the eyes. Everywhere there were signs of age and of long occupation. The stone steps leading up out of the road to the doors of the houses had been worn by human feet for hundreds of years. The houses themselves were old, and as if suffering from the universal depression—gates broken, gardens disordered, and woodwork black and blistered for want of paint. But if the habitations were neglected, there was no neglect in the fields. Sugar cane alternated with sweet potatoes and yams and other strange things the names of which I heard and forgot; but there was not a weed to be seen or broken fence where fence was needed. The soil was clean every inch of it, as well hoed and trenched as in a Middlesex market garden. Salt fish and flour, which is the chief food of the blacks, is imported; but vegetables enough are raised in Barbadoes to keep the cost of living incredibly low; and, to my uninstructed eyes, it seemed that even if sugar and wages did fail there could be no danger of any sudden famine. The people were thick as rabbits in a warren; women with loaded baskets on their heads laughing and chirruping, men driving donkey carts, four donkeys abreast, smoking their early pipes as if they had not a care in the world, as, indeed, they have not.

On we went, the Colonel's horses stepping out twelve miles an hour, and I wondered privately what was to become of our breakfast. We were striking right across the island, along the coral ridge which forms the backbone of it. We found ourselves at length in a grove of orange trees and shaddocks, at the old church of St. John's, which stands upon a perpendicular cliff; Codrington College on the level under our feet, and beyond us the open Atlantic and the everlasting breakers from the trade winds fringing the shore with foam. Far out were the white sails of the fishing smacks. The Barbadians are careless of weather, and the best of boat sailors. It was very pretty in the bright morning, and the church itself was not the least interesting part of the scene. The door was wide open. We went in, and I seemed to be in a parish church in England as parish churches used to be when I was a child. There were the old-fashioned seats, the old unadorned communion table, the old pulpit and reading desk and the clerk's desk below, with the lion and the unicorn conspicuous above the chancel arch. The white tablets on the wall bore familiar names dating back into the last century. On the floor were flagstones still older with armorial bearings and letters cut in stone, half effaced by the feet of the generations who had trodden up the same aisles till they, too, lay down and rested there. And there was this, too, to be remembered—that these Barbadian churches, old as they might seem, had belonged always to the Anglican communion. No mass had ever been said at that altar. It was a milestone on the high road of time, and was venerable to me at once for its antiquity and for the era at which it had begun to exist.

At the porch was an ancient slab on which was a coat of arms, a crest with a hand and sword, and a motto, 'Sic nos, sic nostra tuemur.' The inscription said that it was in memory of Michael Mahon, 'of the kingdom of Ireland,' erected by his children and grandchildren. Who was Michael Mahon? Some expatriated, so-called rebel, I suppose, whose sword could not defend him from being Barbados'd with so many other poor wretches who were sent the same road—victims of the tragi-comedy of the English government of Ireland. There were plenty of them wandering about in Labat's time, ready, as Labat observes, to lend a help to the French, should they take a fancy to land a force in the island.

The churchyard was scarcely so home-like. The graves were planted with tropical shrubs and flowers. Palms waved over the square stone monuments—stephanotis and jessamine crept about the iron railings. The primroses and hyacinths and violets, with which we dress the mounds under which our friends are sleeping, will not grow in the tropics. In the place of them are the exotics of our hot-houses. We too are, perhaps, exotics of another kind in these islands, and may not, after all, have a long abiding place in them.

Colonel ——, who with his secular duties combined serious and spiritual feeling, was a friend of the clergyman of St. John's, and hoped to introduce me to him. This gentleman, however, was absent from home. Our round was still but half completed; we had to mount again and go another seven miles to inspect a police station. The police themselves were, of course, blacks—well-grown fine men, in a high state of discipline. Our visit was not expected, but all was as it should be; the rooms well swept and airy, the horses in good condition, stables clean, harness and arms polished and ready for use. Serious as might be the trials of the Barbadians and decrepit the financial condition, there were no symptoms of neglect either on the farms or in the social machinery.

Altogether we drove between thirty and forty miles that morning. We were in time for breakfast after all, and I had seen half the island. It is like the Isle of Thanet, or the country between Calais and Boulogne. One characteristic feature must not be forgotten: there are no rivers and no waterpower; steam engines have been introduced, but the chief motive agent is still the never-ceasing trade wind. You see windmills everywhere, as it was in the time of Labat. The planters are reproached as being behind the age; they are told that with the latest improvements they might still defy their beetroot enemy. It may be so, but a wind which never rests is force which costs little, and it is possible that they understand their own business best.

Another morning excursion showed me the rest of the country, and introduced me to scenes and persons still more interesting. Sir Graham Briggs[9] is perhaps the most distinguished representative of the old Barbadian families. He is, or was, a man of large fortune, with vast estates in this and other islands. A few years ago, when prospects were brighter, he was an advocate of the constitutional development so much recommended from England. The West Indian Islands were to be confederated into a dominion like that of Canada, to take over the responsibilities of government, and to learn to stand alone. The decline in the value of property, the general decay of the white interest in the islands, and the rapid increase of the blacks, taught those who at one time were ready for the change what the real nature of it would be. They have paused to consider; and the longer they consider the less they like it.

Sir Graham had called upon me at Government House, and had spoken fully and freely about the offered American sugar treaty. As a severe sufferer he was naturally irritated at the rejection of it; and in the mood in which I found him, I should think it possible that if the Americans would hold their hands out with an offer of admission into the Union, he and a good many other gentlemen would meet them halfway. He did not say so—I conjecture only from natural probabilities, and from what I should feel myself if I were in their position. Happily the temptation cannot fall in their way. An American official laconically summed up the situation to me: 'As satellites, sir, as much as you please; but as parts of the primary—no, sir.' The Americans will not take them into the Union; they must remain, therefore, with their English primary and make the best of it; neither as satellites, for they have no proper motion of their own, nor as incorporated in the British Empire, for they derive no benefit from their connection with it, but as poor relations distantly acknowledged. I did not expect that Sir Graham would have more to say to me than he had said already: but he was a cultivated and noteworthy person, his house was said to be the most splendid of the old Barbadian merchant palaces, and I gratefully accepted an invitation to pay him a short visit.

I started as before in the early morning, before the sun was above the trees. The road followed the line of the shore. Originally, I believe, Barbadoes was like the Antilles, covered with forest. In the interior little remains save cabbage palms and detached clumps of mangy-looking mahogany trees. The forest is gone, and human beings have taken the place of it. For ten miles I was driving through a string of straggling villages, each cottage or cabin having its small vegetable garden and clump of plantains. Being on the western or sheltered side of the island, the sea was smooth and edged with mangrove, through which at occasional openings we saw the shining water and the white coral beach, and fishing boats either drawn up upon it or anchored outside with their sails up. Trees had been planted for shade among the houses. There were village greens with great silk-cotton trees, banyans and acacias, mangoes and oranges, and shaddocks with their large fruit glowing among the leaves like great golden melons. The people swarmed, children tumbling about half naked, so like each other that one wondered whether their mothers knew their own from their neighbours'; the fishermen's wives selling flying fish, of which there are infinite numbers. It was an innocent, pretty scene. One missed green fields with cows upon them. Guinea grass, which is all that they have, makes excellent fodder, but is ugly to look at; and is cut and carried, not eaten where it grows. Of animal life there were innumerable donkeys—no black man will walk if he can find a donkey to carry him—infinite poultry, and pigs, familiar enough, but not allowed a free entry into the cabins as in Ireland. Of birds there was not any great variety. The humming birds preferred less populated quarters. There were small varieties of finches and sparrows and buntings, winged atoms without beauty of form or colour; there were a few wild pigeons; but the prevailing figure was the Barbadian crow, a little fellow no bigger than a blackbird, a diminutive jackdaw, who gets his living upon worms and insects and parasites, and so tame that he would perch upon a boy's head if he saw a chance of finding anything eatable there. The women dress ill in Barbadoes, for they imitate English ladies; but no dress can conceal the grace of their forms when they are young. It struck Père Labat two centuries ago, and time and their supposed sufferings as slaves have made no difference. They work harder than the men, and are used as beasts of burden to fetch and carry, but they carry their loads on their heads, and thus from childhood have to stand upright with the neck straight and firm. They do not spoil their shapes with stays, or their walk with high-heeled shoes. They plant their feet firmly on the ground. Every movement is elastic and rounded, and the grace of body gives, or seems to give, grace also to the eyes and expression. Poor things! it cannot compensate for their colour, which now when they are free is harder to bear than when they were slaves. Their prettiness, such as it is, is short-lived. They grow old early, and an old negress is always hideous.

After keeping by the sea for an hour we turned inland, and at the foot of a steep hill we met my host, who transferred me to his own carriage. We had still four or five miles to go through cane fields and among sugar mills. At the end of them we came to a grand avenue of cabbage palms, a hundred or a hundred and twenty feet high. How their slim stems with their dense coronet of leaves survive a hurricane is one of the West Indian marvels. They escape destruction by the elasticity with which they yield to it. The branches, which in a calm stand out symmetrically, forming a circle of which the stem is the exact centre, bend round before a violent wind, are pressed close together, and stream out horizontally like a horse's tail.

The avenue led up to Sir Graham's house, which stands 800 feet above the sea. The garden, once the wonder of the island, was running wild, though rare trees and shrubs survived from its ancient splendour. Among them were two Wellingtonias as tall as the palms, but bent out of shape by the trade winds. Passing through a hall, among a litter of Carib curiosities, we entered the drawing-room, a magnificent saloon extending with various compartments over the greater part of the ground-floor story. It was filled with rare and curious things, gathered in the days when sugar was a horn of plenty, and selected with the finest taste; pictures, engravings, gems, antiquarian relics, books, maps, and manuscripts. There had been fine culture in the West Indies when all these treasures were collected. The English settlers there, like the English in Ireland, had the tastes of a grand race, and by-and-by we shall miss both of them when they are overwhelmed, as they are likely to be, in the revolutionary tide. Sir Graham was stemming it to the best of his ability, and if he was to go under would go under like a gentleman. A dining room almost as large had once been the scene of hospitalities like those which are celebrated by Tom Cringle. A broad staircase led up from the hall to long galleries, out of which bedrooms opened; with cool deep balconies and the universal green blinds. It was a palace with which Aladdin himself might have been satisfied, one of those which had stirred the envying admiration of foreign travellers in the last century, one of many then, now probably the last surviving representative of Anglo-West Indian civilisation. Like other forms of human life, it has had its day and could not last for ever. Something better may grow in the place of it, but also something worse may grow. The example of Hayti ought to suggest misgivings to the most ardent philonegro enthusiast.

West Indian cookery was famous over the world. Père Labat devotes at least a thousand pages to the dishes compounded of the spices and fruits of the islands, and their fish and fowl. Carib tradition was developed by artists from London and Paris. The Caribs, according to Labat, only ate one another for ceremony and on state occasions; their common diet was as excellent as it was innocent; and they had ascertained by careful experience the culinary and medicinal virtues of every animal and plant around them. Tom Cringle is eloquent on the same subject, but with less scientific knowledge. My own unfortunately is less than his, and I can do no justice at all to Sir Graham's entertainment of me; I can but say that he treated me to a West Indian banquet of the old sort, infinite in variety, and with subtle differences of flavour for which no language provides names. The wine—laid up consule Planco, when Pitt was prime minister, and the days of liberty as yet were not—was as admirable as the dishes, and the fruit more exquisite than either. Such pineapples, such shaddocks, I had never tasted before, and shall never taste again.

Hospitable, generous, splendid as was Sir Graham's reception of me, it was nevertheless easy to see that the prospects of the island sat heavy upon him. We had a long conversation when breakfast was over, which, if it added nothing new to what I had heard before, deepened and widened the impression of it.

The English West Indies, like other parts of the world, are going through a silent revolution. Elsewhere the revolution, as we hope, is a transition state, a new birth; a passing away of what is old and worn out, that a fresh and healthier order may rise in its place. In the West Indies the most sanguine of mortals will find it difficult to entertain any such hope at all. We have been a ruling power there for two hundred and fifty years; the whites whom we planted as our representatives are drifting into helplessness, and they regard England and England's policy as the principal cause of it. The blacks whom, in a fit of virtuous benevolence, we emancipated, do not feel that they are particularly obliged to us. They think, if they think at all, that they were ill treated originally, and have received no more than was due to them, and that perhaps it was not benevolence at all on our part, but a desire to free ourselves from the reproach of slaveholding. At any rate, the tendencies now in operation are loosening the hold which we possess on the islands, and the longer they last the looser that hold will become. French influence is in no danger of dying out in Martinique and Guadaloupe. The Spanish race is not dying in Cuba and Puerto Rico. England will soon be no more than a name in Barbadoes and the Antilles. Having acquitted our conscience by emancipation, we have left our West Indian interest to sink or swim. Our principle has been to leave each part of our empire (except the East Indies) to take care of itself: we give the various inhabitants liberty, and what we understand by fair play; that we have any further moral responsibilities towards them we do not imagine, even in our dreams, when they have ceased to be of commercial importance to us; and we assume that the honour of being British subjects will suffice to secure their allegiance. It will not suffice, as we shall eventually discover. We have decided that if the West Indies are to become again prosperous they must recover by their own energy. Our other colonies can do without help; why not they? We ought to remember that they are not like the other colonies. We occupied them at a time when slavery was considered a lawful institution, profitable to ourselves and useful to the souls of the negroes, who were brought by it within reach of salvation.[10] We became ourselves the chief slave dealers in the world. We peopled our islands with a population of blacks more dense by far in proportion to the whites than France or Spain ever ventured to do. We did not recognise, as the French and Spaniards did, that if our western colonies were permanently to belong to us, we must occupy them ourselves. We thought only of the immediate profit which was to be gathered out of the slave gangs; and the disproportion of the two races—always dangerously large—has increased with ever-gathering velocity since the emancipation. It is now beyond control on the old lines. The scanty whites are told that they must work out their own salvation on equal terms with their old servants. The relation is an impossible one. The independent energy which we may fairly look for in Australia and New Zealand is not to be looked for in Jamaica and Barbadoes; and the problem must have a new solution.

Confederation is to be the remedy, we are told. Let the islands be combined under a constitution. The whites collectively will then be a considerable body, and can assert themselves successfully. Confederation is, as I said before of the movement in Trinidad, but a turn of the kaleidoscope, the same pieces with a new pattern. A West Indian self-governed Dominion is possible only with a full negro vote. If the whites are to combine, so will the blacks. It will be a rule by the blacks and for the blacks. Let a generation or two pass by and carry away with them the old traditions, and an English governor-general will be found presiding over a black council, delivering the speeches made for him by a black prime minister; and how long could this endure? No English gentleman would consent to occupy so absurd a situation. The two races are not equal and will not blend. If the white people do not depart of themselves, black legislation will make it impossible for any of them to stay who would not be better out of the way. The Anglo-Irish Protestants will leave Ireland if there is an Irish Catholic parliament in College Green; the whites, for the same reason, will leave the West Indies; and in one and the other the connection with the British Empire will disappear along with them. It must be so; only politicians whose horizon does not extend beyond their personal future, and whose ambition is only to secure the immediate triumph of their party, can expect anything else.

Before my stay at Barbadoes ended, I had an opportunity of meeting at dinner a negro of pure blood who has risen to eminence by his own talent and character. He has held the office of attorney-general. He is now chief justice of the island. Exceptions are supposed proverbially to prove nothing, or to prove the opposite of what they appear to prove. When a particular phenomenon occurs rarely, the probabilities are strong against the recurrence of it. Having heard the craniological and other objections to the supposed identity of the negro and white races, I came to the opinion long ago in Africa, and I have seen no reason to change it, that whether they are of one race or not there is no original or congenital difference of capacity between them, any more than there is between a black horse and a black dog and a white horse and a white dog. With the same chances and with the same treatment, I believe that distinguished men would be produced equally from both races, and Mr. ——'s well-earned success is an additional evidence of it. But it does not follow that what can be done eventually can be done immediately, and the gulf which divides the colours is no arbitrary prejudice, but has been opened by the centuries of training and discipline which have given us the start in the race. We set it down to slavery. It would be far truer to set it down to freedom. The African blacks have been free enough for thousands, perhaps for tens of thousands of years, and it has been the absence of restraint which has prevented them from becoming civilised. Generation has followed generation, and the children are as like their father as the successive generations of apes. The whites, it is likely enough, succeeded one another with the same similarity for a long series of ages. It is now supposed that the human race has been upon the planet for a hundred thousand years at least, and the first traces of civilisation cannot be thrown back at farthest beyond six thousand. During all those ages mankind went on treading in the same steps, century after century making no more advance than the birds and beasts. In Egypt or in India or one knows not where, accident or natural development quickened into life our moral and intellectual faculties; and these faculties have grown into what we now experience, not in the freedom in which the modern takes delight, but under the sharp rule of the strong over the weak, of the wise over the unwise. Our own Anglo-Norman race has become capable of self-government only after a thousand years of civil and spiritual authority. European government, European instruction, continued steadily till his natural tendencies are superseded by a higher instinct, may shorten the probation period of the negro. Individual blacks of exceptional quality, like Frederick Douglas in America, or the Chief Justice of Barbadoes, will avail themselves of opportunities to rise, and the freest opportunities ought to be offered them. But it is as certain as any future event can be that if we give the negroes as a body the political powers which we claim for ourselves, they will use them only to their own injury. They will slide back into their old condition, and the chance will be gone of lifting them to the level to which we have no right to say that they are incapable of rising.

Chief Justice R—— owes his elevation to his English environment and his English legal training. He would not pretend that he could have made himself what he is in Hayti or in Dahomey. Let English authority die away, and the average black nature, such as it now is, be left free to assert itself, and there will be no more negroes like him in Barbadoes or anywhere.

Naturally, I found him profoundly interested in the late revelations of the state of Hayti. Sir Spenser St. John, an English official, after residing for twelve years in Port au Prince, had in a published narrative with many details and particulars, declared that the republic of Toussaint l'Ouverture, the idol of all believers in the new gospel of liberty, had, after ninety years of independence, become a land where cannibalism could be practised with impunity. The African Obeah, the worship of serpents and trees and stones, after smouldering in all the West Indies in the form of witchcraft and poisoning, had broken out in Hayti in all its old hideousness. Children were sacrificed as in the old days of Moloch and were devoured with horrid ceremony, salted limbs being preserved and sold for the benefit of those who were unable to attend the full solemnities.

That a man in the position of a British resident should have ventured on a statement which, if untrue, would be ruinous to himself, appeared in a high degree improbable. Yet one had to set one incredibility against another. Notwithstanding the character of the evidence, when I went out to the West Indies I was still unbelieving. I could not bring myself to credit that in an island nominally Catholic, where the French language was spoken, and there were cathedrals and churches and priests and missionaries, so horrid a revival of devil-worship could have been really possible. All the inquiries which I had been able to make, from American and other officers who had been in Hayti, confirmed Sir S. St. John's story. I had hardly found a person who entertained a doubt of it. I was perplexed and uncertain, when the Chief Justice opened the subject and asked me what I thought. Had I been convinced I should have turned the conversation, but I was not convinced and I was not afraid to say so. I reminded him of the universal conviction through Europe that the Jews were habitually guilty of sacrificing children also. There had been detailed instances. Alleged offenders had been brought before courts of justice at any time for the last six hundred years. Witnesses had been found to swear to facts which had been accepted as conclusive. Wretched creatures in Henry III.'s time had been dragged by dozens at horses' tails through the streets of London, broken on the wheel, or torn to pieces by infuriated mobs. Even within the last two years, the same accusation had been brought forward in Russia and Germany, and had been established apparently by adequate proof. So far as popular conviction of the guilt of the Jews was an evidence against them, nothing could be stronger; and no charge could be without foundation on ordinary principles of evidence which revived so often and in so many places. And yet many persons, I said, and myself among them, believed that although the accusers were perfectly sincere, the guilt of the Jews was from end to end an hallucination of hatred. I had looked into the particulars of some of the trials. They were like the trials for witchcraft. The belief had created the fact, and accusation was itself evidence. I was prepared to find these stories of child murder in Hayti were bred similarly of anti-negro prejudice.

Had the Chief Justice caught at my suggestion with any eagerness I should have suspected it myself. His grave diffidence and continued hesitation in offering an opinion confirmed me in my own. I told him that I was going to Hayti to learn what I could on the spot. I could not expect that I, on a flying visit, could see deeper into the truth than Sir Spenser St. John had seen, but at least I should not take with me a mind already made up, and I was not given to credulity. He took leave of me with an expression of passionate anxiety that it might be found possible to remove so black a stain from his unfortunate race.

FOOTNOTES:

[9]

As I correct the proofs I learn, to my great sorrow, that Sir Graham is dead. I have lost in him a lately made but valued friend; and the colony has lost the ablest of its legislators.

[10]

It was on this ground alone that slavery was permitted in the French islands. Labat says:

C'est une loi très-ancienne que les terres soumises aux rois de France rendent libres tous ceux qui s'y peuvent retirer. C'est ce qui fit que le roi Louis XIII, de glorieuse mémoire, aussi pieux qu'il étoit sage, eut toutes les peines du monde à consentir que les premiers habitants des isles eussent des esclaves: et ne se rendit enfin qu'aux pressantes sollicitations qu'on luy faisoit de leur octroyer cette permission que parce qu'on lui remontra que c'étoit un moyen infaillible et l'unique qu'il y eût pour inspirer le culte du vrai Dieu aux Africains, les retirer de l'idolâtrie, et les faire persévérer jusqu'à la mort dans la religion chrétienne qu'on leur feroit embrasser.—Vol. iv. p. 14.

CHAPTER X.

Leeward and Windward Islands—The Caribs of Dominica—Visit of Père Labat—St. Lucia—The Pitons—The harbour at Castries—Intended coaling station—Visit to the administrator—The old fort and barracks—Conversation with an American—Constitution of Dominica—Land at Roseau.

Beyond all the West Indian Islands I had been curious to see Dominica.[11] It was the scene of Rodney's great fight on April 12. It was the most beautiful of the Antilles and the least known. A tribe of aboriginal Caribs still lingered in the forests retaining the old look and the old language, and, except that they no longer ate their prisoners, retaining their old habits. They were skilful fishermen, skilful basket makers, skilful in many curious arts.

The island lies between Martinique and Guadaloupe, and is one of the group now called Leeward Islands, as distinguished from St. Lucia, St. Vincent, Grenada, c., which form the Windward. The early geographers drew the line differently and more rationally. The main direction of the trade winds is from east to west. To them the Windward Islands were the whole chain of the Antilles, which form the eastern side of the Caribbean Sea. The Leeward were the great islands on the west of it—Cuba, St. Domingo, Puerto Rico, and Jamaica. The modern division corresponds to no natural phenomenon. The drift of the trades is rather from the north-east than from the south-east, and the names serve only now to describe our own not very successful political groupings.

Dominica cuts in two the French West Indian possessions. The French took it originally from the Spaniards, occupied it, colonised it, planted in it their religion and their language, and fought desperately to maintain their possession. Lord Rodney, to whom we owe our own position in the West Indies, insisted that Dominica must belong to us to hold the French in check, and regarded it as the most important of all our stations there. Rodney made it English, and English it has ever since remained in spite of the furious efforts which France made to recover an island which she so highly valued during the Napoleon wars. I was anxious to learn what we had made of a place which we had fought so hard for.

Though Dominica is the most mountainous of all the Antilles, it is split into many valleys of exquisite fertility. Through each there runs a full and ample river, swarming with fish, and yielding waterpower enough to drive all the mills which industry could build. In these valleys and on the rich levels along the shore the French had once their cane fields and orange gardens, their pineapple beds and indigo plantations.

Labat, who travelled through the island at the close of the seventeenth century, found it at that time chiefly occupied by Caribs. With his hungry appetite for knowledge, he was a guest in their villages, acquainted himself with their characters and habits, and bribed out of them by lavish presents of brandy the secrets of their medicines and poisons. The Père was a clever, curious man, with a genial human sympathy about him, and was indulgent to the faults which the poor coloured sinners fell into from never having known better. He tried to make Christians of them. They were willing to be baptised as often as he liked for a glass of brandy. But he was not very angry when he found that the Christianity went no deeper. Moral virtues, he concluded charitably, could no more be expected out of a Carib than reason and good sense out of a woman.

At Roseau, the capital, he fell in with the then queen of Dominica, a Madame Ouvernard, a Carib of pure blood, who in her time of youth and beauty had been the mistress of an English governor of St. Kitts. When Labat saw her she was a hundred years old with a family of children and grandchildren. She was a grand old lady, unclothed almost absolutely, bent double, so that under ordinary circumstances nothing of her face could be seen. Labat, however, presented her with a couple of bottles of eau de vie, under the influence of which she lifted up to him a pair of still brilliant eyes and a fair mouthful of teeth. They did very well together, and on parting they exchanged presents in Homeric fashion, she loading him with baskets of fruit, he giving a box in return full of pins and needles, knives and scissors.

Labat was a student of languages before philology had become a science. He discovered from the language of the Caribs that they were North American Indians. They called themselves Banari, which meant 'come from over sea.' Their dialect was almost identical with what he had heard spoken in Florida. They were cannibals, but of a peculiar kind. Human flesh was not their ordinary food; but they 'boucanned' or dried the limbs of distinguished enemies whom they had killed in, battle, and handed them round to be gnawed at special festivals. They were a light-hearted, pleasant race, capital shots with bows and arrows, and ready to do anything he asked in return for brandy. They killed a hammer shark for his amusement by diving under the monster and stabbing him with knives. As to their religion, they had no objection to anything. But their real belief was in a sort of devil.

Soon after Labat's visit the French came in, drove the Caribs into the mountains, introduced negro slaves, and an ordered form of society. Madame Ouvernard and her court went to their own place. Canes were planted, and indigo and coffee. A cathedral was built at Roseau, and parish churches were scattered about the island. There were convents of nuns and houses of friars, and a fort at the port with a garrison in it. The French might have been there till now had not we turned them out some ninety years ago; English enterprise then setting in that direction under the impulse of Rodney's victories. I was myself about to see the improvements which we had introduced into an acquisition which had cost us so dear.

I was to be dropped at Roseau by the mail steamer from Barbadoes to St. Thomas's. On our way we touched at St. Lucia, another once famous possession of ours. This island was once French also. Rodney took it in 1778. It was the only one of the Antilles which was left to us in the reverses which followed the capitulation of York Town. It was in the harbour at Castries, the chief port, that Rodney collected the fleet which fought and won the great battle with the Count de Grasse. At the peace of Versailles, St. Lucia was restored to France; but was retaken in 1796 by Sir Ralph Abercrombie, and, like Dominica, has ever since belonged to England. This, too, is a beautiful mountainous island, twice as large as Barbadoes, in which even at this late day we have suddenly discovered that we have an interest. The threatened Darien canal has awakened us to a sense that we require a fortified coaling station in those quarters. St. Lucia has the greatest natural advantages for such a purpose, and works are already in progress there, and the long-deserted forts and barracks which had been made over to snakes and lizards, are again to be occupied by English troops.

We sailed one evening from Barbadoes. In the grey of the next morning we were in the passage between St. Lucia and St. Vincent just under the 'Pitons,' which were soaring grandly above us in the twilight. The Pitons are two conical mountains rising straight out of the sea at the southern end of St. Lucia, one of them 3,000 feet high, the other a few feet lower, symmetrical in shape like sugar loaves, and so steep as to be inaccessible to any one but a member of the Alpine Club. Tradition says that four English seamen, belonging to the fleet, did once set out to climb the loftier of the two. They were watched in their ascent through a telescope. When halfway up one of them was seen to drop, while three went on; a few hundred feet higher a second dropped, and afterwards a third; one had almost reached the summit, when he fell also. No account of what had befallen them ever reached their ship. They were supposed to have been bitten by the fer de lance, the deadliest snake in St. Lucia and perhaps in the world, who had resented and punished their intrusion into regions where they had no business. Such is the local legend, born probably out of the terror of a reptile which is no legend at all, but a living and very active reality.

I had gone on deck on hearing where we were, and saw the twin grey peaks high above me in the sky, the last stars glimmering over their tops and the waves washing against the black precipices at their base. The night had been rough, and a considerable sea was running, which changed, however, to an absolute calm when we had passed the Pitons and were under the lee of the island. I could then observe the peculiar blue of the water which I was told that I should find at St. Lucia and Dominica. I have seen the sea of very beautiful colours in several parts of the world, but I never saw any which equalled this. I do not know the cause. The depth is very great even close to the shore. The islands are merely volcanic mountains with sides extremely steep. The coral insect has made anchorages in the bays and inlets; elsewhere you are out of soundings almost immediately. As to St. Lucia itself, if I had not seen Grenada, if I had not known what I was about to see in Dominica, I should have thought it the most exquisite place which nature had ever made, so perfect were the forms of the forest-clothed hills, the glens dividing them and the high mountain ranges in the interior still draped in the white mist of morning. Here and there along the shore there were bright green spots which meant cane fields. Sugar cane in these countries is always called for brevity cane.

Here, as elsewhere, the population is almost entirely negro, forty thousand blacks and a few hundred whites, the ratio altering every year to white disadvantage. The old system has not, however, disappeared as completely as in other places. There are still white planters with large estates, which are not encumbered as in Barbadoes. They are struggling along, discontented of course, but not wholly despondent. The chief complaint is the somewhat weary one of the laziness of the blacks, who they say will work only when they please, and are never fully awake except at dinner time. I do not know that they have a right to expect anything else from poor creatures whom the law calls human, but who to them are only mechanical tools, not so manageable as tools ought to be, with whom they have no acquaintance and no human relations, whose wages are but twopence an hour and are diminished by fines at the arbitrary pleasure of the overseer.

Life and hope and energy are the qualities most needed. When the troops return there will be a change, and spirit may be put into them again. Castries, the old French town, lies at the head of a deep inlet which runs in among the mountains like a fiord. This is to be the future coaling station. The mouth of the bay is narrow with a high projecting 'head' on either side of it, and can be easily and cheaply fortified. There is little or no tide in these seas. There is depth of water sufficient in the greater part of the harbour for line-of-battle ships to anchor and turn, and the few coral shoals which would be in the way are being torn up with dredging machines. The island has borrowed seventy thousand pounds on Government security to prepare for the dignity which awaits it and for the prosperity which is to follow. There was real work actively going on, a rare and perhaps unexampled phenomenon in the English West Indies.

We brought up alongside of a wharf to take in coal. It was a strange scene; cocoa-nut palms growing incongruously out of coal stores, and gorgeous flowering creepers climbing over the workmen's sheds. Volumes of smoke rose out of the dredging engines and hovered over the town. We had come back to French costume again; we had left the white dresses behind at Barbadoes, and the people at Castries were bright as parrots in crimsons and blues and greens; but fine colours looked oddly out of place by the side of the grimy reproduction of England.

I went on shore and fell in with the engineer of the works, who kindly showed me his plans of the harbour, and explained what was to be done. He showed me also some beautiful large bivalves which had been brought up in the scrapers out of the coral. They were new to me and new to him, though they may be familiar enough to more experienced naturalists. Among other curiosities he had a fer de lance, lately killed and preserved in spirits, a rat-tailed, reddish, powerful-looking brute, about four feet long and as thick as a child's wrist. Even when dead I looked at him respectfully, for his bite is fatal and the effect almost instantaneous. He is fearless, and will not, like most snakes, get out of your way if he hears you coming, but leaves you to get out of his. He has a bad habit, too, of taking his walks at night; he prefers a path or a road to the grass, and your house or your garden to the forest; while if you step upon him you will never do it again. They have introduced the mongoose, who has cleared the snakes out of Jamaica, to deal with him; but the mongoose knows the creature that he has to encounter, and as yet has made little progress in extirpating him.

St. Lucia is under the jurisdiction of Barbadoes. It has no governor of its own, but only an administrator indifferently paid. The elective principle has not yet been introduced into the legislature, and perhaps will not be introduced since we have discovered the island to be of consequence to us, unless as part of some general confederation. The present administrator—Mr. Laborde, a gentleman, I suppose, of French descent—is an elderly official, and resides in the old quarters of the general of the forces, 900 feet above the sea. He has large responsibilities, and, having had large experience also, seems fully equal to the duties which attach to him. He cannot have the authority of a complete governor, or undertake independent enterprises for the benefit of the island, as a Rajah Brooke might do, but he walks steadily on in the lines assigned to him. St. Lucia is better off in this respect than most of the Antilles, and may revive perhaps into something like prosperity when the coaling station is finished and under the command of some eminent engineer officer.

Mr. Laborde had invited us to lunch with him. Horses were waiting for us, and we rode up the old winding track which led from the town to the barracks. The heat below was oppressive, but the air cooled as we rose. The road is so steep that resting places had been provided at intervals, where the soldiers could recover breath or shelter themselves from the tropical cataracts of rain which fall without notice, as if the string had been pulled of some celestial shower bath. The trees branched thickly over it, making an impenetrable shade, till we emerged on the plateau at the top, where we were on comparatively level ground, with the harbour immediately at our feet. The situation had been chosen by the French when St. Lucia was theirs. The general's house, now Mr. Laborde's residence, is a long airy building with a deep colonnade, the drawing and dining rooms occupying the entire breadth of the ground floor, with doors and windows on both sides for coolness and air. The western front overlooked the sea. Behind were wooded hills, green valleys, a mountain range in the background, and the Pitons blue in the distance. As we were before our time, Mr. Laborde walked me out to see the old barracks, magazines, and water tanks. They looked neglected and dilapidated, the signs of decay being partly hid by the creepers with which the walls were overgrown. The soldiers' quarters were occupied for the time by a resident gentleman, who attended to the essential repairs and prevented the snakes from taking possession as they were inclined to do. I forget how many of the fer de lance sort he told me he had killed in the rooms since he had lived in them.

In the war time we had maintained a large establishment in St. Lucia; with what consequences to the health of the troops I could not clearly make out. One informant told me that they had died like flies of yellow fever, and that the fields adjoining were as full of bodies as the Brompton cemetery; another that yellow fever had never been known there or any dangerous disorder; and that if we wanted a sanitary station this was the spot for it. Many thousands of pounds will have to be spent there before the troops can return; but that is our way with the colonies—to change our minds every ten years, to do and undo, and do again, according to parliamentary humours, while John Bull pays the bill patiently for his own irresolution.

The fortress, once very strong, is now in ruins, but, I suppose, will be repaired and rearmed unless we are to trust to the Yankees, who are supposed to have established a Pax Dei in these waters and will permit no aggressive action there either by us or against us. We walked round the walls; we saw the hill a mile off from which Abercrombie had battered out the French, having dragged his guns through a roadless forest to a spot to which there seemed no access except on wings. The word 'impossible' was not known in those days. What Englishmen did once they may do again perhaps if stormy days come back. The ruins themselves were silently impressive. One could hear the note of the old bugles as they sounded the reveille and the roaring of the feu de joie when the shattered prizes were brought in from the French fleet. The signs of what once had been were still visible in the parade ground, in the large mangoes which the soldiers had planted, in the English grass which they had introduced and on which cattle were now grazing. There was a clump of guavas, hitherto only known to me in preserves. I gathered a blossom as a remembrance, white like a large myrtle flower, but heavily scented—too heavily, with an odour of death about it.

Mr. Laborde's conversation was instructive. His entertainment of us was all which our acquired West Indian fastidiousness could desire. The inevitable cigars followed, and Mr. L. gave me a beating at billiards. There were some lively young ladies in the party, and two or three of the ship's officers. The young ones played lawn tennis, and we old ones looked on and wished the years off our shoulders. So passed the day. The sun was setting when we mounted to ride down. So short is the twilight in these latitudes, that it was dark night when we reached the town, and we required the light of the stars to find our boat.

When the coaling process was finished, the ship had been washed down in our absence and was anchored off beyond the reach of the dirt; but the ports were shut; the windsails had been taken down; the air in the cabins was stifling; so I stayed on deck till midnight with a clever young American, who was among our fellow-passengers, talking of many things. He was ardent, confident, self-asserting, but not disagreeably either one or the other. It was rather a pleasure to hear a man speak in these flabby uncertain days as if he were sure of anything, and I had to notice again, as I had often noticed before, how well informed casual American travellers are on public affairs, and how sensibly they can talk of them. He had been much in the West Indies and seemed to know them well. He said that all the whites in the islands wished at the bottom of their hearts to be taken into the Union; but the Union Government was too wise to meddle with them. The trade would fall to America of itself. The responsibility and trouble might remain where it was. I asked him about the Canadian fishery dispute. He thought it would settle itself in time, and that nothing serious would come of it. 'The Washington Cabinet had been a little hard on England,' he admitted; 'but it was six of one and half a dozen of the other.' 'Honours were easy; neither party could score.' 'We had been equally hard on them about Alaska.'

He was less satisfied about Ireland. The telegraph had brought the news of Mr. Goschen's defeat at Liverpool, and Home Rule, which had seemed to have been disposed of, was again within the range of probabilities. He was watching with pitying amusement, like most of his countrymen, the weakness of will with which England allowed herself to be worried by so contemptible a business; but he did seem to fear, and I have heard others of his countrymen say the same, that if we let it go on much longer the Americans may become involved in the thing one way or another, and trouble may rise about it between the two countries.

We weighed; and I went to bed and to sleep, and so missed Pigeon Island, where Rodney's fleet lay before the action, and the rock from which, through his telescope, he watched De Grasse come out of Martinique, and gave his own signal to chase. We rolled as usual between the islands. At daylight we were again in shelter under

Martinique, and again in classic regions; for close to us was Diamond Rock—once his Majesty's ship 'Diamond,' commissioned with crew and officers—one of those curious true incidents, out of which a legend might have grown in other times, that ship and mariners had been turned to stone. The rock, a lonely pyramid six hundred feet high, commanded the entrance to Port Royal in Martinique. Lord Howe took possession of it, sent guns up in slings to the top, and left a midshipman with a handful of men in charge. The gallant little fellow held his fortress for several months, peppered away at the French, and sent three of their ships of war to the bottom. He was blockaded at last by an overwhelming force. No relief could be spared for him. Escape was impossible, as he had not so much as a boat, and he capitulated to famine.

We stayed two hours under Martinique. I did not land. It has been for centuries a special object of care on the part of the French Government. It is well looked after, and, considering the times, prosperous. It has a fine garrison, and a dockyard well furnished, with frigates in the harbours ready for action should occasion arise. I should infer from what I heard that in the event of war breaking out between England and France, Martinique, in the present state of preparation on both sides, might take possession of the rest of the Antilles with little difficulty. Three times we took it, and we gave it back again. In turn, it may one day, perhaps, take us, and the English of the West Indies become a tradition like the buccaneers.

The mountains of Dominica are full in sight from Martinique. The channel which separates them is but thirty miles across, and the view of Dominica as you approach it is extremely grand. Grenada, St. Vincent, St. Lucia, Martinique are all volcanic, with lofty peaks and ridges; but Dominica was at the centre of the force which lifted the Antilles out of the ocean, and the features which are common to all are there in a magnified form. The mountains range from four to five thousand feet in height. Mount Diablot, the highest of them, rises to between five and six thousand feet. The mountains being the tallest in all the group, the rains are also the most violent, and the ravines torn out by the torrents are the wildest and most magnificent. The volcanic forces are still active there. There are sulphur springs and boiling water fountains, and in a central crater there is a boiling lake. There are strange creatures there besides: great snakes—harmless, but ugly to look at; the diablot—from which the mountain takes its name—a great bird, black as charcoal, half raven, half parrot, which nests in holes in the ground as puffins do, spends all the day in them, and flies down to the sea at night to fish for its food. There were once great numbers of these creatures, and it was a favourite amusement to hunt and drag them out of their hiding places. Labat says that they were excellent eating. They are confined now in reduced numbers to the inaccessible crags about the peak which bears their name.

Martinique has two fine harbours. Dominica has none. At the north end of the island there is a bay, named after Prince Rupert, where there is shelter from all winds but the south, but neither there nor anywhere is there an anchorage which can be depended upon in dangerous weather.

Roseau, the principal or only town, stands midway along the western shore. The roadstead is open, but as the prevailing winds are from the east the island itself forms a breakwater. Except on the rarest occasions there is neither surf nor swell there. The land shelves off rapidly, and a gunshot from shore no cable can find the bottom, but there is an anchorage in front of the town, and coasting smacks, American schooners, passing steamers bring up close under the rocks or alongside of the jetties which are built out from the beach upon piles.

The situation of Roseau is exceedingly beautiful. The sea is, if possible, a deeper azure even than at St. Lucia; the air more transparent; the forests of a lovelier green than I ever saw in any other country. Even the rain, which falls in such abundance, falls often out of a clear sky as if not to interrupt the sunshine, and a rainbow almost perpetually hangs its arch over the island. Roseau itself stands on a shallow promontory. A long terrace of tolerable-looking houses faces the landing place. At right angles to the terrace, straight streets strike backwards at intervals, palms and bananas breaking the lines of roof. At a little distance, you see the towers of the old French Catholic cathedral, a smaller but not ungraceful-looking Anglican church, and to the right a fort, or the ruins of one, now used as a police barrack, over which flies the English flag as the symbol of our titular dominion. Beyond the fort is a public garden with pretty trees in it along the brow of a precipitous cliff, at the foot of which, when we landed, lay at anchor a couple of smart Yankee schooners and half a dozen coasting cutters, while rounding inwards behind was a long shallow bay dotted over with the sails of fishing boats. White negro villages gleamed among the palms along the shore, and wooded mountains rose immediately above them. It seemed an attractive, innocent, sunny sort of place, very pleasant to spend a few days in, if the inner side of things corresponded to the appearance. To a looker-on at that calm scene it was not easy to realise the desperate battles which had been fought for the possession of it, the gallant lives which had been laid down under the walls of that crumbling castle. These cliffs had echoed the roar of Rodney's guns on the day which saved the British Empire, and the island I was gazing at was England's Salamis.

The organisation of the place, too, seemed, so far as I could gather from official books, to have been carefully attended to. The constitution had been touched and retouched by the home authorities as if no pains could be too great to make it worthy of a spot so sacred. There is an administrator, which is a longer word than governor. There is an executive council, a colonial secretary, an attorney-general, an auditor-general, and other such 'generals of great charge.' There is a legislative assembly of fourteen members, seven nominated by the Crown and seven elected by the people. And there are revenue officers and excise officers, inspectors of roads, and civil engineers, and school boards, and medical officers, and registrars, and magistrates. Where would political perfection be found if not here with such elaborate machinery?

The results of it all, in the official reports, seemed equally satisfactory till you looked closely into them. The tariff of articles on which duties were levied, and the list of articles raised and exported, seemed to show that Dominica must be a beehive of industry and productiveness. The revenue, indeed, was a little startling as the result of this army of officials. Eighteen thousand pounds was the whole of it, scarcely enough to pay their salaries. The population, too, on whose good government so much thought had been expended, was only 30,000; of these 30,000 only a hundred were English. The remaining whites, and those in scanty numbers, were French and principally Catholics. The soil was as rich as the richest in the world. The cultivation was growing annually less. The inspector of roads was likely to have an easy task, for except close to the town there were no roads at all on which anything with wheels could travel, the old roads made by the French having dropped into horse tracks, and the horse tracks into the beds of torrents. Why in an island where the resources of modern statesmanship had been applied so lavishly and with the latest discoveries in political science, the effect should have so ill corresponded to the means employed, was a problem into which it would be curious to inquire.

The steamer set me down upon the pier and went on upon its way. At the end of a fortnight it would return and pick me up again. Meanwhile, I was to make the best of my time. I had been warned beforehand that there was no hotel in Roseau where an Englishman with a susceptible skin and palate could survive more than a week; and as I had two weeks to provide for, I was uncertain what to do with myself. I was spared the trial of the hotels by the liberality of her Majesty's representative in the colony. Captain Churchill, the administrator of the island, had heard that I was coming there, and I was met on the landing stage by a message from him inviting me to be his guest during my stay. Two tall handsome black girls seized my bags, tossed them on their heads, and strode off with a light step in front of me, cutting jokes with their friends; I following, and my mind misgiving me that I was myself the object of their wit.

I was anxious to see Captain Churchill, for I had heard much of him. The warmest affection had been expressed for him personally, and concern for the position in which he was placed. Notwithstanding 'the latest discoveries of political science,' the constitution was still imperfect. The administrator, to begin with, is allowed a salary of only 500l. a year. That is not much for the chief of such an army of officials; and the hospitalities and social civilities which smooth the way in such situations are beyond his means. His business is to preside at the council, where, the official and the elected members being equally balanced and almost invariably dividing one against the other, his duty is to give the casting vote. He cannot give it against his own officers, and thus the machine is contrived to create the largest amount of friction, and to insure the highest amount of unpopularity to the administrator. His situation is the more difficult because the European element in Roseau, small as it is at best, is more French than English. The priests, the sisterhoods, are French or French-speaking. A French patois is the language of the blacks. They are almost to a man Catholics, and to the French they look as their natural leaders. England has done nothing, absolutely nothing, to introduce her own civilisation; and thus Dominica is English only in name. Should war come, a boatload of soldiers from Martinique would suffice to recover it. Not a black in the whole island would draw a trigger in defence of English authority, and, except the Crown officials, not half a dozen Europeans. The administrator can do nothing to improve this state of things. He is too poor to open Government House to the Roseau shopkeepers and to bid for social popularity. He is no one. He goes in and out unnoticed, and flits about like a bat in the twilight. He can do no good, and from the nature of the system on the construction of which so much care was expended, no one else can do any good.

The maximum of expense, the minimum of benefit to the island, is all that has come of it.

Meanwhile the island drifts along, without credit to borrow money and therefore escaping bankruptcy. The blacks there, as everywhere, are happy with their yams, and cocoa nuts and land crabs. They desire nothing better than they have, and do not imagine that they have any rulers unless agitated by the elected members. These gentlemen would like the official situations for themselves as in Trinidad, and they occasionally attempt a stir with partial success; otherwise the island goes on in a state of torpid content. Captain Churchill, quiet and gentlemanlike, gives no personal offence, but popularity he cannot hope for, having no means of recommending himself. The only really powerful Europeans are the Catholic bishop and the priests and sisterhoods. They are looked up to with genuine respect. They are reaping the harvest of the long and honourable efforts of the French clergy in all their West Indian possessions to make the blacks into Catholic Christians. In the Christian part of it they have succeeded but moderately; but such religion as exists in the island is mainly what they have introduced and taught, and they have a distinct influence which we ourselves have not tried to rival.

But we have been too long toiling up the paved road to Captain Churchill's house. My girl-porter guides led me past the fort, where they exchanged shots with the lounging black police, past the English church, which stood buried in trees, the churchyard prettily planted with tropical flowers. The sun was dazzling, the heat was intense, and the path which led through it, if not apparently much used, looked shady and cool.

A few more steps brought us to the gate of the Residence, where Captain Churchill had his quarters in the absence of the Governor-in-Chief of the Leeward Islands, whose visits were few and brief. In the event of the Governor's arrival he removed to a cottage in the hills. The house was handsome, the gardens well kept; a broad walk led up to the door, a hedge of lime trees closely clipt on one side of it, on the other a lawn with orange trees, oleanders, and hibiscus, palms of all varieties and almond trees, which in Dominica grow into giants, their broad leaves turning crimson before they fall, like the Virginia creeper. We reached the entrance of the house by wide stone steps, where countless lizards were lazily basking. Through the bars of the railings on each side of them there were intertwined the runners of the largest and most powerfully scented stephanotis which I have ever seen. Captain Churchill (one of the Marlborough Churchills) received me with more than cordiality. Society is not abundant in his Barataria, and perhaps as coming from England I was welcome to him in his solitude. His wife, an English Creole—that is, of pure English blood, but born in the island—was as hospitable as her husband. They would not let me feel that I was a stranger, and set me at my ease in a moment with a warmth which was evidently unassumed. Captain C. was lame, having hurt his foot. In a day or two he hoped to be able to mount his horse again, when we were to ride together and see the curiosities. Meanwhile, he talked sorrowfully enough of his own situation and the general helplessness of it. A man whose feet are chained and whose hands are in manacles is not to be found fault with if he cannot use either. He is not intended to use either. The duty of an administrator of Dominica, it appears, is to sit still and do nothing, and to watch the flickering in the socket of the last remains of English influence and authority. Individually he was on good terms with everyone, with the Catholic bishop especially, who, to his regret and mine, was absent at the time of my visit.

His establishment was remarkable; it consisted of two black girls—a cook and a parlourmaid—who 'did everything;' and 'everything,' I am bound to say, was done well enough to please the most fastidious nicety. The cooking was excellent. The rooms, which were handsomely furnished, were kept as well and in as good order as in the Churchills' ancestral palace at Blenheim. Dominica has a bad name for vermin. I had been threatened with centipedes and scorpions in my bedroom. I had been warned there, as everywhere in the West Indies, never to walk across the floor with bare feet, lest a land crab should lay hold of my toe or a jigger should bite a hole in it, lay its eggs there, and bring me into the hands of the surgeon. Never while I was Captain C.'s guest did I see either centipede, or scorpion, or jigger, or any other unclean beast in any room of which these girls had charge. Even mosquitoes did not trouble me, so skilfully and carefully they arranged the curtains. They were dressed in the fashion of the French islands, something like the Moorish slaves whom one sees in pictures of Eastern palaces. They flitted about silent on their shoeless feet, never stumbled, or upset chairs or plates or dishes, but waited noiselessly like a pair of elves, and were always in their place when wanted. One had heard much of the idleness and carelessness of negro servants. In no part of the globe have I ever seen household work done so well by two pairs of hands. Of their morals I know nothing. It is usually said that negro girls have none. They appeared to me to be perfectly modest and innocent. I asked in wonder what wages were paid to these black fairies, believing that at no price at all could the match of them be found in England. I was informed that they had three shillings a week each, and 'found themselves,' i.e. found their own food and clothes. And this was above the usual rate, as Government House was expected to be liberal. The scale of wages may have something to do with the difficulty of obtaining labour in the West Indies. I could easily believe the truth of what I had been often told, that free labour is more economical to the employer than slave labour.

The views from the drawing room windows were enchantingly beautiful. It is not the form only in these West Indian landscapes, or the colour only, but form and colour seen through an atmosphere of very peculiar transparency. On one side we looked up a mountain gorge, the slopes covered with forest; a bold lofty crag jutting out from them brown and bare, and the mountain ridge behind half buried in mist. From the other window we had the Botanical Gardens, the bay beyond them sparkling in the sunshine, and on the farther side of it, a few miles off, an island fortress which the Marquis de Bouillé, of Revolution notoriety, took from the English in 1778. The sea stretched out blue and lovely under the fringe of sand, box trees, and almonds which grew along the edge of the cliff. The air was perfumed by white acacia flowers sweeter than orange blossom.

Captain C. limped down with me into the gardens for a fuller look at the scene. Dusky fishermen were busy with their nets catching things like herrings, which come in daily to the shore to escape the monsters which prey upon them. Canoes on the old Carib pattern were slipping along outside, trailing lines for kingfish and bonitos. Others were setting baskets, like enormous lobster pots or hoop nets—such as we use to catch tench in English ponds—these, too, a legacy from the Caribs, made of strong tough cane. At the foot of the cliff were the smart American schooners which I had seen on landing—broad-beamed, shallow, low in the water with heavy spars, which bring Yankee 'notions' to the islands and carry back to New York bananas and limes and pineapples. There they were, models of Tom Cringle's 'Wave,' airy as English yachts, and equal to anything from a smuggling cruise to a race for a cup. I could have gazed for ever, so beautiful, so new, so like a dream it was, had I not been brought back swiftly to prose and reality. Suddenly out of a clear sky, without notice, and without provocation, first a few drops of rain fell, and then a deluge which set the gutters running. We had to scuttle home under our umbrellas. I was told, and I discovered afterwards by fuller experience, that this was the way in Dominica, and that if I went out anywhere I must be prepared for it. In our retreat we encountered a distinguished-looking abbé with a collar and a gold cross, who bowed to my companion. I would gladly have been introduced to him, but neither he nor we had leisure for courtesies in the torrent which was falling upon us.

FOOTNOTES:

[11

Not to be confounded with St. Domingo, which is called after St. Domenic, where the Spaniards first settled, and is now divided into the two black republics of St. Domingo and Hayti. Dominica lies in the chain of the Antilles between Martinique and Guadaloupe, and was so named by Columbus because he discovered it on a Sunday.

CHAPTER XI.

Curiosities in Dominica—Nights in the tropics—English and Catholic churches—The market place at Roseau—Fishing extraordinary—A storm—Dominican boatmen—Morning walks—Effects of the Leeward Islands Confederation—An estate cultivated as it ought to be—A mountain ride—Leave the island—Reflections.

There was much to be seen in Dominica of the sort which travellers go in search of. There was the hot sulphur spring in the mountains; there was the hot lake; there was another volcanic crater, a hollow in the centre of the island now filled with water and surrounded with forest; there were the Caribs, some thirty families of them living among thickets, through which paths must be cut before we could reach them. We could undertake nothing till Captain C. could ride again. Distant expeditions can only be attempted on horses. They are bred to the work. They climb like cats, and step out safely where a fall or a twisted ankle would be the probable consequence of attempting to go on foot. Meanwhile, Roseau itself was to be seen and the immediate neighbourhood, and this I could manage for myself.

My first night was disturbed by unfamiliar noises and strange imaginations. I escaped mosquitoes through the care of the black fairies. But mosquito curtains will not keep out sounds, and when the fireflies had put out their lights there began the singular chorus of tropical midnight. Frogs, lizards, bats, croaked, sang, and whistled with no intermission, careless whether they were in discord or harmony. The palm branches outside my window swayed in the land breeze, and the dry branches rustled crisply, as if they were plates of silver. At intervals came cataracts of rain, and above all the rest the deep boom of the cathedral bell tolling out the hours like a note of the Old World. The Catholic clergy had brought the bells with them as they had brought their faith into these new lands. It was pathetic, it was ominous music; for what had we done and what were we doing to set beside it in the century for which the island had been ours? Towards morning I heard the tinkle of the bell of the convent adjoining the garden calling the nuns to matins. Happily in the tropics hot nights do not imply an early dawn. The darkness lingers late, sleep comes at last and drowns our fancies in forgetfulness.

The swimming bath was immediately under my room. I ventured into it with some trepidation. The basement story in most West Indian houses is open, to allow the air free passage under them. The space thus left vacant is used for lumber and rubbish, and, if scorpions or snakes are in the neighbourhood, is the place where one would look for them. There the bath was. I had been advised to be careful, and as it was dark this was not easy. The fear, however, was worse than the reality. Awkward encounters do happen if one is long in these countries; but they are rare, and seldom befall the accidental visitor; and the plunge into fresh water is so delicious that one is willing to risk the chance.

I wandered out as soon as the sun was over the horizon. The cool of the morning is the time to see the people. The market girls were streaming into the town with their baskets of vegetables on their heads. The fishing boats were out again on the bay. Our Anglican church had its bell too as well as the cathedral. The door was open, and I went in and found a decent-looking clergyman preparing a flock of seven or eight blacks and mulattoes for the Communion. He was taking them through their catechism, explaining very properly, that religion meant doing one's duty, and that it was not enough to profess particular opinions. Dominica being Roman Catholic, and Roman Catholics not generally appreciating or understanding the claims of Anglicans to the possession of the sacraments, he pointed out where the difference lay. He insisted that we had priests as well as they; we had confession; we had absolution; only our priests did not claim, as the Catholics did, a direct power in themselves to forgive sins. Their office was to tell sinners that if they truly and sincerely repented and amended their lives God would forgive them. What he said was absolutely true; but I could not see in the dim faces of the catechumens that the distinction was particularly intelligible to them. If they thought at all, they probably reflected that no divinely constituted successor of the Apostles was needed to communicate a truism which every sensible person was equally able and entitled to tell them. Still the good earnest man meant well, and I wished him more success in his missionary enterprise than he was likely to find.

From the Church of England to the great rival establishment was but a few minutes' walk. The cathedral was five times as large, at least, as the building which I had just left—old in age, old in appearance, with the usual indifferent pictures or coloured prints, with the usual decorated altar, but otherwise simple and venerable. There was no service going on, for it was a week-day; a few old men and women only were silently saying their prayers. On Sundays I was told that it was overflowing.

The negro morals are as emancipated in Dominica as in the rest of the West Indies. Obeah is not forgotten; and along with the Catholic religion goes on an active belief in magic and witchcraft. But their religion is not necessarily a sham to them; it was the same in Europe in the ages of faith. Even in enlightened Protestant countries people calling themselves Christians believe that the spirits of the dead can be called up to amuse an evening party. The blacks in this respect are no worse than their white kinsmen. The priests have a genuine human hold upon them; they baptize the children; they commit the dead to the cemetery with the promise of immortality; they are personally loved and respected: and when a young couple marry, as they seldom but occasionally do, it is to the priest that they apply to tie them together.

From the cathedral I wandered through the streets of Roseau; they had been well laid out; the streets themselves, and the roads leading to them from the country, had been carefully paved, and spoke of a time when the town had been full of life and vigour. But the grass was growing between the stones, and the houses generally were dilapidated and dirty. A few massive stone buildings there were, on which time and rain had made no impression; but these probably were all French—built long ago, perhaps in the days of Labat and Madame Ouvernard. The English hand had struck the island with paralysis. The British flag was flying over the fort, but for once I had no pride in looking at it. The fort itself was falling to pieces, like the fort at Grenada. The stones on the slope on which it stands had run with the blood which we spilt in the winning of it. Dominica had then been regarded as the choicest jewel in the necklace of the Antilles. For the last half-century we have left it to desolation, as a child leaves a plaything that it is tired of.

In Roseau, as in most other towns, the most interesting spot is the market. There you see the produce of the soil; there you see the people that produce it; and you see them, not on show, as in church on Sundays, but in their active working condition. The market place at Roseau is a large square court close to the sea, well paved, surrounded, by warehouses, and luxuriantly shaded by large overhanging trees. Under these trees were hundreds of black women, young and old, with their fish and fowls, and fruit and bread, their yams and sweet potatoes, their oranges and limes and plantains. They had walked in from the country five or ten miles before sunrise with their loaded baskets on their heads. They would walk back at night with flour or salt fish, or oil, or whatever they happened to want. I did not see a single sullen face among them. Their figures were unconscious of lacing, and their feet of the monstrosities which we call shoes. They moved with the lightness and elasticity of leopards. I thought that I had never seen in any drawing room in London so many perfectly graceful forms. They could not mend their faces, but even in some of these there was a swarthy beauty. The hair was hopeless, and they knew it, but they turn the defect into an ornament by the coloured handkerchief which they twist about their heads, leaving the ends flowing. They chattered like jackdaws about a church tower. Two or three of the best looking, seeing that I admired them a little, used their eyes and made some laughing remarks. They spoke in their French patois, clipping off the first and last syllables of the words. I but half understood them, and could not return their bits of wit. I can only say that if their habits were as loose as white people say they are, I did not see a single licentious expression either in face or manner.

They seemed to me light-hearted, merry, innocent young women, as free from any thought of evil as the peasant girls in Brittany.

Two middle-aged dames were in a state of violent excitement about some subject on which they differed in opinion. A ring gathered about them, and they declaimed at one another with fiery volubility. It did not go beyond words; but both were natural orators, throwing their heads back, waving their arms, limbs and chest quivering with emotion. There was no personal abuse, or disposition to claw each other. On both sides it was a rhetorical outpouring of emotional argument. One of them, a tall pure blood negress, black as if she had just landed from Guinea, began at last to get the best of it. Her gesticulations became more imposing. She shook her finger. Mandez this, she said, and mandez that, till she bore her antagonist down and sent her flying. The audience then melted away, and I left the conqueror standing alone shooting a last volley at the retreating enemy and making passionate appeals to the universe. The subject of the discussion was a curious one. It was on the merits of race. The defeated champion had a taint of white blood in her. The black woman insisted that blacks were of pure breed, and whites were of pure breed. Mulattoes were mongrels, not creatures of God at all, but creatures of human wickedness. I do not suppose that the mulatto was convinced, but she accepted her defeat. The conqueror, it was quite clear, was satisfied that she had the best of the discussion, and that the hearers were of the same opinion.

MORNING WALK, DOMINICA.
MORNING WALK, DOMINICA.

From the market I stepped back upon the quay, where I had the luck to witness a novel form of fishing, the most singular I have ever fallen in with. I have mentioned the herring-sized white fish which come in upon the shores of the island. They travel, as most small fish do, in enormous shoals, and keep, I suppose, in the shallow waters to avoid the kingfish and bonitos, who are good judges in their way, and find these small creatures exceptionally excellent. The wooden pier ran out perhaps a hundred and fifty feet into the sea. It was a platform standing on piles, with openings in several places from which stairs led down to landing stages. The depth at the extremity was about five fathoms. There is little or no tide, the difference between high water and low being not more than a couple of feet. Looking down the staircases, I saw among the piles in the brilliantly clear water unnumbered thousands of the fish which I have described. The fishermen had carried a long net round the pier from shore to shore, completely inclosing it. The fish were shut in, and had no means of escape except at the shore end, where boys were busy driving them back with stones; but how the net was to be drawn among the piles, or what was to be done next, I was curious to learn. I was not left long to conjecture. A circular bag net was produced, made of fine strong thread, coloured a light green, and almost invisible in the sea. When it was spread, one side could be left open and could be closed at will by a running line from above. This net was let carefully down between the piles, and was immediately swollen out by the current which runs along the coast into a deep bag. Two young blacks then dived; one saw them swimming about under water like sharks, hunting the fish before them as a dog would hunt a flock of sheep. Their companions, who were watching from the platform, waited till they saw as many driven into the purse of the inner net as they could trust the meshes to bear the weight of. The cord was then drawn. The net was closed. Net and all that it contained were hoisted into a boat, carried ashore and emptied. The net itself was then brought back and spread again for a fresh haul. In this way I saw as many fish caught as would have filled a large cart. The contrivance, I believe, is one more inheritance from the Caribs, whom Labat describes as doing something of a similar kind.

Another small incident happened a day or two after, which showed the capital stuff of which the Dominican boatmen and fishermen are made. They build their own vessels large and small, and sail them themselves, not afraid of the wildest weather, and doing the local trade with Martinique and Guadaloupe. Four of these smacks, cutter rigged, from ten to twenty tons burden, I had seen lying at anchor one evening with an American schooner under the gardens. In the night, the off-shore wind rose into one of those short violent tropical storms which if they lasted longer would be called hurricanes, but in these winter months are soon over. It came on at midnight, and lasted for two hours. The noise woke me, for the house shook, and the roar was like Niagara. It was too dark, however, to see anything. The tempest died away at last, and I slept till daybreak. My first thought on waking was for the smacks and the schooner Had they sunk at their moorings? Had they broken loose, or what had become of them? I got up and went down to the cliff to see. The damage to the trees had been less than I expected. A few torn branches lay on the lawn and the leaves were cast about, but the anchorage was empty. Every vessel of every sort and size was gone. There was still a moderate gale blowing. As the wind was off-shore the sea was tolerably smooth for a mile or two, but outside the waves were breaking violently, and the foam scuds were whirling off their crests. The schooner was about four miles off, beating back under storm canvas, making good weather of it and promising in a tack or two to recover the moorings. The smacks, being less powerful vessels, had been driven farther out to sea. Three of them I saw labouring heavily in the offing. The fourth I thought at first had disappeared altogether, but finally I made out a white speck on the horizon which I supposed to be the missing cutter. One of the first three presently dropped away to leeward, and I lost sight of her. The rest made their way back in good time. Towards the afternoon when the wind had gone down the two that remained came in after them, and before night they were all in their places again.

The gale had struck them at about midnight. Their cables had parted, and they had been blown away to sea. The crews of the schooner and of three of the cutters were all on board. They got their vessels under command, and had been in no serious danger. In the fourth there was no one but a small black boy of the island. He had been asleep, and woke to find himself driving before the wind. In an hour or two he would have been beyond the shelter of the land, and in the high seas which were then running must have been inevitably swamped. The little fellow contrived in the darkness—no one could tell how—to set a scrap of his mainsail, get his staysail up, and in this condition to lie head to the wind. So handled, small cutters, if they have a deck over them, can ride out an ordinary gale in tolerable security. They drift, of course; in a hurricane the only safety is in yielding to it; but they make fair resistance, and the speed is checked. The most practical seaman could have done no better than this boy. He had to wait for help in the morning. He was not strong enough to set his canvas properly, and work his boat home. He would have been driven out at last, and as he had neither food nor water would have been starved had he escaped drowning. But his three consorts saw him. They knew how it was, and one of them went back to his assistance.

I have known the fishing boys of the English Channel all my life; they are generally skilful, ready, and daring beyond their years; but I never knew one lad not more than thirteen or fourteen years old who, if woke out of his sleep by a hurricane in a dark night and alone, would have understood so well what to do, or have it done so effectually. There are plenty more of such black boys in Dominica, and they deserve a better fate than to be sent drifting before constitutional whirlwinds back into barbarism, because we, on whom their fate depends, are too ignorant or too careless to provide them with a tolerable government.

The kind Captain Churchill, finding himself tied to his chair, and wishing to give me every assistance towards seeing the island, had invited a creole gentleman from the other side of it to stay a few days with us. Mr. F——, a man about thirty, was one of the few survivors from among the planters; he had never been out of the West Indies, but was a man of honesty and intelligence, could use his eyes, and form sound judgments on subjects which immediately concerned him. I had studied Roseau for myself. With Mr. F—— for a companion, I made acquaintance with the environs. We started for our walks at daybreak, in the cool of the morning. We climbed cliffs, we rambled on the rich levels about the river, once amply cultivated, and even now the soil is luxuriant in neglect; a few canefields still survive, but most of them are turned to other uses, and you pass wherever you go the ruins of old mills, the massive foundations of ancient warehouses, huge hewn stones built and mortared well together, telling what once had been; the mango trees, which the owners had planted, waving green over the wrecks of their forgotten industry. Such industry as is now to be found is, as elsewhere in general, the industry of the black peasantry. It is the same as in Grenada: the whites, or the English part of them, have lost heart, and cease to struggle against the stream. A state of things more helplessly provoking was never seen. Skill and capital and labour have only to be brought to bear together, and the land might be a Garden of Eden. All precious fruits, and precious spices, and gums, and plants of rarest medicinal virtues will spring and grow and flourish for the asking. The limes are as large as lemons, and in the markets of the United States are considered the best in the world.

As to natural beauty, the West Indian Islands are like Scott's novels, where we admire most the one which we have read the last. But Dominica bears the palm away from all of them. One morning Mr. F—— took me a walk up the Roseau river, an ample stream even in what is called the dry season, with deep pools full of eels and mullet. We entered among the hills which were rising steep above us. The valley grew deeper, or rather there were a series of valleys, gorges dense with forest, which had been torn out by the cataracts. The path was like the mule tracts of the Alps, cut in other days along the sides of the precipices with remnants of old conduits which supplied water to the mills below. Rich odorous acacias bent over us. The flowers, the trees, the birds, the insects, were a maze of perfume and loveliness.

Occasionally some valley opposite the sun would be spanned by a rainbow as the rays shone through a morning shower out of the blue sky. We wandered on and on, wading through tributary brooks, stopping every minute to examine some new fern or plant, peasant women and children meeting us at intervals on their way into the town. There were trees to take shelter under when indispensable, which even the rain of Dominica could not penetrate. The levels at the bottom of the valleys and the lower slopes, where the soil was favourable, were carelessly planted with limes which were in full bearing. Small black boys and girls went about under the trees, gathering the large lemon-shaped fruit which lay on the ground thick as apples in a West of England orchard. Here was all this profusion of nature, lavish beyond example, and the enterprising youth of England were neglecting a colony which might yield them wealth beyond the treasures of the old sugar planters, going to Florida, to Texas, to South America, taking their energy and their capital to the land of the foreigner, leaving Dominica, which might be the garden of the world, a precious emerald set in the ring of their own Antilles, enriched by the sacred memories of glorious English achievements, as if such a place had no existence. Dominica would surrender herself to-morrow with a light heart to France, to America, to any country which would accept the charge of her destinies. Why should she care any more for England, which has so little care for her? Beauties conscious of their charms do not like to be so thrown aside. There is no dislike to us among the blacks; they are indifferent, but even their indifference would be changed into loyalty if we made the slightest effort to recover it. The poor black was a faithful servant as long as he was a slave. As a freeman he is conscious of his inferiority at the bottom of his heart, and would attach himself to a rational white employer with at least as much fidelity as a spaniel. Like the spaniel, too, if he is denied the chance of developing under guidance the better qualities which are in him, he will drift back into a mangy cur.

In no country ought a government to exist for which respect is impossible, and English rule as it exists in Dominica is a subject for a comedy. The Governor-General of the Leeward Islands resides in Antigua, and in theory ought to go on progress and visit in turn his subordinate dominions. His visits are rare as those of angels. The eminent person, who at present holds that high office, has been once in Nevis; and thrice in Dominica, but only for the briefest stay there. Perhaps he has held aloof in consequence of an adventure which befell a visiting governor some time ago on one of these occasions. When there is a constitution there is an opposition. If there are no grievances the opposition manufacture them, and the inhabitants of Roseau were persuaded that they were an oppressed people and required fuller liberties. I was informed that His Excellency had no sooner landed and taken possession of the Government House, than a mob of men and women gathered in the market place under the leadership of their elected representative. The girls that I had admired very likely made a part of it. They swarmed up into the gardens, they demonstrated under the windows, laughing, shouting, and petitioning. His Excellency first barricaded the doors, then opened them and tried a speech, telling the dear creatures how much he loved and respected them. Probably they did not understand him, as few of them speak English. Producing no effect, he retreated again, barred the door once more, slipped out at a back entrance down a lane to the port, took refuge on board his steamer, and disappeared. So the story was told me—not by the administrator, who was not a man to turn English authority into ridicule—but by some one on the spot, who repeated the current report of the adventure. It may be exaggerated in some features, but it represents, at any rate, the feeling of the place towards the head representative of the existing government.

I will mention another incident, said to have occurred still more recently to one of these great persons, very like what befell Sancho Panza in Barataria. This, too, may have been wickedly turned, but it was the subject of general talk and general amusement on board the steamers which make the round of the Antilles. Universal belief is a fact of its kind, and though it tends to shape itself in dramatic form more completely than the facts justify, there is usually some truth at the bottom of it. The telegrams to the West Indies pass through New York, and often pick up something on the way. A warning message reached a certain colony that a Yankee-Irish schooner with a Fenian crew was coming down to annex the island, or at least to kidnap the governor. This distinguished gentleman ought perhaps to have suspected that a joke was being played upon his fears; but he was a landlord. A governor-general had been threatened seriously in Canada, why not he in the Antilles? He was as much agitated as Sancho himself. All these islands were and are entirely undefended save by a police which cannot be depended on to resist a serious invasion. They were called out. Rumour said that in half the rifles the cartridges were found afterwards inverted. The next day dispelled the alarm. The schooner was the creation of some Irish telegraph clerk, and the scare ended in laughter. But under the jest lies the wretched certainty that the Antilles have no protection except in their own population, and so little to thank England for that scarcely one of the inhabitants, except the officials, would lift a finger to save the connection.

Once more, I tell these stories not as if they were authenticated facts, but as evidence of the scornful feeling towards English authority. The current belief in them is a fact of a kind and a very serious one.

The confederation of the Leeward Islands may have been a convenience to the Colonial Office, and may have allowed a slight diminution in the cost of administration. The whole West Indies might be placed under a single governor with only good results if he were a real one like the Governor-General at Calcutta. But each single island has lost from the change, so far, more than it has gained. Each ship of war has a captain of its own and officers of its own trained specially for the service. If the Antilles are ever to thrive, each of them also should have some trained and skilful man at its head, unembarrassed by local elected assemblies. The whites have become so weak that they would welcome the abolition of such assemblies. The blacks do not care for politics, and would be pleased to see them swept away to-morrow if they were governed wisely and fairly. Of course, in that case it would be necessary to appoint governors who would command confidence and respect. But let governors be sent who would be governors indeed, like those who administer the Indian presidencies, and the white residents would gather heart again, and English and American capitalists would bring their money and their enterprise, and the blacks would grow upwards instead of downwards. Let us persist in the other line, let us use the West Indian governments as asylums for average worthy persons who have to be provided for, and force on them black parliamentary institutions as a remedy for such persons' inefficiency, and these beautiful countries will become like Hayti, with Obeah triumphant, and children offered to the devil and salted and eaten, till the conscience of mankind wakes again and the Americans sweep them all away.

I had an opportunity of seeing what can really be done in Dominica by an English gentleman who has gone the right way to work there. Dr. Nicholls came out a few years ago to Roseau as a medical officer. He was described to me as a man not only of high professional skill, but with considerable scientific attainments. Either by purchase or legacy (I think the latter) he had become possessed of a small estate on a hillside a mile or two from the town. He had built a house upon it. He was cultivating the soil on scientific principles, and had politely sent me an invitation to call on him and see what he was about. I was delighted to avail myself of such an opportunity.

I do not know the exact extent of the property which was under cultivation; perhaps it was twenty-five or thirty acres. The chief part of it was planted with lime trees, the limes which I saw growing being as large as moderate-sized lemons; most of the rest was covered with Liberian coffee, which does not object to the moist climate, and was growing with profuse luxuriance. Each tree, each plant had been personally attended to, pruned when it needed pruning, supported by bamboos if it was overgrowing its strength, while the ground about the house was consecrated to botanical experiments, and specimens were to be seen there of every tropical flower, shrub, or tree, which was either remarkable for its beauty or valuable for its chemical properties. His limes and coffee went principally to New York, where they had won a reputation, and were in special demand; but ingenuity tries other tracks besides the beaten one. Dr. Nicholls had a manufactory of citric acid which had been found equally excellent in Europe. Everything which he produced was turning to gold, except donkeys, seven or eight of which were feeding under his windows, and which multiplied so fast that he could not tell what to do with them.

Industries so various and so active required labour, and I saw many of the blacks at work on the grounds. In apparent contradiction to the general West Indian experience, he told me that he had never found a difficulty about it. He paid them fair wages, and paid them regularly without the overseer's fines and drawbacks. He knew one from the other personally could call each by his name, remembered where he came from, where he lived, and how, and could joke with him about his wife or mistress. They in consequence clung to him with an innocent affection, stayed with him all the week without asking for holidays, and worked with interest and goodwill. Four years only had elapsed since Dr. Nicholls commenced his undertakings, and he already saw his way to clearing a thousand pounds a year on that one small patch of acres. I may mention that, being the only man in the island of really superior attainments, he had tried in vain to win one of the seats in the elective part of the legislature.

There was nothing particularly favourable in the situation of his land. All parts of Dominica would respond as willingly to similar treatment. What could be the reason, Dr. Nicholls asked me, why young Englishmen went planting to so many other countries, went even to Ceylon and Borneo, while comparatively at their own doors, within a fortnight's sail of Plymouth, there was this island immeasurably more fertile than either? The explanation, I suppose, is the misgiving that the West Indies are consigned by the tendencies of English policy to the black population, and that a local government created by representatives of the negro vote would make a residence there for an energetic and self-respecting European less tolerable than in any other part of the globe. The republic of Hayti not only excludes a white man from any share of the administration, but forbids his acquisition or possession of real property in any form. Far short of such extreme provisions, the most prosperous industry might be blighted by taxation. Self-government is a beautiful subject for oratorical declamation. If the fact corresponded to the theory and if the possession of a vote produced the elevating effects upon the character which are so noisily insisted upon, it would be the welcome panacea for political and social disorder. Unfortunately the fact does not correspond to the theory. The possession of a vote never improved the character of any human being and never will.

There are many islands in the West Indies, and an experiment might be ventured without any serious risk. Let the suffrage principle be applied in its fullness where the condition of the people seems best to promise success. In some one of them—Dominica would do as well as any other—let a man of ability and character with an ambition to distinguish himself be sent to govern with a free hand. Let him choose his own advisers, let him be untrammelled, unless he falls into fatal and inexcusable errors, with interference from home. Let him have time to carry out any plans which he may form, without fear of recall at the end of the normal period. After ten or fifteen years, let the results of the two systems be compared side by side. I imagine the objection to such a trial would be the same which was once made in my hearing by an Irish friend of mine, who was urging on an English statesman the conversion of Ireland into a Crown colony. 'You dare not try it,' he said, 'for if you did, in twenty years we would be the most prosperous island of the two, and you would be wanting to follow our example.'

We had exhausted the neighbourhood of Roseau. After a few days Captain C. was again able to ride, and we could undertake more extended expeditions. He provided me with a horse or pony or something between both, a creature that would climb a stone staircase at an angle of forty-five, or slide down a clay slope soaked by a tropical shower, with the same indifference with which it would canter along a meadow. In the slave times cultivation had been carried up into the mountains. There were the old tracks through the forest engineered along the edges of precipices, torrents roaring far down below, and tall green trees standing in hollows underneath, whose top branches were on a level with our eyes. We had to ride with mackintosh and umbrella, prepared at any moment to have the floods descend upon us. The best costume would be none at all. While the sun is above the horizon the island seems to lie under the arches of perpetual rainbows. One gets wet and one dries again, and one is none the worse for the adventure. I had heard that it was dangerous. It did no harm to me. A very particular object was to reach the crest of the mountain ridge which divides Dominica down the middle. We saw the peaks high above us, but it was useless to try the ascent if one could see nothing when one arrived, and mists and clouds hung about so persistently that we had to put off our expedition day after day.

A tolerable morning came at last. We started early. A faithful black youth ran alongside of the horses to pick us up if we fell, and to carry the indispensable luncheon basket. We rode through the town, over the bridge and by the foot of Dr. Nicholls's plantations. We passed through lime and banana gardens rising slowly along the side of a glen above the river. The road had been made by the French long ago, and went right across the island. It had once been carefully paved, but wet and neglect had loosened the stones and tumbled them out of their places. Trees had driven their roots through the middle of the track. Mountain streams had taken advantage of convenient cuttings and scooped them into waterways. The road commissioner on the official staff seemed a merely ornamental functionary. We could only travel at a foot pace and in single file. Happily our horses were used to it. Along this road in 1805 Sir George Prevost retreated with the English garrison of Roseau, when attacked in force from Martinique; saved his men and saved the other part of the island till relief came and the invaders were driven out again. That was the last of the fighting, and we have been left since in undisturbed possession. Dominica was then sacred as the scene of Rodney's glories. Now I suppose, if the French came again, we should calculate the mercantile value of the place to us, and having found it to be nothing at all, might conclude that it would be better to let them keep it.

We went up and up, winding round projecting spurs of mountain, here and there coming on plateaus where pioneering blacks were clearing patches of forest for their yams and coffee. We skirted the edge of a valley several miles across, on the far side of which we saw the steaming of the sulphur springs, and beyond and above it a mountain peak four thousand feet high and clothed with timber to the summit. In most countries the vegetation grows thin as you rise into the higher altitudes. Here the bush only seems to grow denser, the trees grander and more self-asserting, the orchids and parasites on the boughs more variously brilliant. There were tree ferns less splendid than those in New Zealand and Australia, but larger than any one can see in English hot-houses, wild oranges bending under the weight of ripe fruit which was glowing on their branches, wild pines, wild begonias scattered along the banks, and a singularly brilliant plant which they call the wild plantain, but it is not a plantain at all, with large broad pointed leaves radiating out from a centre like an aloe's, and a crimson flower stem rising up straight in the middle. It was startling to see such insolent beauty displaying itself indifferently in the heart of the wilderness with no human eye to look at it unless of some passing black or wandering Carib.

The track had been carried across hot streams fresh from boiling springs, and along the edge of chasms where there was scarcely foothold for the horses. At length we found ourselves on what was apparently the highest point of the pass. We could not see where we were for the trees and bushes which surrounded us, but the path began to descend on the other side. Near the summit was a lake formed in an old volcanic crater which we had come specially to look at. We descended a few hundred feet into a hollow among the hills where the lake was said to be. Where was it, then? I asked the guide, for I could discover nothing that suggested a lake or anything like one. He pointed into the bush where it was thicker with tropical undergrowth than a wheatfield with ears of corn. If I cared to creep below the branches for two hundred yards at the risk of meeting snakes, scorpions, and other such charming creatures, I should find myself on the water's edge.

To ride up a mountain three thousand feet high, to be near a wonder which I could not see after all, was not what I had proposed to myself. There was a traveller's rest at the point where we halted, a cool damp grotto carved into the sand-stone. We picketed our horses, cutting leafy boughs off the trees for them, and making cushions for ourselves out of the ferns. We were told that if we walked on for half a mile we should see the other side of the island, and if we were lucky we might catch a glimpse of the lake. Meanwhile clouds rolled, down off the mountains, filled the hollow where we stood, and so wrapped us in mist, that the question seemed rather how we were to return than whether we should venture farther.

While we were considering what to do, we heard steps approaching through the fog, and a party of blacks came up on their way to Roseau with a sick companion whom they were carrying in a palanquin. We were eating our luncheon in the grotto, and they stopped to talk to our guide and stare at us. Two of them, a lad and a girl, came up closer to me than good manners would have allowed if they had possessed such things; the 'I am as good as you, and you will be good enough to know it,' sort of tone which belongs to these democratic days showing itself rather notably in the rising generation in parts of these islands. I defended myself with producing a sketch book and proceeding to take their likenesses, on which they fled precipitately.

Our sandwiches finished, we were pensively consuming our cigars, I speculating on Sir George Prevost and his party of redcoats who must have bivouacked on that very spot, when the clouds broke and the sun came out. The interval was likely to be a short one, so we hurried to our feet, walked rapidly on, and at a turn of the path where a hurricane had torn a passage through the trees, we caught a sight of our lake as we had been told that perhaps we might do. It lay a couple of hundred feet beneath us deep and still, winding away round a promontory under the crags and woods of the opposite hills: they call it a crater, and I suppose it may have been one, for the whole island shows traces of violent volcanic disturbance, but in general a crater is a bowl, and this was like a reach of a river, which lost itself before one could see where it ended. They told us that in old times, when troops were in the fort, and the white men of the island went about and enjoyed themselves, there were boats on this lake, and parties came up and fished there. Now it was like the pool in the gardens of the palace of the sleeping princess, guarded by impenetrable thickets, and whether there are fish there, or enchanted princesses, or the huts of some tribe of Caribs, hiding in those fastnesses from negroes whom they hate, or from white men whom they do not love, no one knows or cares to know. I made a hurried pencil sketch, and we went on.

A little farther and we were out of the bush, at a rocky terrace on the rim of the great valley which carries the rainfall on the eastern side of the mountains down into the Atlantic. We were 3,000 feet above the sea. Far away the ocean stretched out before us, the horizon line where sky met water so far distant that both had melted into mist at the point where they touched. Mount Diablot, where Labat spent a night catching the devil birds, soared up on our left hand. Below, above, around us, it was forest everywhere; forest, and only forest, a land fertile as Adam's paradise, still waiting for the day when 'the barren woman shall bear children.' Of course it was beautiful, if that be of any consequence—mountain peaks and crags and falling waters, and the dark green of the trees in the foreground, dissolving from tint to tint to grey, violet, and blue in the far-off distance. Even at the height where we stood, the temperature must have been 70°. But the steaming damp of the woods was gone, the air was clear and exhilarating as champagne. What a land! And what were we doing with it? This fair inheritance, won by English hearts and hands for the use of the working men of England, and the English working men lying squalid in the grimy alleys of crowded towns, and the inheritance turned into a wilderness. Visions began to rise of what might be, but visions which were taken from me before they could shape themselves. The curtain of vapour fell down over us again, and all was gone, and of that glorious picture nothing was left but our own two selves and the few yards of red rock and soil on which we were standing.

There was no need for haste now. We return slowly to our horses, and our horses carried us home by the way that we had come. Captain C. went carelessly in front through the fog, over boulders and watercourses and roots of fallen trees. I followed as I could, expecting every moment to find myself flying over my horse's head; stumbling, plunging, sliding, but getting through with it somehow. The creature had never seen me before, but was as careful of my safety as if I had been an old acquaintance and friend. Only one misadventure befell me, if misadventure it may be called. Shaken, and damp with heat, I was riding under a wild orange tree, the fruit within reach of my hand. I picked an orange and plunged my teeth into the skin, and I had to remember my rashness for days. The oil in the rind, pungent as aromatic salts, rushed on my palate, and spurted on my face and eyes. The smart for the moment half blinded me. I bethought me, however, that oranges with such a flavour would be worth something, and a box of them which was sent home for me was converted into marmalade with a finer flavour than ever came from Seville.

What more can I say of Dominica? I stayed with the hospitable C.'s for a fortnight. At the appointed time the returning steamer called for me. I left Capt. C. with a warm hope that he might not be consigned for ever to a post which an English gentleman ought not to be condemned to occupy; that if matters could not be mended for him where he stood, he might find a situation where his courage and his understanding might be turned to useful purpose. I can never forget the kindness both of himself and his clever, good, graceful lady. I cannot forget either the two dusky damsels who waited upon me like spirits in a fairy tale. It was night when I left. The packet came alongside the wharf. We took leave by the gleaming of her lights. The whistle screamed, and Dominica, and all that I had seen, faded into a memory. All that I had seen, but not all that I had thought. That island was the scene of the most glorious of England's many famous actions. It had been won for us again and again by the gallantry of our seamen and soldiers. It had been secured at last to the Crown by the genius of the greatest of our admirals. It was once prosperous. It might be prosperous again, for the resources of the soil are untouched and inexhaustible. The black population are exceptionally worthy. They are excellent boatmen, excellent fishermen, excellent mechanics, ready to undertake any work if treated with courtesy and kindness. Yet in our hands it is falling into ruin. The influence of England there is gone. It is nothing. Indifference has bred indifference in turn as a necessary consequence. Something must be wrong when among 30,000 of our fellow-subjects not one could be found to lift a hand for us if the island were invaded, when a boat's crew from Martinique might take possession of it without a show of resistance.

If I am asked the question, What use is Dominica to us? I decline to measure it by present or possible marketable value; I answer simply that it is part of the dominions of the Queen. If we pinch a finger, the smart is felt in the brain. If we neglect a wound in the least important part of our persons, it may poison the system. Unless the blood of an organised body circulates freely through the extremities, the extremities mortify and drop off, and the dropping off of any colony of ours will not be to our honour and may be to our shame. Dominica seems but a small thing, but our larger colonies are observing us, and the world is observing us, and what we do or fail to do works beyond the limits of its immediate operation. The mode of management which produces the state of things which I have described cannot possibly be a right one. We have thought it wise, with a perfectly honest intention, to leave our dependencies generally to work out their own salvation. We have excepted India, for with India we dare not run the risk. But we have refused to consider that others among our possessions may be in a condition analogous to India, and we have allowed them to drift on as they could. It was certainly excusable, and it may have been prudent, to try popular methods first, but we have no right to persist in the face of a failure so complete. We are obliged to keep these islands, for it seems that no one will relieve us of them; and if they are to remain ours, we are bound so to govern them that our name shall be respected and our sovereignty shall not be a mockery. Am I asked what shall be done? I have answered already. Among the silent thousands whose quiet work keeps the Empire alive, find a Rajah Brooke if you can, or a Mr. Smith of Scilly. If none of these are attainable, even a Sancho Panza would do. Send him out with no more instructions than the knight of La Mancha gave Sancho—to fear God and do his duty. Put him on his mettle. Promise him the respect and praise of all good men if he does well; and if he calls to his help intelligent persons who understand the cultivation of soils and the management of men, in half a score of years Dominica would be the brightest gem of the Antilles. From America, from England, from all parts of the world, admiring tourists would be flocking there to see what Government could do, and curious politicians with jealous eyes admitting reluctantly unwelcome conclusions.

Woman! no mortal o'er the widespread earth
Can find a fault in thee; thy good report
Doth reach the widespread heaven, as of some prince
Who, in the likeness of a god, doth rule
O'er subjects stout of heart and strong of hand;
And men speak greatly of him, and his land
Bears wheat and rye, his orchards bend with fruit,
His flocks breed surely, the sea yields her fish,
Because he guides his folk with wisdom.
In grace and manly virtue.[12]

Because 'He guides with wisdom.' That is the whole secret. The leading of the wise few, the willing obedience of the many, is the beginning and the end of all right action. Secure this, and you secure everything. Fail to secure it, and be your liberties as wide as you can make them, no success is possible.

FOOTNOTES:

[12]

ὦ γύναι, οὐκ ἄν τίς σε βροτῶν ἐπ' ἀπείρονα γαῖαν
νεικέοι; ἦγάρ σευ κλέος οὐρανὸν εὐρὺν ἱκάνει;
ὥστε τευ ἢ βασιλῆος ἀμύμονος, ὅστε θεουδὴς
  ἀνδράσιν ἐν πολλοῖσι καὶ ἰφθίμοισιν ἀνάσσων,
  εὐδικίας ἀνέχῃσι; φέρῃσι δέ γαῖα μέλαινα
πυροὺς καὶ κριθάς, βρίθῃσι δὲ δένδρεα καρπῷ,
τίκτει δ' ἔμπεδα μῆλα, θάλασσα δὲ παρέχει ἰχθῦς,
ἐξ εὐηγεσίης; ἀρετῶσι δὲ λαοὶ ὑπ' αὐτοῦ.—Odyssey, xix. 107.

CHAPTER XII.

The Darien canal—Jamaica mail packet—Captain W.—Retrospect of Jamaican history—Waterspout at sea—Hayti—Jacmel—A walk through the town—A Jamaican planter—First sight of the Blue Mountains—Port Royal—Kingston—The Colonial Secretary—Gordon riots—Changes in the Jamaican constitution.

Once more to Barbadoes, but merely to change there from steamer to steamer. My course was now across the Caribbean Sea to the great islands at the bottom of it. The English mail, after calling and throwing off its lateral branches at Bridgetown, pursues its direct course to Hayti and Jamaica, and so on to Vera Cruz and the Darien canal. This wonderful enterprise of M. Lesseps has set moving the loose negro population of the Antilles and Jamaica. Unwilling to work as they are supposed to be, they have swarmed down to the isthmus, and are still swarming thither in tens of thousands, tempted by the dollar or dollar and a half a day which M. Lesseps is furnishing. The vessel which called for us at Dominica was crowded with them, and we picked up more as we went on. Their average stay is for a year. At the end of a year half of them have gone to the other world. Half go home, made easy for life with money enough to buy a few acres of land and 'live happy ever after.' Heedless as schoolboys they plunge into the enterprise, thinking of nothing but the harvest of dollars. They might earn as much or more at their own doors if there were any one to employ them, but quiet industry is out of joint, and Darien has seized their imaginations as an Eldorado.

If half the reports which reached me are correct, in all the world there is not perhaps now concentrated in any single spot so much foul disease, such a hideous dungheap of moral and physical abomination, as in the scene of this far-famed undertaking of nineteenth-century engineering. By the scheme, as it was first propounded, six-and-twenty millions of English money were to unite the Atlantic and Pacific Oceans, to form a highway for the commerce of the globe, and enrich with untold wealth the happy owners of original shares. The thrifty French peasantry were tempted by the golden bait, and poured their savings into M. Lesseps's lottery box. All that money and more besides, I was told, had been already spent, and only a fifth of the work was done. Meanwhile the human vultures have gathered to the spoil. Speculators, adventurers, card sharpers, hell keepers, and doubtful ladies have carried their charms to this delightful market. The scene of operations is a damp tropical jungle, intensely hot, swarming with mosquitoes, snakes, alligators, scorpions, and centipedes; the home, even as nature made it, of yellow fever, typhus, and dysentery, and now made immeasurably more deadly by the multitudes of people who have crowded thither. Half buried in mud lie about the wrecks of costly machinery, consuming by rust, sent out under lavish orders, and found unfit for the work for which they were intended. Unburied altogether lie also skeletons of the human machines which have broken down there.[13] Everything which imagination can conceive that is ghastly and loathsome seems to be gathered into that locality just now. I was pressed to go on and look at the moral surroundings of 'the greatest undertaking of our age,' but my curiosity was less strong than my disgust. I did not see the place and the description which I have given is probably too highly coloured. The accounts which reached me, however, were uniform and consistent. Not one person whom I met and who could speak from personal knowledge had any other story to tell.

We looked again into St. Lucia on our way. The training squadron was lying outside, and the harbour was covered with boats full of blue-jackets. The big ships were rolling heavily. They could have eaten up Rodney's fleet. The great 'Ville de Paris' would have been a mouthful to the smallest of them. Man for man, officers and crew were as good as Rodney ever commanded. Yet, somehow, they produce small effect on the imagination of the colonists. The impression is that they are meant more for show than for serious use. Alas! the stars and stripes on a Yankee trader have more to say in the West Indies than the white ensigns of a fleet of British iron-clads.

At Barbadoes there was nothing more for me to do or see. The English mail was on the point of sailing, and I hastened on board. One does not realise distance on maps. Jamaica belongs to the West Indies, and the West Indies are a collective entity. Yet it is removed from the Antilles by the diameter of the Caribbean Sea, and is farther off than Gibraltar from Southampton. Thus it was a voyage of several days, and I looked about to see who were to be my companions. There were several Spaniards, one or two English tourists, and some ladies who never left their cabins. The captain was the most remarkable figure: an elderly man with one eye lost or injured, the other as peremptory as I have often seen in a human face; rough and prickly on the outside as a pineapple, internally very much resembling the same fruit, for at the bottom he was true, genuine, and kindly hearted, very amusing, and intimately known to all travellers on the West Indian line, in the service of which he had passed forty years of his life. In his own ship he was sovereign and recognised no superior. Bishops, colonial governors, presidents of South American republics were, so far as their office went, no more to him than other people, and as long as they were on board were chattels of which he had temporary charge. Peer and peasant were alike under his orders, which were absolute as the laws of Medes and Persians. On the other hand, his eye was quick to see if there was any personal merit in a man, and if you deserved his respect you would have it. One particular merit he had which I greatly approved. He kept his cabin to himself, and did not turn it into a smoking room, as I have known captains do a great deal too often.

All my own thoughts were fixed upon Jamaica. I had read so much about it, that my memory was full of persons and scenes and adventures of which Jamaica was the stage or subject. Penn and Venables and the Puritan conquest, and Morgan and the buccaneers; Port Royal crowded with Spanish prizes; its busy dockyards, and English frigates and privateers fitting out there for glorious or desperate enterprises. The name of Jamaica brought them crowding up with incident on incident; and behind the history came Tom Cringle and the wild and reckless, yet wholesome and hearty, planter's life in Kingston; the dark figures of the pirates swinging above the mangroves at Gallows Point; the balls and parties and the beautiful quadroons, and the laughing, merry innocent children of darkness, with the tricks of the middies upon them. There was the tragic side of it, too, in slavery, the last ugly flash out of the cloud being not two decades distant in the Eyre and Gordon time. Interest enough there was about Jamaica, and things would be strangely changed in Kingston if nothing remained of the society which was once so brilliant. There, if anywhere, England and English rule were not yet a vanished quantity. There was a dockyard still, and a commodore in command, and a guardship and gunboats, and English regiments and West Indian regiments with English officers. Some representatives, too, I knew were to be found of the old Anglo-West Indians, men whose fathers and grandfathers were born in the island, and whose fortunes were bound up in it. Aaron Bang! what would not one have given to meet Aaron? The real Aaron had been gathered to his fathers, and nature does not make two such as he was; but I might fall in with something that would remind me of him. Paul Gelid and Pepperpot Wagtail, and Peter Mangrove, better than either of them—the likeness of these might be surviving, and it would be delightful to meet and talk to them. They would give fresh flavour to the immortal 'Log.' Even another Tom was not impossible; some middy to develop hereafter into a frigate captain and to sail again into Port Royal with his prizes in tow.

Nature at all events could not be changed. The white rollers would still be breaking on the coral reefs. The palms would still be waving on the sand ridge which forms the harbour, and the amber mist would be floating round the peaks of the Blue Mountains. There were English soldiers and sailors and English people. The English language was spoken there by blacks as well as whites. The religion was English. Our country went for something, and there would be some persons, at least, to whom the old land was more than a stepmother, and who were not sighing in their hearts for annexation to the American Union. The governor, Sir Henry Norman, of Indian fame, I was sorry to learn, was still absent; he had gone home on some legal business. Sir Henry had an Imperial reputation. He had been spoken of to me in Barbadoes as able, if he were allowed a chance, to act as Viceroy of all the islands, and to set them on their feet again. I could well believe that a man of less than Sir Henry's reputed power could do it—for in the thing itself there was no great difficulty—if only we at home were once disenchanted; though all the ability in the world would be thrown away as long as the enchantment continued. I did see Sir Henry, as it turned out, but only for a few hours.

Our voyage was without remarkable incident; as voyages are apt to be in these days of powerful steamboats. One morning there was a tropical rain storm which was worth seeing. We had a strong awning over the quarter-deck, so I could stand and watch it. An ink-black cloud came suddenly up from the north which seemed to hang into the sea, the surface of the water below being violently agitated. According to popular belief, the cloud on these occasions is drawing up water which it afterwards discharges. Were this so the water discharged would be salt, which it never is. The cause of the agitation is a cyclonic rotation of air or local whirlwind. The most noticeable feature was the blackness of the cloud itself. It became so dark that it would have been difficult to read any ordinary print. The rain, when it burst, fell not in drops but in torrents. The deck was flooded, and the scuttle-holes ran like jets from a pump. The awning was ceasing to be a shelter, for the water was driven bodily through it; but the downpour passed off as suddenly as it had risen. There was no lightning and no wind. The sea under our side was glassy smooth, and was dashed into millions of holes by the plunging of the rain pellets.

The captain in his journeys to and fro had become acquainted with the present black President of Hayti, Mr. Salomon. I had heard of this gentleman as an absolute person, who knew how to make himself obeyed, and who treated opposition to his authority in a very summary manner. He seemed to be a favourite of the captain's. He had been educated in France, had met with many changes of fortune, and after an exile in Jamaica had become quasi-king of the black republic. I much wished to see this paradise of negro liberty; we were to touch at Jacmel, which is one of the principal ports, to leave the mails, and Captain W—— was good enough to say that, if I liked, I might go ashore for an hour or two with the officer in charge.

Hayti, as everyone knows who has studied the black problem, is the western portion of Columbus's Española, or St. Domingo, the largest after Cuba and the most fertile in natural resources of all the islands of the Caribbean Sea. It was the earliest of the Spanish settlements in the New World. The Spaniards found there a million or two of mild and innocent Indians, whom in their first enthusiasm they intended to convert to Christianity, and to offer as the first fruits of their discovery to the Virgin Mary and St. Domenic. The saint gave his name to the island, and his temperament to the conquerors. In carrying out their pious design, they converted the Indians off the face of the earth, working them to death in their mines and plantations. They filled their places with blacks from Africa, who proved of tougher constitution. They colonised, they built cities; they throve and prospered for nearly two hundred years; when Hayti, the most valuable half of the island, was taken from them by the buccaneers and made into a French province. The rest which keeps the title of St. Domingo, continued Spanish, and is Spanish still—a thinly inhabited, miserable, Spanish republic. Hayti became afterwards the theatre of the exploits of the ever-glorious Toussaint l'Ouverture. When the French Revolution broke out, and Liberty and the Rights of Man became the new gospel, slavery could not be allowed to continue in the French dominions. The blacks of the colony were emancipated and were received into the national brotherhood. In sympathy with the Jacobins of France, who burnt the chateaux of the nobles and guillotined the owners of them, the liberated slaves rose as soon as they were free, and massacred the whole French population, man, woman, and child. Napoleon sent an army to punish the murderers and recover the colony. Toussaint, who had no share in the atrocities, and whose

fault was only that he had been caught by the prevailing political epidemic and believed in the evangel of freedom, surrendered and was carried to France, where he
died or else was made an end of. The yellow fever avenged him, and secured for
his countrymen the opportunity of trying out to the uttermost the experiment of negro self-government. The French troops perished in tens of thousands. They were
reinforced again and again, but it was like pouring water into a sieve. The climate
won a victory to the black man which he could not win for himself. They abandoned
their enterprise at last, and Hayti was free. We English tried our hand to recover it
afterwards, but we failed also, and for the same reason.

Hayti has thus for nearly a century been a black independent state. The negro race
have had it to themselves and have not been interfered with. They were equipped
when they started on their career of freedom with the Catholic religion, a civilised
language, European laws and manners, and the knowledge of various arts and occupations which they had learnt while they were slaves. They speak French still; they
are nominally Catholics still; and the tags and rags of the gold lace of French civilisation continue to cling about their institutions. But in the heart of them has revived
the old idolatry of the Gold Coast, and in the villages of the interior, where they
are out of sight and can follow their instincts, they sacrifice children in the serpent's
honour after the manner of their forefathers. Perhaps nothing better could be expected from a liberty which was inaugurated by assassination and plunder. Political
changes which prove successful do not begin in that way.

The Bight of Leogane is a deep bay carved in the side of the island, one arm of
which is a narrow ridge of high mountains a hundred and fifty miles long and from
thirty to forty wide. At the head of this bay, to the north of the ridge, is Port au
Prince, the capital of this remarkable community. On the south, on the immediately
opposite side of the mountains and facing the Caribbean Sea, is Jacmel, the town next
in importance. We arrived off it shortly after daybreak. The houses, which are white,
looked cheerful in the sunlight. Harbour there was none, but an open roadstead into
which the swell of the sea sets heavily, curling over a long coral reef which forms
a partial shelter. The mountain range rose behind, sloping off into rounded woody
hills. Here were the feeding grounds of the herds of wild cattle which tempted the
buccaneers into the island, and from which they took their name. The shore was
abrupt; the land broke off in cliffs of coral rock tinted brilliantly with various colours.
One rather striking white-cliff, a ship's officer assured me, was chalk; adding flint
when I looked incredulous. His geological education was imperfect. We brought up
a mile outside the black city. The boat was lowered. None of the other passengers
volunteered to go with me; the English are out of favour in Hayti just now; the captain
discouraged landings out of mere curiosity; and, indeed, the officer with the mails
had to reassure himself of Captain W——'s consent before he would take me. The
presence of Europeans in any form is barely tolerated. A few only are allowed to
remain about the ports, just as the Irish say they let a few Danes remain in Dublin
and Waterford after the battle of Clontarf, to attend to the ignoble business of trade.

The country after the green of the Antilles looked brown and parched. In the
large islands the winter months are dry. As we approached the reef we saw the
long hills of water turn to emerald as they rolled up the shoal, then combing and

breaking in cataracts of snow-white foam. The officer in charge took me within oar's length of the rock to try my nerves, and the sea, he did not fail to tell me, swarmed with sharks of the worst propensities. Two steamers were lying inside, one of which, belonging to an English company, had 'happened a misfortune,' and was breaking up as a deserted wreck. A Yankee clipper schooner had just come in with salt fish and crackers—a singularly beautiful vessel, with immense beam, which would have startled the builders of the Cowes racers. It was precisely like the schooner which Tom Cringle commanded before the dockyard martinets had improved her into ugliness, built on the lines of the old pirate craft of the islands, when the lives and fortunes of men hung on the extra speed, or the point which they could lie closer to the wind. Her return cargo would be coffee and bananas.

Englishmen move about in Jacmel as if they were ashamed of themselves among their dusky lords and masters. I observed the Yankee skipper paddling himself off in a canoe with his broad straw hat and his cigar in his mouth, looking as if all the world belonged to him, and as if all the world, and the Hayti blacks in particular, were aware of the fact. The Yankee, whether we like it or not, is the acknowledged sovereign in these waters.

The landing place was, or had been, a jetty built on piles and boarded over. Half the piles were broken; the planks had rotted and fallen through. The swell was rolling home, and we had to step out quickly as the boat rose on the crest of the wave. A tattered crowd of negroes were loafing about variously dressed, none, however, entirely without clothes of some kind. One of them did kindly give me a hand, observing that I was less light of foot than once I might have been. The agent's office was close by. I asked the head clerk—a Frenchman—to find me a guide through the town. He called one of the bystanders whom he knew, and we started together, I and my black companion, to see as much as I could in the hour which was allowed me. The language was less hopeless than at Dominica. We found that we could understand each other—he, me, tolerably; I, him, in fragments, for his tongue went as fast as a shuttle. Though it was still barely eight o'clock the sun was scalding. The streets were filthy and the stench abominable. The houses were of white stone, and of some pretensions, but ragged and uninviting—paint nowhere, and the woodwork of the windows and verandahs mouldy and worm-eaten. The inhabitants swarmed as in a St. Giles's rookery. I suppose they were all out of doors. If any were left at home Jacmel must have been as populous as an African ants' nest. As I had looked for nothing better than a Kaffir kraal, the degree of civilisation was more than I expected. I expressed my admiration of the buildings; my guide was gratified, and pointed out to me with evident pride a new hotel or boarding house kept by a Madame Somebody who was the great lady of the place. Madame Ellemême was sitting in a shady balcony outside the first-floor windows. She was a large menacing-looking mulatto, like some ogress of the 'Arabian Nights,' capable of devouring, if she found them palatable, any number of salt babies. I took off my hat to this formidable dame, which she did not condescend to notice, and we passed on. A few houses in the outskirts stood in gardens with inclosures about them. There is some trade in the place, and there were evidently families, negro or European, who lived in less squalid style than the generality. There was a governor there, my guide informed me—an ornamental personage, much respected. To my question whether he had any soldiers, I was answered 'No,' the Haytians didn't like soldiers. I was to understand, however, that they were not common blacks. They aspired to be a commonwealth with public rights and alliances. Hayti a republic, France a republic: France and Hayti good friends now. They had a French bishop and French priests and a French currency. In spite of their land laws, they were proud of their affinity with the great nation; and I heard afterwards, though not from my Jacmel companion, that the better part of the Haytians would welcome back the French dominion if they were not afraid that the Yankees would disapprove.

My guide persisted in leading me outside the town, and as my time was limited, I tried in various ways to induce him to take me back into it. He maintained, however, that he had been told to show me whatever was most interesting, and I found that I was to see an American windmill-pump which had been just erected to supply Jacmel with fresh water. It was the first that had been seen in the island, and was a wonder of wonders. Doubtless it implied 'progress,' and would assist in the much-needed ablution of the streets and kennels. I looked at it and admired, and having thus done homage, I was allowed my own way.

It was market day. The Yankee cargo had been unloaded, and a great open space in front of the cathedral was covered with stalls or else blankets stretched on poles to keep the sun off, where hundreds of Haytian dames were sitting or standing disposing of their wares—piles of salt fish, piles of coloured calicoes, knives, scissors, combs, and brushes. Of home produce there were great baskets of loaves, fruit, vegetables, and butcher's meat on slabs. I looked inquisitively at these last; but I acknowledge that I saw no joints of suspicious appearance. Children were running about in thousands, not the least as if they were in fear of being sacrificed, and babies hung upon their mothers as if natural affection existed in Jacmel as much as in other places. I asked no compromising questions, not wishing to be torn in pieces. Sir Spenser St. John's book has been heard of in Hayti, and the anger about it is considerable. The scene was interesting enough, but the smell was unendurable. The wild African black is not filthy in his natural state. He washes much, as wild animals do, and at least tries to keep himself clear of vermin. The blacks in Jacmel appeared (like the same animals as soon as they are domesticated) to lose the sense which belongs to them in their wild condition. My prejudices, if I have any, had not blinded me to the good qualities of the men and women in Dominica. I do not think it was prejudice wholly which made me think the faces which I saw in Hayti the most repulsive which I had ever seen in the world, or Jacmel itself, taken for all in all, the foulest, dirtiest, and nastiest of human habitations. The dirt, however, I will do them the justice to say did not seem to extend to their churches. The cathedral stood at the upper end of the market place. I went in. It was airy, cool, and decent-looking. Some priests were saying mass, and there was a fairly large congregation. I wished to get a nearer sight of the altar and the images and pictures, imagining that in Hayti the sacred persons might assume a darker colour than in Europe; but I could not reach the chancel without disturbing people who were saying their prayers, and, to the disappointment of my companion, who beckoned me on, and would have cleared a way for me, I controlled my curiosity and withdrew.

My hour's leave of absence was expired. I made my way back to the landing place, where the mail steamer's boat was waiting for me. On the steamer herself the passengers were waiting impatiently for breakfast, which had been put off on our account. We hurried on board at our best speed; but before breakfast could be thought of, or any other thing, I had to strip and plunge into a bath and wash away the odour of the great negro republic of the West which clung to my clothes and skin.

Leaving Jacmel and its associations, we ran all day along the land, skirting a range of splendid mountains between seven and eight thousand feet high; past the Isle à Vache; past the bay of Cayes, once famous as the haunt of the sea-rovers; past Cape Tubiron, the Cape of Sharks. At evening we were in the channel which divides St. Domingo from Jamaica. Captain —— insisted to me that this was the scene of Rodney's action, and he pointed out to me the headland under which the British fleet had been lying. He was probably right in saying that it was the scene of some action of Rodney's, for there is hardly a corner of the West Indies where he did not leave behind him the print of his cannon shot; but it was not the scene of the great fight which saved the British Empire. That was below the cliffs of Dominica; and Captain W——, as many others have done, was confounding Dominica with St. Domingo.

The next morning we were to anchor at Port Royal. We had a Jamaica gentleman of some consequence on board. I had failed so far to make acquaintance with him, but on this last evening he joined me on deck, and I gladly used the opportunity to learn something of the present condition of things. I was mistaken in expecting to find a more vigorous or more sanguine tone of feeling than I had left at the Antilles. There was the same despondency, the same sense that their state was hopeless, and that nothing which they could themselves do would mend it. He himself, for instance, was the owner of a large sugar estate which a few years ago was worth 60,000l. It was not encumbered. He was his own manager, and had spared no cost in providing the newest machinery. Yet, with the present prices and with the refusal of the American Commercial Treaty, it would not pay the expense of cultivation. He held on, for it was all that he could do. To sell was impossible, for no one would buy even at the price of the stock on the land. It was the same story which I had heard everywhere. The expenses of the administration, this gentleman said, were out of all proportion to the resources of the island, and were yearly increasing. The planters had governed in the old days as the English landlords had governed Ireland. They had governed cheaply and on their own resources. They had authority; they were respected; their word was law. Now their power had been taken from them, and made over to paid officials, and the expense was double what it used to be. Between the demands made on them in the form of taxation and the fall in the value of their produce their backs were breaking, and the 'landed interest' would come to an end. I asked him, as I had asked many persons without getting a satisfactory answer, what he thought that the Imperial Government could do to mend matters. He seemed to think that it was too late to do anything. The blacks were increasing so fast, and the white influence was diminishing so fast, that Jamaica in a few years would be another Hayti.

In this gentleman, too, I found to my sorrow that there was the same longing for admission to the American Union which I had left behind me at the Antilles. In spite of soldiers and the naval station, the old country was still looked upon as a stepmother, and of genuine loyalty there was, according to him, little or nothing. If the West Indies were ever to become prosperous again, it could only be when they were annexed to the United States. For the present, at least, he admitted that annexation was impossible. Not on account of any possible objection on the part of the British Government; for it seems to be assumed by every one that the British Government cares nothing what they do; nor wholly on account of the objections of the Americans, though he admitted that the Americans were unwilling to receive them; but because in the existing state of feeling such a change could not be carried out without civil war. In Jamaica, at least, the blacks and mulattoes would resist. There were nearly 700,000 of them, while of the whites there were but 15,000, and the relative numbers were every year becoming more unfavourable. The blacks knew that under England they had nothing to fear. They would have everything more and more their own way, and in a short time they expected to have the island to themselves. They might collect arms; they might do what they pleased, and no English officer dared to use rough measures with them; while, if they belonged to the Union, the whites would recover authority one way or another. The Americans were ready with their rifles on occasions of disorder, and their own countrymen did not call them to account for it as we did. The blacks, therefore, preferred the liberty which they had and the prospects to which they looked forward, and they and the mulattoes also would fight, and fight desperately, before they would allow themselves to be made American citizens.

The prospect which Mr. —— laid before me was not a beautiful one, and was coming a step nearer at each advance that was made in the direction of constitutional self-government; for, like every other person with whom I spoke on the subject, he said emphatically that Europeans would not remain to be ruled under a black representative system; nor would they take any part in it when they would be so overwhelmingly outvoted and outnumbered. They would sooner forfeit all that they had in the world and go away. An effective and economical administration on the Indian pattern might have saved all a few years ago. It was too late now, and Jamaica was past recovery. At this rate it was a sadly altered Jamaica since Tom Cringle's time, though his friend Aaron even then had seen what was probably coming. But I could not accept entirely all that Mr. —— had been saying, and had to discount the natural irritation of a man who sees his fortune sliding out of his hands. Moreover, for myself, I never listen much to a desponding person. Even when a cause is lost utterly, and no rational hope remains, I would still go down, if it had to be so, with my spirit unbroken and my face to the enemy. Mr. —— perhaps would recover heart if the price of sugar mended a little. For my own part, I do not care much whether it mends or not. The economics of the islands ought not to depend exclusively on any single article of produce. I believe, too, in spite of gloomy prognostics, that a loyal and prosperous Jamaica is still among the possibilities of the future, if we will but study in earnest the character of the problem. Mr. ——, however, did most really convey to me the convictions of a large and influential body of West Indians—convictions on which they are already acting, and will act more and more. With Hayti so close, and with opinion in England indifferent to what becomes of them, they will clear out while they have something left to lose, and will not wait till ruin is upon them or till they are ordered off the land by a black legislature. There is a saying in Hayti that the white man has no rights which the blacks are bound to recognise.

I walked forward after we had done talking. We had five hundred of the poor creatures on board on their way to the Darien pandemonium. The vessel was rolling with a heavy beam sea. I found the whole mass of them reduced into the condition of the pigs who used to occupy the foredeck in the Cork and Bristol packets. They were lying in a confused heap together, helpless, miserable, without consciousness apparently, save a sense in each that he was wretched. Unfortunate brothers-in-law! following the laws of political economy, and carrying their labour to the dearest market, where, before a year was out, half of them were to die. They had souls, too, some of them, and honest and kindly hearts. I observed one man who was suffering less than the rest reading aloud to a prostrate group a chapter of the New Testament; another was reading to himself a French Catholic book of devotion.

The dawn was breaking in the east when I came on deck in the morning. The Blue Mountains were hanging over us on our right hand, the peaks buried in white mist which the unrisen sun was faintly tinting with orange. We had passed Morant Bay, the scene of Gordon's rash attempt to imitate Toussaint l'Ouverture. As so often in the Antilles, a level plain stretched between the sea and the base of the hills, formed by the debris washed down by the rivers in the rainy season. Among cane fields and cocoa-nut groves we saw houses and the chimneys of the sugar factories; and, as we came nearer, we saw men and horses going to their early work. Presently Kingston itself came in sight, and Up Park Camp, and the white barracks high up on the mountain side, of which one had read and heard so much. Here was actually Tom Cringle's Kingston, and between us and the town was the long sand spit which incloses the lagoon at the head of which Kingston is built. How this natural breakwater had been deposited I could find no one to tell me. It is eight miles long, rising but a few feet above the water-line, in places not more than thirty yards across—nowhere, except at the extremity, more than sixty or a hundred.

PORT ROYAL, JAMAICA.

PORT ROYAL, JAMAICA.

The thundering swell of the Caribbean Sea breaks upon it from year's end to year's end, and never washes it any thinner. Where the sand is dry, beyond the reach of the waves, it is planted thickly all along with palms, and appears from the sea a soft green line, over which appear the masts and spars of the vessels at anchor in the harbour, and the higher houses of Kingston itself. To reach the opening into the lagoon you have to run on to the end of the sandbank, where there is a peninsula on which is built the Port Royal so famous in West Indian story. Halfway down among the palms the lighthouse stands, from which a gun was fired as we passed, to give notice that the English mail was coming in. Treacherous coral reefs rise out of the deep water for several miles, some under water and visible only by the breakers over them, others forming into low wooded islands. Only local pilots can take a ship safely through these powerful natural defence works. There are but two channels through which the lagoon can be approached. The eastern passage, along which we were steaming, runs so near the shore that an enemy's ship would be destroyed by the batteries among the sandhills long before it could reach the mouth. The western passage is less intricate, but that also is commanded by powerful forts. In old times Kingston was unattackable, so strong had the position been made by nature and art combined. It could be shelled now over the spit from the open sea. It might be destroyed, but even so could not easily be taken.

I do not know that I have ever seen any scene more interesting than that which broke upon my eyes as we rounded the point, and the lagoon opened out before me. Kingston, which we had passed half an hour, before, lay six miles off at the head of the bay, now inside the sand, ridge, blue and hazy in the distance. At the back were the mountains. The mist had melted off, standing in shadowy grey masses with the sun rising behind them. Immediately in front were the dockyards, forts, and towers of Port Royal, with the guardship, gunboats, and tenders, with street and terrace, roof and turret and glistening vane, all clearly and sharply defined in the exquisite transparency of the air. The associations of the place no doubt added to the impression. Before the first hut was run up in Kingston, Port Royal was the rendezvous of all English ships which, for spoil or commerce, frequented the West Indian seas. Here the buccaneers sold their plunder and squandered their gains in gambling and riot. Here in the later century of legitimate wars, whole fleets were gathered to take in stores, or refit when shattered by engagements. Here Nelson had been, and Collingwood and Jervis, and all our other naval heroes. Here prizes were brought in for adjudication, and pirates to be tried and hanged. In this spot more than in any other, beyond Great Britain herself, the energy of the Empire once was throbbing. The 'Urgent,' an old two-decker, and three gunboats were all that were now floating in the once crowded water; the 'Urgent,' no longer equipped for active service, imperfectly armed, inadequately manned, but still flaunting the broad white ensign, and as if grandly watching over the houses which lay behind her. There were batteries at the point, and batteries on the opposite shore. The morning bugle rang out clear and inspiriting from the town, and white coats and gold and silver lace glanced in and out as men and officers were passing to parade. Here, at any rate, England was still alive.

The channel at the entrance is a mile in width. The lagoon (the open part of it) may be seven or eight miles long and half as many broad. It forms the mouth of the Cobre river, one of the largest in Jamaica, on which, ten miles up, stands the original seat of government established by the Spaniards, and called after them Spanish Town. The fashion of past times, as old as the times of Thucydides, and continued on till the end of the last century, was to choose the sites for important towns in estuaries, at a distance from the sea, to be out of the reach of pirates. The Cobre, running down from Spanish Town, turns the plain through which it flows into a swamp. The swamp covers itself with mangroves, and the mangroves fringe the shore of the lagoon itself for two-thirds of its circuit. As Jamaica grew in wealth and population the trade was carried from Port Royal deeper into the bay. Another town sprang up there, called King's Town, or shortly 'Kingston.' The administration was removed thither for convenience, and though fallen away from its old consequence, Kingston, with its extended suburbs, its churches and warehouses, and large mansions overhung with trees, looks at a distance like a place of consideration. Many ships lay along the wharves, or anchored a few cables' distance off. Among them were a couple of Spanish frigates, which remain there in permanence on the watch for refugees from Cuba. On the slopes behind the town, as far as eye could see, were the once splendid estates of the sugar princes of the last century. One of them was pointed out to me as the West Indian home of the author of 'Tom Cringle.'

We had to stop for a few minutes as the officer of the port came alongside for the mails. We then went on at reduced speed. The lagoon is generally shoal. A deep water channel runs along the side of it which is farthest from the sea; made, I suppose, by the river, for as usual there is little tide or none. Halfway up we passed under the walls of Fort Augusta, now a ruin and almost deserted, but once mounting a hundred guns. The money which we spent on the defence of Jamaica in the old times was not always laid out wisely, as will be seen in an account which I shall have to give of this remarkable structure; but, at any rate, we were lavish of it.

Of the sharks with which the water used to swarm we saw none. Port Royal Jack and his kindred are said to have disappeared, driven or frightened out by the screws of the steamers. But it is not a place which I should choose for a swim. Nor did the nigger boys seem as anxious as I had seen them in other spots to dive for sixpences under the ship's side.

No account is made of days when you come into port after a voyage. Cargoes have to be landed, or coal has to be taken in. The donkey engines are at work, hoisting packing cases and luggage out of the hold. Stewards run to and fro, and state-room doors are opened, and busy figures are seen through each, stuffing their portmanteaus and preparing for departure. The church bells at Kingston, ringing for early service, reminded me that it was Sunday. We brought up at a jetty, and I cannot say that, close at hand, the town was as attractive as it had appeared when first I saw it. The enchantment was gone. The blue haze of distance gave place to reality. The water was so fetid under the ship's side that it could not be pumped into the baths. Odours, not Arabian, from open drains reminded me of Jacmel. The streets, up which I could see from the afterdeck, looked dirty and the houses shabby. Docks and wharves, however, are never the brightest part of any town, English or foreign. There were people enough at any rate, and white faces enough among them. Gangways were rigged from the ship to the shore, and ladies and gentlemen rushed on board to meet their friends. The companies' agents appeared in the captain's cabin. Porters were scrambling for luggage; pushing, shoving, and swearing. Passengers who had come out with us, and had never missed attendance at the breakfast table, were hurrying home unbreakfasted to their wives and families. My own plans were uncertain. I had no friends, not even an acquaintance. I knew nothing of the hotels and lodging houses, save that they had generally a doubtful reputation. I had brought with me a letter of introduction to Sir H. Norman, the governor, but Sir Henry had gone to England. On the whole, I thought it best to inclose the letter to Mr. Walker, the Colonial Secretary, who I understood was in Kingston, with a note asking for advice. This I sent by a messenger. Meanwhile I stayed on board to look about me from the deck. The ship was to go on the next morning to the canal works at Darien. Time was precious. Immediately on arriving she had begun to take in coal, Sunday though it might be, and a singular spectacle it was. The coal yard was close by, and some hundreds of negroes, women and men, but women, in four times the number, were hard at work. The entire process was by hand and basket, each basket holding from eighty to a hundred pounds weight. Two planks were laid down at a steep incline from the ship's deck to the yard. Swinging their loads on their heads, erect as statues, and with a step elastic as a racehorse's, they marched up one of the planks, emptied their baskets into the coal bunkers, and ran down the other. Round and round they went under the blazing sun all the morning through, and round and round they would continue to go all the afternoon. The men took it comparatively easy. The women flew along, laughing, and clamouring, as if not knowing what weariness was—willing beasts of burden, for they had the care upon them of their children; the men disclaiming all responsibilities on that score, after the babies have been once brought into the world. The poor women are content with the arrangement, which they prefer to what they would regard as legal bondage. They earn at this coaling work seven or eight shillings a day. If they were wives, their husbands would take it from them and spend it in rum. The companion who is not a wife can refuse and keep her earnings for her little ones. If black suffrage is to be the rule in Jamaica, I would take it away from the men and would give it to the superior sex. The women are the working bees of the hive. They would make a tolerable nation of black amazons, and the babies would not be offered to Jumbi.

When I had finished my meditations on the coaling women, there were other black creatures to wonder at; great boobies or pelicans, old acquaintances of the Zoological Gardens, who act as scavengers in these waters. We had perhaps a couple of dozen of them round us as large as vultures, ponderous and sleepy to look at when squatting on rocks or piles, over-weighted by their enormous bills. On the wing they were astonishingly swift, wheeling in circles, till they could fix their prey with their eyes, then pouncing upon it with a violent slanting plunge. I suppose their beaks might be broken if they struck directly, but I never saw one miss its aim. Nor do they ever go below the surface, but seize always what is close to it. I was told—I do not know how truly—that like the diablots in Dominica, they nest in the mountains and only come down to the sea to feed.

Hearing that I was in search of quarters, a Miss Burton, a handsome mulatto woman, came up and introduced herself to me. Hotels in the English West Indies are generally detestable. This dame had set up a boarding house on improved principles, or rather two boarding houses, between which she invited me to take my choice, one in the suburbs of Kingston, one on the bank of a river in a rocky gorge in the Blue Mountains. In either of these she promised that she would make me happy, and I do not doubt that she would have succeeded, for her fame had spread through all Jamaica, and her face was as merry as it was honest. As it turned out I was provided for elsewhere, and I lost the chance of making an acquaintance which I should have valued. When she spoke to me she seemed a very model of vigour and health. She died suddenly while I was in the island.

The day was still early. When the vessel was in some order again, and those who were going on shore had disappeared, the rest of us were called down to breakfast to taste some of those Jamaica delicacies on which Paul Gelid was so eloquent. The fruit was the chief attraction: pineapples, of which one can eat as much as one likes in these countries with immunity from after suffering; oranges, more excellent than even those of Grenada and Dominica; shaddocks, admirable as that memorable one which seduced Adam; and for the first time mangoes, the famous Number Eleven of which I had heard such high report, and was now to taste. The English gardeners can do much, but they cannot ripen a Number Eleven, and it is too delicate to bear carriage. It must be eaten in the tropics or nowhere. The mango is the size and shape of a swan's egg, of a ruddy yellow colour when ripe, and in flavour like an exceptionally good apricot, with a very slight intimation of resin. The stone is disproportionately large. The flesh adheres to it, and one abandons as hopeless the attempt to eat mangoes with clean lips and fingers. The epicures insist that they should be eaten only in a bath.

The heat was considerable, and the feast of fruit was the more welcome. Soon after the Colonial Secretary politely answered my note in person. In the absence of the governor of a colony, the colonial secretary, as a rule, takes his place. In Jamaica, and wherever we have a garrison, the commander of the forces becomes acting governor; I suppose because it is not convenient to place an officer of high military rank under the orders of a civilian who is not the direct representative of the sovereign. In the gentleman who now called on me I found an old acquaintance whom I had known as a boy many years ago. He told me that, if I had made no other arrangements, Colonel J——, who was the present chief, was expecting me to be his guest at the 'King's House' during my stay in Jamaica. My reluctance to trespass on the hospitality of an entire stranger was not to be allowed. Soldiers who have distinguished themselves are, next to lawyers, the most agreeable people to be met with, and when I was convinced that I should really be welcome, I had no other objection. An aide-de-camp, I was told, would call for me in the afternoon. Meanwhile the secretary stayed with me for an hour or two, and I was able to learn something authentic from him as to the general condition of things. I had not given entire credit to the representations of my planter friend of the evening before. Mr. Walker took a more cheerful view, and, although the prospects were not as bright as they might be, he saw no reason for despondency. Sugar was down of course. The public debt had increased, and taxation was heavy. Many gentlemen in Jamaica, as in the Antilles, were selling, or trying to sell, their estates and go out of it. On the other hand, expenses of government were being reduced, and the revenue showed a surplus. The fruit trade with the United States was growing, and promised to grow still further. American capitalists had come into the island, and were experimenting on various industries. The sugar treaty with America would naturally have been welcome; but Jamaica was less dependent on its sugar crop, and the action of the British Government was less keenly resented. In the Antilles, the Colonial Secretary admitted, there might be a desire for annexation to the United States, and Jamaican landowners had certainly expressed the same wish to myself. Mr. Walker, however, assured me that, while the blacks would oppose it unanimously, the feeling, if it existed at all among the whites, was confined as yet to a very few persons. They had been English for 230 years, and the large majority of them wished to remain English. There had been suffering among them; but there had been suffering in other places besides Jamaica. Better times might perhaps be coming with the opening of the

Darien canal, when Kingston might hope to become again the centre of a trade. Of the negroes, both men and women, Mr. Walker spoke extremely favourably. They were far less indolent than they were supposed to be; they were settling on the waste lands, acquiring property, growing yams and oranges, and harming no one; they had no grievance left; they knew it, and were perfectly contented.

As Mr. Walker was an official, I did not ask him about the working of the recent changes in the constitution; nor could he have properly answered me if I had. The state of things is briefly this: Jamaica, after the first settlement, received a parliamentary form of government, modelled on that of Ireland, the colonial liberties being restricted by a law analogous to Poynings' Act. The legislature, so constructed, of course represented the white interest only and was entirely composed of whites. It remained substantially unaltered till 1853, when modifications were made which admitted coloured men to the suffrage, though with so high a franchise as to be almost exclusive. It became generally felt that the franchise would have to be extended. A popular movement, led by Mr. Gordon, who was a member of the legislature, developed into a riot, into bloodshed and panic. Gordon was hanged by a court-martial, and the assembly, aware that, if allowed to exist any longer, it could exist only with the broad admission of the negro vote, pronounced its own dissolution, surrendered its powers to the Crown, and represented formally 'that nothing but a strong government could prevent the island from lapsing into the condition of Hayti.'

The surrender was accepted. Jamaica was administered till within the last four years by a governor, officials, and council all nominated by the Queen. No dissatisfaction had been expressed, and the blacks at least had enjoyed a prosperity and tranquillity which had been unbroken by a single disturbance. If the island has suffered, it has suffered from causes with which political dissatisfaction has had nothing to do, and which, therefore, political changes cannot remove. In 1884 Mr. Gladstone's Government, for reasons which I have not been able to ascertain, revived suddenly the representative system; constructed a council composed equally of nominated and of elected members, and placed the franchise so low as to include practically every negro peasant who possessed a hut and a garden. So long as the Crown retains and exercises its power of nomination, no worse results can ensue than the inevitable discontent when the votes of the elected members are disregarded or overborne. But to have ventured so important an alteration with the intention of leaving it without further extension would have been an act of gratuitous folly, of which it would be impossible to imagine an English cabinet to have been capable. It is therefore assumed and understood to have been no more than an initial step towards passing over the management of Jamaica to the black constituencies. It has been so construed in the other islands, and was the occasion of the agitation in Trinidad which I observed when I was there.

My own opinion as to the wisdom of such an experiment matters little: but I have a right to say that neither blacks nor whites have asked for it; that no one who knows anything of the West Indies and wishes them to remain English sincerely asked for it; that no one has agitated for it save a few newspaper writers and politicians whom it would raise into consequence. If tried at all, it will be tried either with a deliberate intention of cutting Jamaica free from us altogether, or else in deference to English political superstitions, which attribute supernatural virtues to the exercise of the franchise, and assume that a form of self-government which suits us tolerably at home will be equally beneficial in all countries and under all conditions.

FOOTNOTES:

[13]

This has been angrily denied. A gentleman whose veracity I cannot doubt assured me that he had himself seen a dead body lying unburied among some bushes. When he returned to the place a month after it was still there. The frightful mortality among the labourers, at least in the early years of the undertaking, is too notorious to be called in question.

CHAPTER XIII.

The English mails—Irish agitation—Two kinds of colonies—Indian administration—How far applicable in the West Indies—Land at Kingston—Government House—Dinner party—Interesting officer—Majuba Hill—Mountain station—Kingston curiosities—Tobacco—Valley in the Blue Mountains.

I am reminded as I write of an adventure which befell Archbishop Whately soon after his promotion to the see of Dublin. On arriving in Ireland he saw that the people were miserable. The cause, in his mind, was their ignorance of political economy, of which he had himself written what he regarded as an excellent manual. An Irish translation of this manual he conceived would be the best possible medicine, and he commissioned a native Scripture reader to make one. To insure correctness he required the reader to retranslate to him what he had written line by line. He observed that the man as he read turned sometimes two pages at a time. The text went on correctly, but his quick eye perceived that something was written on the intervening leaves. He insisted on knowing what it was, and at last extorted an explanation, 'Your Grace, me and my comrade conceived that it was mighty dry reading, so we have just interposed now and then a bit of a pawem, to help it forward, your Grace.' I am myself imitating the translators, and making sandwiches out of politics and local descriptions.

We had brought the English mails with us. There were letters to read which had been in the ship with us, though out of our reach. There were the newspapers to read. They told me nothing but the weary round of Irish outrages and the rival remedies of Tory or Radical politicians who cared for Ireland less than I did, and considered only how to trim their sails to keep in office or to get it. How sick one is of all that! Half-a-dozen times at least in Anglo-Irish history things have come to the same point. 'All Ireland cannot govern the Earl of Kildare,' said someone in Henry VIII.'s privy council. Then answered Wolsey, in the tone of Mr. Gladstone, 'Let the Earl of Kildare govern all Ireland.' Elizabeth wished to conciliate. Shan O'Neil, Desmond, Tyrone promised in turn to rule Ireland in loyal union with England under Irish ideas. Lord Grey, who was for 'a Mahometan conquest,' was censured and 'girded at:' yet the end was always broken heads. From 1641 to 1649 an Irish parliament sat at Kilkenny, and Charles I. and the Tories dreamt of an alliance between Irish popery and English loyalism. Charles lost his head, and Cromwell had to make an end of Irish self-government at Drogheda and Wexford. Tyrconnell and James II. were to repeal the Act of Settlement and restore the forfeited lands to the old owners. The end of that came at the Boyne and at Aghrim. Grattan would remake the Irish nation. The English Liberals sent Lord Fitzwilliam to help him, and the Saxon mastiff and the Celtic wolf were to live as brothers evermore. The result has been always the same; the wretched country inflated with a dream of independence, and then trampled into mud again. So it has been. So it will be again. Ireland cannot be independent, for England is stronger than she, and cannot permit it. Yet nothing less will satisfy her. And so there has been always a weary round of fruitless concessions leading to demands which cannot be gratified, and in the end we are driven back upon force, which the miserable people lack the courage to encounter like men. Mr. Gladstone's experiment differs only from its antecedents because in the past the English friends of Irish liberty had a real hope that a reconciliation was possible. They believed in what they were trying to do. The present enterprise is the creation of parliamentary faction. I have never met any person acquainted with the minds and motives of the public men of the day who would not confess to me that, if it had suited the interests of the leaders of the present Radical party to adopt the Irish policy of the Long Parliament, their energy and their eloquence would have been equally at the service of the Protestant ascendency, which they have now denounced as a upas tree. They even ask you with wide eyes what else you would expect?

Mr. Sexton says that if England means to govern Ireland she must keep an army there as large as she keeps in India. England could govern Ireland in perfect peace, without an army at all, if there was no faction in the House of Commons. The spirit of party will either destroy the British Empire, or the British nation will make an end of party government on its present lines. There are sounds in the air like the cracking of the ice of the Neva at the incoming of spring, as if a nobler purpose was at last awaking in us. In a few more years there may be no more Radicals and no more Conservatives, and the nation will be all in all.

Here is the answer to the question so often asked, What is the use of the colonies to us? The colonies are a hundredfold multiplication of the area of our own limited islands. In taking possession of so large a portion of the globe, we have enabled ourselves to spread and increase, and carry our persons, our language and our liberties, into all climates and continents. We overflow at home; there are too many of us here already; and if no lands belonged to us but Great Britain and Ireland, we should become a small insignificant power beside the mighty nations which are forming around us. There is space for hundreds of millions of us in the territories of which we and our fathers have possessed ourselves. In Canada, Australia, New Zealand we add to our numbers and our resources. There are so many more Englishmen in the world able to hold their own against the mightiest of their rivals. And we have another function, such as the Romans had. The sections of men on this globe are unequally gifted. Some are strong and can govern themselves; some are weak and are the prey of foreign invaders or internal anarchy; and freedom, which all desire, is only attainable by weak nations when they are subject to the rule of others who are at once powerful and just. This was the duty which fell to the Latin race two thousand years ago. In these modern times it has fallen to ours, and in the discharge of it the highest features in the English character have displayed themselves. Circumstances forced on us the conquest of India; we have given India in return internal peace undisturbed by tribal quarrels or the ambitions of dangerous neighbours, with a law which deals out right to high and low among 250,000,000 human beings.

Never have rulers been less self-seeking than we have been in our Asiatic empire. No 'lex de repetundis' has been needed to punish avaricious proconsuls who had fattened on the provinces. In such positions the English show at their best, and do their best. India has been the training school of our greatest soldiers and greatest administrators. Strike off the Anglo-Indian names from the roll of famous Englishmen, and we shall lose the most illustrious of them all.

In India the rule of England has been an unexampled success, glorious to ourselves and of infinite benefit to our subjects, because we have been upright and disinterested, and have tried sincerely and honourably to do our duty. In other countries belonging to us, where with the same methods we might have produced the same results, we have applied them with a hesitating and less clean hand. We planted Ireland as a colony with our own people, we gave them a parliament of their own, and set them to govern the native Irish for us instead of doing it ourselves, to save appearances and to save trouble. We have not failed altogether. All the good that has been done at all in that poor island has been done by the Anglo-Irish landlords. But it has not been much, as the present condition of things shows. In the West Indies similarly the first settlers carried with them their English institutions. They were themselves a handful. The bulk of the population were slaves, and as long as slavery continued those institutions continued to work tolerably in the interest of the white race. When the slaves were emancipated, the distinction of colour done away with, and the black multitude and their white employers made equal before the law and equally privileged, constitutional government became no longer adapted to the new conditions. The white minority could not be trusted with the exclusive possession of political power. The blacks could not be trusted with the equally dangerous supremacy which their numbers would insure them. Our duty, if we did not and do not mean to abandon them altogether, has been to govern both with the same equity with which we govern at Calcutta. If you choose to take a race like the Irish or like the negroes whom you have forced into an unwilling subjection and have not treated when in that condition with perfect justice—if you take such a race, strike the fetters off them, and arm them at once with all the powers and privileges of loyal citizens, you ought not to be surprised if they attribute your concessions to fear, and if they turn again and rend you. When we are brought in contact with races of men who are not strong enough or brave enough to defend their own independence, and whom our own safety cannot allow to fall under any other power, our right and our duty is to govern such races and to govern them well, or they will have a right in turn to cut our throats. This is our mission. When we have dared to act up to it we have succeeded magnificently; we have failed when we have paltered and trifled; and we shall fail again, and the great empire on which the sun never sets will be shattered to atoms, if we refuse to look facts in the face.

From these meditations, suggested by the batch of newspapers which I had been studying, I was roused by the arrival of the promised aide-de-camp, a good-looking and good-humoured young officer in white uniform (they all wear white in the tropics), who had brought the governor's carriage for me. Government House, or King's

House, as it is called, answering to a 'Queen's House' in Barbadoes, is five miles from Kingston, on the slope which gradually ascends from the sea to the mountains. We drove through the town, which did not improve on closer acquaintance. The houses which front towards the streets are generally insignificant. The better sort, being behind walls or overhung with trees, were imperfectly visible. The roads were deep in white dust, which flies everywhere in whirling clouds from the unceasing wind. It was the dry season. The rains are not constant in Jamaica, as they are in the Antilles. The fields and the sides of the mountains were bare and brown and parched. The blacks, however, were about in crowds in their Sunday finery. Being in a British island, we had got back into the white calicoes and ostrich plumes, and I missed the grace of the women at Dominica; but men and women seemed as if they had not a care in the world. We passed Up Park Camp and the cantonments of the West India regiments, and then through a 'scrub' of dwarf acacia and blue flowered lignum vitae. Handsome villas were spread along the road with lawns and gardens, and the road itself was as excellent as those in Barbadoes. Half an hour's drive brought us to the lodge, and through the park to the King's House itself, which stands among groups of fine trees four hundred feet above the sea.

All the large houses in Jamaica—and this was one of the largest of them—are like those in Barbadoes, with the type more completely developed, generally square, built of stone, standing on blocks, hollow underneath for circulation of air, and approached by a broad flight of steps. On the three sides which the sun touches, deep verandahs or balconies are thrown out on the first and second floors, closed in front by green blinds, which can be shut either completely or partially, so that at a distance they look like houses of cards or great green boxes, made pretty by the trees which shelter them or the creepers which climb over them. Behind the blinds run long airy darkened galleries, and into these the sitting rooms open which are of course still darker with a subdued green light, in which, till you are used to it, you can hardly read. The floors are black, smooth, and polished, with loose mats for carpets. The reader of 'Tom Cringle' will remember Tom's misadventure when he blundered into a party of pretty laughing girls, slipped on one of these floors with a retrospective misadventure, and could not rise till his creole cousin slipped a petticoat over his head. All the arrangements are made to shut out heat and light. The galleries have sofas to lounge upon—everybody smokes, and smokes where he pleases; the draught sweeping away all residuary traces. At the King's House to increase the accommodation a large separate dining saloon has been thrown out on the north side, to which you descend from the drawing room by stairs, and thence along a covered passage. Among the mango trees behind there is a separate suite of rooms for the aides de-camp, and a superb swimming bath sixty feet long and eight feet deep. Altogether it was a sumptuous sort of palace where a governor with 7,000l. a year might spend his term of office with considerable comfort were it not haunted by recollections of poor Eyre. He, it seems, lived in the 'King's House,' and two miles off, within sight of his windows, lived Gordon.

I had a more than gracious welcome from Colonel J—— and his family. In him I found a high-bred soldier, who had served with distinction in India, who had been at the storm of Delhi, and who was close by when Nicholson was shot. No one could have looked fitter for the post which he now temporarily occupied. I felt uncomfortable at being thus thrust upon his hospitality. I had letters of introduction with me to the various governors of the islands, but on Colonel J—— I had no claim at all. I was not even aware of his existence, or he, very likely, of mine. If not he, at any rate the ladies of his establishment, might reasonably look upon me as a bore, and if I had been allowed I should simply have paid my respects and have gone on to my mulatto. But they would not hear of it. They were so evidently hearty in their invitation to me that I could only submit and do my best not to be a bore, the one sin for which there is no forgiveness.

In the circle into which I was thrown I was unlikely to hear much of West Indian politics or problems. Colonel J—— was acting as governor by accident, and for a few months only. He had his professional duties to look after; his term of service in Jamaica had nearly expired; and he could not trouble himself with possibilities and tendencies with which he would have no personal concern. As a spectator he considered probably that we were not making much of the West Indies, and were not on the way to make much. He confirmed the complaint which I had heard so often, that the blacks would not work for wages more than three days in the week, or regularly upon those, preferring to cultivate their own yams and sweet potatoes; but as it was admitted that they did work one way or another at home, I could not see that there was much to complain of. The blacks were only doing as we do. We, too, only work as much as we like or as we must, and we prefer working for ourselves to working for others.

On his special subjects the Colonel was as interesting as he could not help being. He talked of the army and of the recent changes in it without insisting that it was going to the devil. He talked of India and the Russians, and for a wonder he had no Russophobia. He thought that England and Russia might as easily be friends as enemies, and that it would be better for the world if they were. As this had been my own fixed opinion for the last thirty years, I thought him a very sensible man. In the evening there was a small dinner party, made up chiefly of officers from the West Indian regiments at Kingston. The English troops are in the mountains at Newcastle, four or five thousand feet up and beyond common visiting distance. Among those whom I met on this occasion was an officer who struck me particularly. There was a mystery about his origin. He had risen from the ranks, but was evidently a gentleman by birth; he had seen service all over the world; he had been in Chili, and, among his other accomplishments, spoke Spanish fluently; he entered the English army as a private, had been in the war in the Transvaal, and was the only survivor of the regiment which was surprised and shot down by the Boers in an intricate pass where they could neither retreat nor defend themselves. On that occasion he had escaped and saved the colours, for which he was rewarded by a commission. He was acquainted with many of my friends there who had been in the thick of the campaign; knew Sir Owen Lanyon, Sir Morrison Barlow, and Colley. He had surveyed the plateau on Majuba Hill after the action, and had gathered the rumours which were flying many coloured about Colley's death. Friend and foe alike loved Colley, and his already legendary fame is an unconscious tribute to his memory. By whose hand he fell can never be known. We believe as we wish or as we fancy.

Mr. —— was so fine an officer, so clever a man, and so reserved about his personal affairs, that about him too 'myths' were growing. He was credited in the mess room with being the then unknown author of 'Solomon's Mines.' Mr. Haggard will forgive a mistake which, if he knows Mr. ——, he will feel to be a compliment.

From general conversation I gathered that the sanguine views of the Colonial Secretary were not widely shared. The English interest was still something in Jamaica; but the phenomena of the Antilles were present there also, if in a less extreme form. There were 700,000 coloured people in the island, with but 15,000 or 16,000 whites; and the blacks there also were increasing rapidly, and the whites were stationary if not declining. There was the same uneasy social jealousy, and the absence of any social relation between the two races. There were mulattoes in the island of wealth and consequence, and at Government House there are no distinctions; but the English residents of pure colonial blood would not associate with them, social exclusiveness increasing with political equality. The blacks disliked the mulattoes; the mulattoes despised the blacks, and would not intermarry with them. The impression was that the mulatto would die out, that the tendency of the whites and blacks was to a constantly sharpening separation, and that if things went on as they were going for another generation, it was easy to see which of the two colours would then be in the ascendant. The blacks were growing saucy, too; with much else of the same kind. I could but listen and wait to judge for myself.

Meanwhile my quarters were unexceptionable, my kind entertainers leaving nothing undone to make my stay with them agreeable. In hot climates one sleeps lightly; but light sleep is all that one wants, and one wakes early. The swimming bath was waiting for me underneath my window. After a plunge in the clear cold water came coffee, grown and dried and roasted on the spot, and 'made' as such coffee ought to be. Then came the early walk. One missed the tropical luxuriance of Trinidad and Dominica, for the winter months in Jamaica are almost rainless; but it would have been beautiful anywhere else, and the mango trees were in their glory. There was a corner given to orchids, which were hung in baskets and just coming into flower. Lizards swarmed in the sunshine, running up the tree trunks, or basking on the garden seats. Snakes there are none; the mongoose has cleared them all away so completely that there is nothing left for him to eat but the poultry, in which he makes havoc, and, having been introduced to exterminate the vermin, has become a vermin himself.

To drive, to ride, to visit was the employment of the days. I saw the country. I saw what people were doing, and heard what they had to say.

The details are mostly only worth forgetting. The senior aide-de-camp, Captain C——, an officer in the Artillery, was a man of ability and observation. He, too, like the Colonel, was mainly interested in his profession, to which he was anxious to return; but he was watching, too, with serious interest the waning fortunes of the West Indies. He superintended the social part of the governor's business to perfection. Anything which I wished for had only to be mentioned to be provided. He gave me the benefit, though less often than I could have wished, of his shrewd, and not ungenial, observations. He drove me one morning into Kingston. I had passed through it hastily on the day of my landing. There were libraries, museums, public offices, and such like to be seen, besides the town itself. High up on the mountain side, more often in the clouds than out of them, the cantonments of the English regiments were visible from the park at Government House. The slope where they had been placed was so steep that one wondered how they held on. They looked like tablecloths stretched out to dry. I was to ride up there one day. Meanwhile, as we were driving through the park and saw the white spots shining up above us, I asked the aide-de-camp what the privates found to do in such a place. The ground was too steep for athletics; no cricket could be possible there, no lawn tennis, no quoits, no anything. There were no neighbours. Sports there were none. The mongoose had destroyed the winged game, and there was neither hare nor rabbit, pig nor deer; not a wild animal to be hunted and killed. With nothing to do, no one to speak to, and nothing to kill, what could become of them? Did they drink? Well, yes. They drank rum occasionally; but there were no public houses. They could only get it at the canteen, and the daily allowance was moderate. As to beer, it was out of reach altogether. At the foot of the mountains it was double the price which it was in England. At Newcastle the price was doubled again by the cost of carriage to the camp. I inquired if they did not occasionally hang themselves. 'Perhaps they would,' he said, 'if they had no choice, but they preferred to desert, and this they did in large numbers. They slipped down the back of the range, made their way to the sea, and escaped to the United States.' The officers—what became of them? The officers! Oh, well! they gardened! Did they like it? Some did and some didn't. They were not so ill off as the men, as occasionally they could come down on leave.

One wondered what the process had been which had led the authorities to select such a situation. Of course it was for the health of the troops, but the hill country in Jamaica is wide; there were many other places available, less utterly detestable, and ennui and discontent are as mischievous as fever. General ——, a short time ago, went up to hold an inquiry into the desertions, and expressed his wonder how such things could be. With such air, such scenery, such views far and wide over the island, what could human creatures wish for more? 'You would desert yourself, general,' said another officer, 'if you were obliged to stay there a month.'

Captain C—— undertook that I should go up myself in a day or two. He promised to write and make arrangements. Meanwhile we went on to Kingston. It was not beautiful. There was Rodney's statue. Rodney is venerated in Jamaica, as he ought to be; but for him it would have been a Spanish colony again. But there is nothing grand about the buildings, nothing even handsome, nothing even specially characteristic of England or the English mind. They were once perhaps business-like, and business having slackened they are now dingy. Shops, houses, wharves, want brightness and colour. We called at the office of the Colonial Secretary, the central point of the administration. It was an old mansion, plain, unambitious, sufficient perhaps for its purpose, but lifeless and dark. If it represented economy there would be no objection. The public debt has doubled since Jamaica became a Crown colony. In 1876 it was half a million. It is now more than a million and a half. The explanation is the extension of the railway system, and there has been no culpable extravagance. I do not suppose that the re-establishment of a constitution would mend matters. Democracies are always extravagant. The majority, who have little property or none, regulate the expenditure. They lay the taxes on the minority, who have to find the money, and have no interest in sparing them.

Ireland when it was governed by the landowners, Jamaica in the days of slavery, were administered at a cost which seems now incredibly small. The authority of the landowners and of the planters was undisputed. They were feared and obeyed, and magistrates unpaid and local constables sufficed to maintain tolerable order. Their authority is gone. Their functions are transferred to the police, and every service has to be paid for. There may be fewer serious crimes, but the subordination is immeasurably less, the expense of administration is immeasurably greater. I declined to be taken over sugar mills, or to be shown the latest improvements. I was too ignorant to understand in what the improvements consisted, and could take them upon trust. The public bakery was more interesting. In tropical climates a hot oven in a small house makes an inconvenient addition to the temperature. The bread for Kingston, and for many miles around it, is manufactured at night by a single company and is distributed in carts in the morning. We saw the museum and public library. There were the usual specimens of island antiquities—of local fish, birds, insects, reptiles, plants, geological formations, and such like. In the library were old editions of curious books at the West Indies, some of them unique, ready to yield ampler pictures of the romance of the old life there than we at present possess. I had but leisure to glance at title-pages and engravings. The most noticeable relic preserved there, if it be only genuine, is the identical bauble which Cromwell ordered to be taken away from the Speaker's table in the House of Commons. Explanations are given of the manner in which it came to Jamaica. The evidence, so far as I could understand it, did not appear conclusive.

Among the new industries in the island in the place of sugar was, or ought to be, tobacco. A few years ago I asked Sir J. Hooker, the chief living authority in such matters, why Cuba was allowed the monopoly of delicate cigar tobacco—whether there were no other countries where it could be grown equally good. He said that at the very moment cigars, as fine as the finest Havanas, were being produced in Jamaica. He gave me an excellent specimen with the address of the house which supplied it; and for a year or two I was able to buy from it what, if not perfect, was more than tolerable. The house acquired a reputation; and then, for some reason or other, perhaps from weariness of the same flavour, perhaps from a falling off in the character of the cigars, I, and possibly others, began to be less satisfied. Here on the spot I wished to make another experiment. Captain C—— introduced me to a famous manufacturer, a Spaniard, with a Spanish manager under him who had been trained at Havana. I bespoke his good will by adjuring him in his own tongue not to disappoint me; and I believe that he gave me the best that he had. But, alas! it is with tobacco as with most other things. Democracy is king; and the greatest happiness of the greatest number is the rule of modern life. The average of everything is higher than it used to be; the high quality which rises above mediocrity is rare or is non-existent. We are swept away by the genius of the age, and must be content with such other blessings as it has been pleased to bring with it.

Why should I murmur thus and vainly moan?

The Gods will have it so—their will be done.[14]

The earth is patient also, and allows the successive generations of human creatures to play their parts upon her surface as they please. She spins on upon her own course; and seas and skies, and crags and forests, are spiritual and beautiful as ever.

Gordon's Town is a straggling village in the Blue Range underneath Newcastle. Colonel J—— had a villa there, and one afternoon he took me over to see it. You pass abruptly from the open country into the mountains. The way to Gordon's Town was by the side of the Hope river, which cuts its way out of them in a narrow deep ravine. The stream was now trickling faintly among the stones; the enormous boulders in the bed were round as cannon balls, and, weighing hundreds of tons, show what its power must be in the coming down of the floods. Within the limits of the torrent, which must rise at such times thirty feet above its winter level, the rocks were bare and stern, no green thing being able to grow there. Above the line the tropical vegetation was in all its glory: ferns and plantains waving in the moist air; cedars, tamarinds, gum trees, orange trees striking their roots among the clefts of the crags, and hanging out over the abysses below them. Aloes flung up their tall spiral stems; flowering shrubs and creepers covered bank and slope with green and blue and white and yellow, and above and over our heads, as we drove along, frowned the great limestone blocks which thunder down when loosened by the rain. Farther up the hill sides, where the slopes are less precipitous, the forest has been burnt off by the unthrifty blacks, who use fire to clear the ground for their yam gardens, and destroy the timber over a dozen acres when they intend to cultivate but a single one. The landscape suffers less than the soil. The effect to the eye is merely that the mountains in Jamaica, as in temperate climates, become bare at a moderate altitude, and their outlines are marked more sharply against the sky.

Introduced among scenery of this kind, we followed the river two or three miles, when it was crossed by a bridge, above which stood my friend Miss Burton's lodging house, where she had designed entertaining me. At Gordon's Town, which is again a mile farther on, the valley widens out, and there are cocoa and coffee plantations. Through an opening we saw far above our heads, like specks of snow against the mountain side, the homes or prisons of our unfortunate troops. Overlooking the village through which we were passing, and three hundred feet above it, was perched the Colonel's villa on a projecting spur where a tributary of the Hope river has carved out a second ravine. We drove to the door up a steep winding lane among coffee bushes, which scented the air with their jessamine-like blossom, and wild oranges on which the fruit hung untouched, glowing like balls of gold. We were now eleven hundred feet above the sea. The air was already many degrees cooler than at Kingston. The ground in front of the house was levelled for a garden. Ivy was growing about the trellis work, and scarlet geraniums and sweet violets and roses which cannot be cultivated in the lower regions, were here in full bloom. Elsewhere in the grounds there was a lawn tennis court to tempt the officers down from their eyrie in the clouds. The house was empty, in charge of servants. From the balcony in front of the drawing room we saw peak rising behind peak, till the highest, four thousand feet above us, was lost in the white mist. Below was the valley of the Hope river with its gardens and trees and scattered huts, with buildings here and there of higher pretensions. On the other side the tributary stream rushed down its own ravine, while the breeze among the trees and the sound of the falling waters swayed up to us in intermittent pulsations.

VALLEY IN THE BLUE MOUNTAINS, JAMAICA.

VALLEY IN THE BLUE MOUNTAINS, JAMAICA.

The place had been made, I believe, in the days of plantation prosperity. What would become of it all, if Jamaica drifted after her sisters in the Antilles, as some persons thought that she was drifting, and became, like Grenada, an island of small black proprietors? Was such a fate really hanging over her? Not necessarily, not by any law of nature. If it came, it would come from the dispiritment, the lack of energy and hope in the languid representatives of the English colonists; for the land even in the mountains will grow what it is asked to grow, and men do not live by sugar alone; and my friend Dr. Nicholl in Dominica and Colonel Duncan in Grenada itself were showing what English energy could do if it was alive and vigorous. The pale complaining beings of whom I saw too many, seemed as if they could not be of the same race as the men who ruled in the days of the slave trade. The question to be asked in every colony is, what sort of men is it rearing? If that cannot be answered satisfactorily, the rest is not worth caring for. The blacks do not deserve the ill that is spoken of them. Colonel J——'s house is twelve miles from Kingston. He told me that a woman would walk in with a load for him, and return on the same day with another, for a shilling. With such material of labour wisely directed, whites and blacks might live and prosper together; but even the poor negro will not work when he is regarded only as a machine to bring grist to his master's mill.

FOOTNOTES:

[14]

Euripides.

CHAPTER XIV.

Visit to Port Royal—Dockyard—Town—Church—Fort Augusta—The eyrie in the mountains—Ride to Newcastle—Society in Jamaica—Religious bodies—Liberty and authority.

A new fort was being built at the mouth of the harbour. New batteries were being armed on the sandbanks at Port Royal. Colonel J—— had to inspect what was going on, and he allowed me to go with him. We were to lunch with the commodore of the station at the Port Royal dockyard. I could then see the town—or what was left of it, for the story went that half of it had been swallowed up by an earthquake. We ran out in a steam launch from Kingston, passing under the sterns of the Spanish frigates. I was told that there were always one or more Spanish ships of war stationed there, but no one knew anything about them except generally that they were on the look-out for Cuban conspirators. There was no exchange of courtesies between their officers and ours, nor even official communication beyond what was formally necessary. I thought it strange, but it was no business of mine. My surprise, however, was admitted to be natural. As the launch drew little water, we had no occasion to follow the circuitous channel, but went straight over the shoals. We passed close by Gallows Point, where the Johnny crows used to pick the pirates' bones. In the mangrove swamp adjoining, it was said that there was an old Spanish cemetery; but the swamp was poisonous, and no one had ever seen it. At the dockyard pier the commodore was waiting for us. I found that he was an old acquaintance whom I had met ten years before at the Cape. He was a brisk, smart officer, quiet and sailor-like in his manners, but with plenty of talent and cultivation. He showed us his stores and his machinery, large engines, and engineers to work them, ready for any work which might be wanted, but apparently with none to do. We went over the hospital, airy and clean, with scarcely a single occupant, so healthy has now been made a spot which was once a nest of yellow fever. Naval stores soon become antiquated; and parts of the great square were paved with the old cannon balls which had become useless on the introduction of rifled guns. The fortifications were antiquated also, but new works were being thrown up armed with the modern monster cannon. One difficulty struck me; Port Royal stood upon a sandbank. In such a place no spring of fresh water could be looked for. On the large acreage of roofs there were no shoots to catch the rain and carry it into cisterns. Whence did the water come for the people in the town? How were the fleets supplied which used to ride there? How was it in the old times when Port Royal was crowded with revelling crews of buccaneers? I found that every drop which is consumed in the place, or which is taken on board either of merchant ship or man-of-war, is brought in a steam tug from a spring ten miles off upon the coast. Before steam came in, it was fetched in barges rowed by hand. Nothing could be easier than to save the rain which falls in abundance. Nothing could be easier than to lay pipes along the sand-spit to the spring. But the tug plies daily to and fro, and no one thinks more about the matter.

A West Indian regiment is stationed at Port Royal. After the dockyard we went through the soldiers' quarters and then walked through the streets of the once famous station. It is now a mere hamlet of boatmen and fishermen, squalid and wretched, without and within. Half-naked children stared at us from the doors with their dark, round eyes. I found it hard to call up the scenes of riot, and confusion, and wild excitement which are alleged to have been witnessed there. The story that it once covered a far larger area has been, perhaps, invented to account for the incongruity. Old plans exist which seem to show that the end of the spit could never have been of any larger dimensions than it is at present. There is proof enough, however, that in the sand there lie the remains of many thousand English soldiers and seamen, who ended their lives there for one cause or other. The bones lie so close that they are turned up as in a country churchyard when a fresh grave is dug. The walls of the old church are inlaid thickly with monuments and monumental tablets to the memory of officers of either service, young and old; some killed by fever, some by accidents of war or sea; some decorated with the honours which they had won in a hundred fights, some carried off before they had gathered the first flower of fame. The costliness of many of these memorials was an affecting indication how precious to their families those now resting there once had been. One in high relief struck me as a characteristic specimen of Rubillac's workmanship. It was to a young lieutenant who had been killed by the bursting of a gun. Flame and vapour were rushing out of the breech. The youth himself was falling backwards, with his arms spread out, and a vast preternatural face—death, judgment, eternity, or whatever it was meant to be—was glaring at him through the smoke. Bad art, though the execution was remarkable; but better, perhaps, than the weeping angels now grown common among ourselves.

After luncheon the commodore showed us his curiosities, especially his garden, which, considering the state of his water supply, he had created under unfavourable conditions. He had a very respectable collection of tropical ferns and flowers, with palms and plantains to shade and shelter them. He was an artist besides, within the lines of his own profession. Drawings of ships and boats of all sorts and in all attitudes by his own brush or pencil were hanging on the walls of his working room. He was good enough to ask me to spend a day or two with him at Port Royal before I left the island, and I looked forward with special pleasure to becoming closer acquainted with such a genuine piece of fine-grained British oak.

There were the usual ceremonies to be attended to. The officers of the guard-ship and gunboats had to be called on. The forts constructed, or in the course of construction, were duly inspected. I believe that there is a real serious intention to strengthen Port Royal in view of the changes which may come about through the opening, if that event ever takes place, of the Darien canal.

Our last visit was to a fort deserted, or all but deserted—the once too celebrated Fort Augusta, which deserves particular description. It stands on the inner side of the lagoon commanding the deep-water channel at the point of the great mangrove swamp at the mouth of the Cobre river. For the purpose for which it was intended no better situation could have been chosen, had there been nothing else to be con-sidered except the defence of the harbour, for a vessel trying to reach Kingston had to pass close in front of its hundred guns. It was constructed on a scale becoming its importance, with accommodation for two or three regiments, and the regiments were sent thither, and they perished, regiment after regiment, officers and men, from the malarious exhalations of the morass. Whole battalions were swept away. The ranks were filled up by reinforcements from home, and these, too, went the same road. Of one regiment the only survivors, according to the traditions of the place, were a quartermaster and a corporal. Finally it occurred to the authorities at the Horse Guards that a regiment of Hussars would be a useful addition to the garrison. It was not easy to see what Hussars were to do there. There is not a spot where the horses could stand twenty yards beyond the lines; nor could they reach Fort Augusta at all except in barges. However, it was perhaps well that they were sent. Horses and men went the way of the rest. The loss of the men might have been supplied, but horses were costly, and the loss of them was more serious. Fort Augusta was gradually abandoned, and is now used only as a powder magazine. A guard is kept there of twenty blacks from the West Indian force, but even these are changed every ten days—so deadly the vapour of that malarious jungle is now understood to be.

I never saw so spectral a scene as met my eyes when we steamed up to the landing place—ramparts broken down, and dismantled cannon lying at the foot of the wall overgrown by jungle. The sentinel who presented arms was like a corpse in uniform. He was not pale, for he was a negro—he was green, and he looked like some ghoul or afrite in a ghastly cemetery. The roofs of the barracks and storehouses had fallen in, the rafters being left standing with the light shining between them as through the bones of skeletons. Great piles of shot lay rusting, as not worth removal; among them conical shot, so recently, had this fatal charnel house been regarded as a fit location for British artillerymen.

I breathed more freely as we turned our backs upon the hideous memorial of parliamentary administration, and steamed away into a purer air. My conservative instincts had undergone a shock. As we look back into the past, the brighter features stand out conspicuously. The mistakes and miseries have sunk in the shade and are forgotten. In the present faults and merits are visible alike. The faults attract chief notice that they may be mended; and as there seem so many of them, the impulse is to conclude that the past was better. It is well to be sometimes reminded what the past really was. In Colonel J—— I found a strong advocate of the late army reforms. Thanks to recovering energy and more distinct conscientiousness, thanks to the all-seeing eye of the Press, such an experiment as that of Fort Augusta could hardly be tried again, or if tried could not be persisted in. Extravagance and absurdities, however, remain, and I was next to witness an instance of them.

Having ceased to quarter our regiments in mangrove swamps, we now build a camp for them among the clouds. I mentioned that Captain C—— had undertaken that I should see Newcastle. He had written to a friend there to say that I was coming up, and the junior aide-de-camp kindly lent his services as a guide. As far as Gordon's Town we drove along the same road which we had followed before. There, at a small wayside inn, we found horses waiting which were accustomed to the mountain. Suspicious mists were hanging about aloft, but the landlord, after a glance at them, promised us a fine day, and we mounted and set off. My animal's merits were not in his appearance, but he had been up and down a hundred times, and might be trusted to accomplish his hundred and first without misfortune. For the first mile or so the road was tolerably level, following the bank of the river under the shade of the forest. It then narrowed into a horse path and zigzagged upwards at the side of a torrent into the deep pools of which we occasionally looked down over the edges of uncomfortable precipices. Then again there was a level, with a village and coffee plantations and oranges and bananas. After this the vegetation changed. We issued out upon open mountain, with English grass, English clover, English gorse, and other familiar acquaintances introduced to make the isolation less intolerable. The track was so rough and narrow that we could ride only in single file, and was often no better than a watercourse; yet by this and no other way every article had to be carried on donkeys' backs or human heads which was required for the consumption of 300 infantry and 100 artillerymen. Artillerymen might seem to imply artillery, but they have only a single small field gun. They are there for health's sake only, and to be fit for work if wanted below. An hour's ride brought us to the lowest range of houses, which were 4,000 feet above the sea. From thence they rose, tier above tier, for 500 feet more. The weather so far had held up, and the views had been glorious, but we passed now into a cloud, through which we saw, dimly, groups of figures listlessly lounging. The hillside was bare, and the slope so steep that there was no standing on it, save where it had been flattened by the spade; and here in this extraordinary place were 400 young Englishmen of the common type of which soldiers are made, with nothing to do and nothing to enjoy—remaining, unless they desert or die of ennui, for one, two, or three years, as their chance may be. Every other day they can see nothing, save each other's forms and faces in the fog; for, fine and bright as the air may be below, the moisture in the air is condensed into cloud by the chill rock and soil of the high ranges. The officers come down now and then on furlough or on duty; the men rarely and hardly at all, and soldiers, in spite of General ——, cannot always be made happy by the picturesque. They are not educated enough to find employment for their minds, and of amusement there is none.

We continued our way up, the track if anything growing steeper, till we reached the highest point of the camp, and found ourselves before a pretty cottage with creepers climbing about it belonging to the major in command. A few yards off was the officers' mess room. They expected us. They knew my companion, and visitors from the under-world were naturally welcome. The major was an active clever man, with a bright laughing Irish wife, whose relations in the old country were friends of my own. The American consul and his lady happened to have ridden up also the same day; so, in spite of fog, which grew thicker every moment, we had a good time. As to seeing, we could see nothing; but then there was nothing to see except views; and panoramic views from mountain tops, extolled as they may be, do not particularly interest me. The officers, so far as I could learn, are less ill off than the privates. Those who are married have their wives with them; they can read, they can draw, they can ride; they have gardens about their houses where they can grow English flowers and vegetables and try experiments. Science can be followed anywhere, and is everywhere a resource. Major —— told me that he had never known what it was to find the day too long. Healthy the camp is at any rate. The temperature never rises above 70° nor sinks often below 60°. They require charcoal fires to keep the damp out and blankets to sleep under; and when they see the sun it is an agreeable change and something to talk about. There are no large incidents, but small ones do instead. While I was there a man came to report that he had slipped by accident and set a stone rolling; the stone had cut a water pipe in two, and it had to be mended, and was an afternoon's work for somebody. Such officers as have no resources in themselves are, of course, bored to extinction. There is neither furred game to hunt nor feathered game to shoot; the mongoose has eaten up the partridges. I suggested that they should import two or three couple of bears from Norway; they would fatten and multiply among the roots and sugar canes, with a black piccaninny now and then for a special delicacy. One of the party extemporised us a speech which would be made on the occasion in Exeter Hall.

We had not seen the worst of the weather. As we mounted to ride back the fog changed to rain, and the rain to a deluge. The track became a torrent. Macintoshes were a vanity, for the water rushed down one's neck, and every crease made itself into a conduit carrying the stream among one's inner garments. Dominica itself had not prepared me for the violence of these Jamaican downpourings. False had proved our prophet down below. There was no help for it but to go on; and we knew by experience that one does not melt on these occasions. At a turn of the road we met another group of riders, among them Lady N——, who, during her husband's absence in England, was living at a country house in the hills. She politely stopped and would have spoken, but it was not weather to stand talking in; the torrent washed us apart.

And now comes the strangest part of the story. A thousand feet down we passed out below the clouds into clear bright sunshine. Above us it was still black as ever. The vapour clung about the peaks and did not leave them. Underneath us and round us it was a lovely summer's day. The farther we descended the fewer the signs that any rain had fallen. When we reached the stables at Gordon's Town, the dust was on the road as we left it, and the horsekeeper congratulated us on the correctness of his forecast. Clothes soon dry in that country, and we drove down home none the worse for our wetting. I was glad to have seen a place of which I had heard so much. On the whole, I hoped that perhaps by-and-by the authorities may discover some camping ground for our poor soldiers halfway between the Inferno of Fort Augusta and the Caucasian cliffs to which they are chained like Prometheus. Malice did say that Newcastle was the property of a certain Sir ——, a high official of a past generation, who wished to part with it, and found a convenient purchaser in the Government.

The hospitalities at Government House were well maintained under the J—— administration. The Colonel was gracious, the lady beautiful and brilliant. There were lawn parties and evening parties, when all that was best in the island was collected; the old Jamaican aristocracy, army and navy officers, civilians, eminent lawyers, a few men among them of high intelligence. The tone was old-fashioned and courteous, with little, perhaps too little, of the go-a-headism of younger colonies, but not the less agreeable on that account. As to prospects, or the present condition of things in the island, there were wide differences of opinion. If there was unanimity about anything, it was about the consequences likely to arise from an extension of the principle of self-government. There, at all events, lay the right road to the wrong place. The blacks had nothing to complain of, and the wrong at present was on the other side. The taxation fell heavily on the articles consumed by the upper classes. The duty on tea, for instance, was a shilling a pound, and the duties on other luxuries in the same proportion. It scarcely touched the negroes at all. They were acquiring land, and some thought that there ought to be a land tax. They would probably object and resist, and trouble would come if it was proposed, for the blacks object to taxes. As long as there are white men to pay them, they will be satisfied to get the benefit of the expenditure; but let not their English friends suppose that when they have the island for their own they will tax themselves for police or schools, or for any other of those educational institutions from which the believers in progress anticipate such glorious results.

As to the planters, it seemed agreed that when an estate was unencumbered and the owner resided upon it and managed it himself, he could still keep afloat. It was agreed also that when the owner was an absentee the cost of management consumed all the profits, and thus the same impulse to sell which had gone so far in the Antilles was showing itself more and more in Jamaica also. Fine properties all about the island were in the market for any price which purchasers could be found to give. Too many even of the old English families were tired of the struggle, and were longing to be out of it at any cost.

At one time we heard much of the colonial Church and the power which it was acquiring, and as it seems unlikely that the political authority of the white race will be allowed to reassert itself, it must be through their minds and through those other qualities which religion addresses that the black race will be influenced by the white, if it is ever to be influenced at all.

I had marked the respect with which the Catholic clergy were treated in Dominica, and even the Hayti Republic still maintains the French episcopate and priesthood. But I could not find that the Church of England in Jamaica either was at present or had ever been more than the Church of the English in Jamaica, respected as long as the English gentry were a dominant power there, but with no independent charm to work on imagination or on superstition. Labat says, as I noted above, that the English clergy in his time did not baptise the black babies, on the curious ground that Christians could not lawfully be held as slaves, and the slaves therefore were not to be made Christians. A Jesuit Father whom I met at Government House told me that even now the clergy refuse to baptise the illegitimate children, and as, according to the official returns, nearly two-thirds of the children that are born in Jamaica come into the world thus irregularly, they are not likely to become more popular than they used to be. Perhaps Father —— was doing what a good many other people do, making a general practice out of a few instances. Perhaps the blacks themselves who wish their children to be Christians carry them to the minister whom they prefer, and that minister may not be the Anglican clergyman. Of Catholics there are not many in Jamaica; of the Moravians I heard on all sides the warmest praise. They, above all the religious bodies in the island, are admitted to have a practical power for good over the limited number of people which belong to them. But the Moravians are but a few. They do not rush to make converts in the highways and hedges, and my observations in Dominica almost led me to wish that, in the absence of other forms of spiritual authority, the Catholics might become more numerous than they are. The priests in Dominica were the only Europeans who, for their own sakes and on independent grounds, were looked up to with fear and respect.

The religion of the future! That is the problem of problems that rises before us at the close of this waning century. The future of the West Indies is a small matter. Yet that, too, like all else, depends on the spiritual beliefs which are to rise out of the present confusion. Men will act well and wisely, or ill and foolishly, according to the form and force of their conceptions of duty. Once before, under the Roman Empire, the conditions were not wholly dissimilar. The inherited creed had become unbelievable, and the scientific intellect was turning materialist. Christianity rose out of the chaos, confounding statesmen and philosophers, and became the controlling power among mankind for 1,800 years. But Christianity found a soil prepared for the seed. The masses of the inhabitants of the Roman world were not materialist. The masses of the people believed already in the supernatural and in penal retribution after death for their sins. Lucretius complains of the misery produced upon them by the terrors of the anticipated Tartarus. Serious and good men were rather turning away from atheism than welcoming it; and if they doubted the divinity of the Olympian gods, it was not because they doubted whether gods existed at all, but because the immoralities attributed to them were unworthy of the exalted nature of the Divine Being. The phenomena are different now. Who is now made wretched by the fear of hell? The tendency of popular thought is against the supernatural in any shape. Far into space as the telescope can search, deep as analysis can penetrate into mind and consciousness or the forces which govern natural things, popular thought finds only uniformity and connection of cause and effect—no sign anywhere of a personal will which is influenced by prayer or moral motive. When a subject is still obscure we are confident that it admits of scientific explanation; we no longer refer 'ad Deum,' whom we regard as a constitutional monarch taking no direct part at all. The new creed, however, not having crystallised as yet into a shape which can be openly professed, and as without any creed at all the flesh and the devil might become too powerful, we maintain the old names and forms, as we maintain the monarchy. We surround both with reverence and majesty, and the reverence, being confined to feeling, continues to exercise a vague but wholesome influence. We row in one way while we look another. In the presence of the marked decay of Protestantism as a positive creed, the Protestant powers of Europe may, perhaps, patch up some kind of reconciliation with the old spiritual organisation which was shattered in the sixteenth century, and has since shown no unwillingness to adapt itself to modern forms of thought. The Olympian gods survived for seven centuries after Aristophanes with the help of allegory and 'economy.' The Church of Rome may survive as long after Calvin and Luther. Carlyle mocked at the possibility when I ventured to say so to him. Yet Carlyle seemed to think that the mass was the only form of faith in Europe which had any sincerity remaining in it.

A religion, at any rate, which will keep the West Indian blacks from falling into devil worship is still to seek. Constitutions and belief in progress may satisfy Europe, but will not answer in Jamaica. In spite of the priests, child murder and cannibalism have reappeared in Hayti; but without them things might have been worse than they are, and the preservation of white authority and influence in any form at all may be better than none.

White authority and white influence may, however, still be preserved in a nobler and better way. Slavery was a survival from a social order which had passed away, and slavery could not be continued. It does not follow that per se it was a crime. The negroes who were sold to the dealers in the African factories were most of them either slaves already to worse masters or were servi, servants in the old meaning of the word, prisoners of war, or else criminals, servati or reserved from death. They would otherwise have been killed; and since the slave trade has been abolished are again killed in the too celebrated 'customs.' The slave trade was a crime when the chiefs made war on each other for the sake of captives whom they could turn into money. In many instances, perhaps in most, it was innocent and even beneficent. Nature has made us unequal, and Acts of Parliament cannot make us equal. Some must lead and some must follow, and the question is only of degree and kind. For myself, I would rather be the slave of a Shakespeare or a Burghley than the slave of a majority in the House of Commons or the slave of my own folly. Slavery is gone, with all that belonged to it; but it will be an ill day for mankind if no one is to be compelled any more to obey those who are wiser than himself, and each of us is to do only what is right in our own eyes. There may be authority, yet not slavery: a soldier is not a slave, a sailor is not a slave, a child is not a slave, a wife is not a slave; yet they may not live by their own wills or emancipate themselves at their own pleasure from positions in which nature has placed them, or into which they have themselves voluntarily entered. The negroes of the West Indies are children, and not yet disobedient children. They have their dreams, but for the present they are dreams only. If you enforce self-government upon them when they are not asking for it, you may turn the dream into a reality, and wilfully drive them back into the condition of their ancestors, from which the slave trade was the beginning of their emancipation.

CHAPTER XV.

The Church of England in Jamaica—Drive to Castleton—Botanical Gardens—Picnic by the river—Black women—Ball at Government House—Mandeville—Miss Roy—Country society—Manners—American visitors—A Moravian missionary—The modern Radical creed.

If I have spoken without enthusiasm of the working of the Church of England among the negroes, I have not meant to be disrespectful. As I lay awake at daybreak on the Sunday morning after my arrival, I heard the sound of church bells, not Catholic bells as at Dominica, but good old English chimes. The Church is disestablished so far as law can disestablish it, but, as in Barbadoes, the royal arms still stand over the arches of the chancel. Introduced with the English conquest, it has been identified with the ruling order of English gentry, respectable, harmless, and useful, to those immediately connected with it.

The parochial system, as in Barbadoes also, was spread over the island. Each parish had its church, its parsonage and its school, its fonts where the white children were baptised—in spite of my Jesuit, I shall hope not whites only; and its graveyard, where in time they were laid to rest. With their quiet Sunday services of the old type the country districts were exact reproductions of English country villages. The church whose bells I had heard was of the more fashionable suburban type, standing in a central situation halfway to Kingston. The service was at the old English hour of eleven. We drove to it in the orthodox fashion, with our prayer books and Sunday costumes, the Colonel in uniform. The gentry of the neighbourhood are antiquated in their habits, and to go to church on Sunday is still regarded as a simple duty. A dozen carriages stood under the shade at the doors. The congregation was upper middle-class English of the best sort, and was large, though almost wholly white. White tablets as at Port Royal covered the walls, with familiar English names upon them. But for the heat I could have imagined myself at home. There were no Aaron Bangs to be seen, or Paul Gelids, with the rough sense, the vigour, the energy, and roystering light-heartedness of our grandfathers. The faces of the men were serious and thoughtful, with the shadow resting on them of an uncertain future. They are good Churchmen still, and walk on in the old paths, wherever those paths may lead. They are old-fashioned and slow to change, and are perhaps belated in an eddy of the great stream of progress; but they were pleasant to see and pleasant to talk to. After service there were the usual shakings of hands among friends outside; arrangements were made for amusements and expeditions in which I was invited to join—which were got up, perhaps, for my own entertainment. I was to be taken to the sights of the neighbourhood. I was to see this; I was to see that; above all, I must see the Peak of the Blue Mountains. The peak itself I could see better from below, for there it stood, never moving, between seven and eight thousand feet high. But I had had mountain riding enough and was allowed to plead my age and infirmities. It was arranged finally that I should be driven the next day to Castleton, seventeen miles off over a mountain pass, to see the Botanical Gardens.

Accordingly early on the following morning we set off; two carriages full of us; Mr. M——, a new friend lately made, but I hope long to be preserved, on the box of his four-in-hand. The road was as good as all roads are in Jamaica and Barbadoes, and more cannot be said in their favour. Forest trees made a roof over our heads as we climbed to the crest of the ridge. Thence we descended the side of a long valley, a stream running below us which gradually grew into a river. We passed through all varieties of cultivation. On the high ground there was a large sugar plantation, worked by coolies, the first whom I had seen in Jamaica. In the alluvial meadows on the river-side were tobacco fields, cleanly and carefully kept, belonging to my Spanish friend in Kingston, and only too rich in leaves. There were sago too, and ginger, and tamarinds, and cocoa, and coffee, and cocoa-nut palms. On the hill-sides were the garden farms of the blacks, which were something to see and remember. They receive from the Government at an almost nominal quit rent an acre or two of uncleared forest. To this as the first step they set light; at twenty different spots we saw their fires blazing. To clear an acre they waste the timber on half a dozen or a dozen. They plant their yams and sweet potatoes among the ashes and grow crops there till the soil is exhausted. Then they move on to another, which they treat with the same recklessness, leaving the first to go back to scrub. Since the Chinaman burnt his house to roast his pig, such waste was never seen. The male proprietors were lounging about smoking. Their wives, as it was market day, were tramping into Kingston with their baskets on their head. We met them literally in thousands, all merry and light-hearted, their little ones with little baskets trudging at their side. Of the lords of the creation we saw, perhaps, one to each hundred women, and he would be riding on mule or donkey, pipe in mouth and carrying nothing. He would be generally sulky too, while the ladies, young and old, had all a civil word for us and curtsied under their loads. Decidedly if there is to be a black constitution I would give the votes only to the women.

We reached Castleton at last. It was in a hot damp valley, said to be a nest of yellow fever. The gardens slightly disappointed me; my expectations had been too much raised by Trinidad. There were lovely flowers of course, and curious plants and trees. Every known palm is growing there. They try hard to grow roses, and they say that they succeed. The roses were not in flower, and I could not judge. Bye the familiar names were all there, and others which were not familiar, the newest im-portations called after the great ladies of the day. I saw one labelled Mabel Morrison. To find the daughter of an ancient college friend and contemporary giving name to a plant in the New World makes one feel dreadfully old; but I expected to find, and I did not find, some useful practical horticulture going on. They ought, for instance, to have been trying experiments with orange trees. The orange in Jamaica is left to nature. They plant the seeds, and leave the result to chance. They neither bud nor graft, and go upon the hypothesis that as the seed is, so will be the tree which comes of it. Yet even thus, so favourable is the soil and climate that the oranges of Jamaica are prized above all others which are sold in the American market. With skill and knowledge and good selection they might produce the finest in the world. 'There are dollars in that island, sir,' as an American gentleman said to me, 'if they look for them in the right way.' Nothing of this kind was going on at Castleton; so much the worse, but perhaps things will mend by-and-by. I was consoled partly by another specimen of the Amherstia nobilis. It was not so large as those which I had seen at Trinidad, but it was in splendid bloom, and certainly is the most gorgeous flowering tree which the world contains.

Wild nature also was luxuriantly beautiful. We picnicked by the river, which here is a full rushing stream with pools that would have held a salmon, and did hold abundant mullet. We found a bower formed by a twisted vine, so thick that neither sun nor rain could penetrate the roof. The floor was of shining shingle, and the air breathed cool from off the water. It was a spot which nymph or naiad may haunt hereafter, when nymphs are born again in the new era. The creatures of imagination have fled away from modern enlightenment. But we were a pleasant party of human beings, lying about under the shade upon the pebbles. We had brought a blanket of ice with us, and the champagne was manufactured into cup by choicest West Indian skill. Figures fall unconsciously at such moments into attitudes which would satisfy a painter, and the scenes remain upon the memory like some fine finished work of art. We had done with the gardens, and I remember no more of them except that I saw a mongoose stalking a flock of turkeys. The young ones and their mother gathered together and showed fight. The old cock, after the manner of the male animal, seemed chiefly anxious for his own skin, though a little ashamed at the same time, as if conscious that more was expected of him. On the way back we met the returning stream of women and children, loaded heavily as before and with the same elastic step. In spite of all that is incorrect about them, the women are the material to work upon; and if they saw that we were in earnest, they would lend their help to make their husbands bestir themselves. A Dutch gentleman once boasted to me of the wonderful prosperity of Java, where everybody was well off and everybody was industrious. He so insisted upon the industry that I ask him how it was brought about. Were the people slaves? 'Oh,' he cried, as if shocked, 'God forbid that a Christian nation should be so wicked as to keep slaves!' 'Do they never wish to be idle?' I asked. 'Never, never,' he said; 'no, no: we do not permit anyone to be idle.'

My stay with Colonel J—— was drawing to a close; one great festivity was impending, which I wished to avoid; but the gracious lady insisted that I must remain. There was to be a ball, and all the neighbourhood was invited. Pretty it was sure to be. Windows and doors, galleries and passages, would be all open. The gardens would be lighted up, and the guests could spread as they pleased. Brilliant it all was; more brilliant than you would see in our larger colonies. A ball in Sydney or Melbourne is like a ball in the north of England or in New York. There are the young men in black coats, and there are brightly dressed young ladies for them to dance with. The chaperons sit along the walls; the elderly gentlemen withdraw to the card room. Here all was different. The black coats in the ball at Jamaica were on the backs of old or middle-aged men, and, except Government officials, there was hardly a young man present in civilian dress. The rooms glittered with scarlet and white and blue and gold lace. The officers were there from the garrison and the fleet; but of men of business, of professional men, merchants, planters, lawyers, c. there were only those who had grown up to middle age in the island, whose fortunes, bad or good, were bound up with it. When these were gone, it seemed as if there would be no one to succeed them. The coveted heirs of great estates were no longer to be found for mothers to angle after. The trades and professions in Kingston had ceased to offer the prospect of an income to younger brothers who had to make their own way. For 250 years generations of Englishmen had followed one upon another, but we seemed to have come to the last. Of gentlemen unconnected with the public service, under thirty-five or forty, there were few to be seen, they were seeking their fortunes elsewhere. The English interest in Jamaica is still a considerable thing. The English flag flies over Government House, and no one so far wishes to remove it. But the British population is scanty and refuses to grow. Ships and regiments come and go, and officers and State employés make what appears to be a brilliant society. But it is in appearance only. The station is no longer a favourite one. They are gone, those pleasant gentry whose country houses were the paradise of middies sixty years ago. All is changed, even to the officers themselves. The drawling ensign of our boyhood, brave as a lion in the field, and in the mess room or the drawing room an idiot, appears also to be dead as the dodo. Those that one meets now are intelligent and superior men—no trace of the frivolous sort left. Is it the effect of the abolition of purchase, and competitive examinations? Is it that the times themselves are growing serious, and even the most empty-headed feel that this is no season for levity?

I had seen what Jamaican life was like in the upper spheres, and I had heard the opinions that were current in them; but I wished to see other parts of the country. I wished to see a class of people who were farther from headquarters, and who might not all sing to the same note. I determined to start off on an independent cruise of my own. In the centre of the island, two thousand feet above the sea, it was reported to me that I should find a delightful village called Mandeville, after some Duke of Manchester who governed Jamaica a hundred years ago. The scenery was said to have a special charm of its own, the air to be exquisitely pure, the land to be well cultivated. Village manners were to be found there of the old-fashioned sort, and a lodging house and landlady of unequalled merit. There was a railway for the first fifty miles. The line at starting crosses the mangrove swamps at the mouth of the Cobre river. You see the trees standing in the water on each side of the road. Rising slowly, it hardens into level grazing ground, stocked with cattle and studded with mangoes and cedars. You pass Spanish Town, of which only the roofs of the old State buildings are visible from the carriages. Sugar estates follow, some of which are still in cultivation, while ruined mills and fallen aqueducts show where others once had been. The scenery becomes more broken as you begin to ascend into the hills. River beds, dry when I saw them, but powerful torrents in the rainy season, are crossed by picturesque bridges. You come to the forest, where the squatters were at their usual work, burning out their yam patches. Columns of white smoke were rising all about us, yet so abundant the timber and so rapid the work of restoration when the devastating swarm has passed, that in this direction they have as yet made no marked impression, and the forest stretches as far as eye can reach. The glens grew more narrow and the trees grander as the train proceeded. After two hours we arrived at the present terminus, an inland town with the singular name of Porus. No explanation is given of it in the local handbooks; but I find a Porus among the companions of Columbus, and it is probably an interesting relic of the first Spanish occupation. The railway had brought business. Mule carts were going about, and waggons; omnibuses stood in the yards, and there were stores of various kinds. But it was all black. There was not a white face to be seen after we left the station. One of my companions in the train was a Cuban engineer, now employed upon the line; a refugee, I conjectured, belonging to the beaten party in the late rebellion, from the bitterness with which he spoke of the Spanish administration.

Porus is many hundred feet above the sea, in a hollow where three valleys meet. Mandeville, to which I was bound, was ten miles farther on, the road ascending all the way. A carriage was waiting for me, but too small for my luggage. A black boy offered to carry up a heavy bag for a shilling, a feat which he faithfully and expeditiously performed. After climbing a steep hill, we came out upon a rich undulating plateau, long cleared and cultivated; green fields with cows feeding on them; pretty houses standing in gardens; a Wesleyan station; a Moravian station, with chapels and parsonages. The red soil was mixed with crumbling lumps of white coral, a ready-made and inexhaustible supply of manure. Great silk-cotton trees towered up in lonely magnificence, the home of the dreaded Jumbi—woe to the wretch who strikes an axe into those sacred stems! Almonds, cedars, mangoes, gum trees spread their shade over the road. Orange trees were everywhere; sometimes in orchards, sometimes growing at their own wild will in hedges and copse and thicket. Finally, at the outskirts of a perfectly English village, we brought up at the door of the lodging house kept by the justly celebrated Miss Roy. The house, or cottage, stood at the roadside, at the top of a steep flight of steps; a rambling one-story building, from which rooms, creeper-covered, had been thrown out as they were wanted. There was the universal green verandah into which they all opened; and the windows looked out on a large common, used of old, and perhaps now, as a race-course; on wooded slopes, with sunny mansions dropped here and there in openings among the woods; on farm buildings at intervals in the distance, surrounded by clumps of palms; and beyond them ranges of mountains almost as blue as the sky against which they were faintly visible. Miss Roy, the lady and mistress of the establishment, came out to meet me: middle-aged, with a touch of the black blood, but with a face in which one places instant and sure dependence, shrewd, quiet, sensible, and entirely good-humoured. A white-haired brother, somewhat infirm and older than she, glided behind her as her shadow. She attends to the business. His pride is in his garden, where he has gathered a collection of rare plants in admired disorder; the night-blowing cereus hanging carelessly over a broken paling, and a palm, unique of its kind, waving behind it. At the back were orange trees and plantains and coffee bushes, with long-tailed humming birds flitting about their nests among the branches. All kinds of delicacies, from fruit and preserves to coffee, Miss Roy grows for her visitors on her own soil, and prepares from the first stage to the last with her own cunning hands.

Having made acquaintance with the mistress, I strolled out to look about me. After walking up the road for a quarter of a mile, I found myself in an exact reproduction of a Warwickshire hamlet before the days of railways and brick chimneys. There were no elms to be sure—there were silk cotton-trees and mangoes where the elms should have been; but there were the boys playing cricket, and a market house, and a modest inn, and a shop or two, and a blacksmith's forge with a shed where horses were standing waiting their turn to be shod. Across the green was the parish church, with its three aisles and low square tower, in which hung an old peal of bells. Parish stocks I did not observe, though, perhaps, I might have had I looked for them; but there was a schoolhouse and parsonage, and, withdrawn at a distance as of superior dignity, what had once perhaps been the squire's mansion, when squire and such-like had been the natural growth of the country. It was as if a branch of the old tree had been carried over and planted there ages ago, and as if it had taken root and become an exact resemblance of the parent stock. The people had black faces; but even they, too, had shaped their manners on the old English models. The men touched their hats respectfully (as they eminently did not in Kingston and its environs). The women smiled and curtsied, and the children looked shy when one spoke to them. The name of slavery is a horror to us; but there must have been something human and kindly about it, too, when it left upon the character the marks of courtesy and good breeding. I wish I could say as much for the effect of modern ideas. The negroes in Mandeville were, perhaps, as happy in their old condition as they have been since their glorious emancipation, and some of them to this day speak regretfully of a time when children did not die of neglect; when the sick and the aged were taken care of, and the strong and healthy were, at least, as well looked after as their owner's cattle.

Slavery could not last; but neither can the condition last which has followed it. The equality between black and white is a forced equality and not a real one, and nature in the long run has her way, and readjusts in their proper relations what theorists and philanthropists have disturbed.

I was not Miss Roy's only guest. An American lady and gentleman were staying there; he, I believe, for his health, as the climate of Mandeville is celebrated. Americans, whatever may be their faults, are always unaffected; and so are easy to get on with. We dined together, and talked of the place and its inhabitants. They had been struck like myself with the manners of the peasants, which were something entirely new to them. The lady said, and without expressing the least disapproval, that she had fallen in with an old slave who told her that, thanks to God, he had seen good times. 'He was bred in a good home, with a master and mistress belonging to him. What the master and mistress had the slaves had, and there was no difference; and his master used to visit at King's House, and his men were all proud of him. Yes, glory be to God, he had seen good times.'

In the evening we sat out in the verandah in the soft sweet air, the husband and I smoking our cigars, and the lady not minding it. They had come to Mandeville, as we go to Italy, to escape the New England winter. They had meant to stay but a few days; they found it so charming that they had stayed for many weeks. We talked on till twilight became night, and then appeared a show of natural pyrotechnics which beat anything of the kind which I had ever seen or read of: fireflies as large as cockchafers flitting round us among the leaves of the creepers, with two long antennæ, at the point of each of which hangs out a blazing lanthorn. The unimaginative colonists call them gig-lamps. Had Shakespeare ever heard of them, they would have played round Ferdinand and Miranda in Prospero's cave, and would have borne a fairer name. The light is bluish-green, like a glowworm's, but immeasurably brighter; and we could trace them far away glancing like spirits over the meadows.

I could not wonder that my new friends had been charmed with the place. The air was exquisitely pure; the temperature ten degrees below that of Kingston, never oppressively hot and never cold; the forest scenery as beautiful as at Arden; and Miss Roy's provision for us, rooms, beds, breakfasts, dinners, absolutely without fault. If ever there was an inspired coffee maker, Miss Roy was that person. The glory of Mandeville is in its oranges. The worst orange I ate in Jamaica was better than the best I ever ate in Europe, and the best oranges of Jamaica are the oranges of Mandeville. New York has found out their merits. One gentleman alone sent twenty thousand boxes to New York last year, clearing a dollar on each box; and this, as I said just now, when Nature is left to produce what she pleases, and art has not begun to help her. Fortunes larger than were ever made by sugar wait for any man, and the blessings of the world along with it, who will set himself to work at orange growing with skill and science in a place where heat will not wither the trees, nor frosts, as in Florida, bite off the blossoms. Yellow fever was never heard of there, nor any dangerous epidemic, nor snake nor other poisonous reptile. The droughts which parch the lowlands are unknown, for an even rain falls all the year and the soil is always moist. I inquired with wonder why the unfortunate soldiers who were perched among the crags at Newcastle were not at Mandeville instead. I was told that water was the difficulty; that there was no river or running stream there, and that it had to be drawn from wells or collected into cisterns. One must applaud the caution which the authorities have at last displayed; but cattle thrive at Mandeville, and sheep, and black men and women in luxuriant abundance. One would like to know that the general who sold the Newcastle estate to the Government was not the same person who was allowed to report as to the capabilities of a spot which, to the common observer, would seem as perfectly adapted for the purpose as the other is detestable.

A few English families were scattered about the neighbourhood, among whom I made a passing acquaintance. They had a lawn-tennis club in the village, which met once a week; they drove in with their pony carriages; a lady made tea under the trees; they had amusements and pleasant society which cost nothing. They were not rich; but they were courteous, simple, frank, and cordial.

Mandeville is the centre of a district which all resembles it in character and extends for many miles. It is famous for its cattle as well as for its fruit, and has excellent grazing grounds. Mr. ——, an officer of police, took me round with him one morning. It was the old story. Though there were still a few white proprietors left, they were growing fewer, and the blacks were multiplying upon them. The smoke of their clearances showed where they were at work. Many of them are becoming well-to-do. We met them on the roads with their carts and mules; the young ones armed, too, in some instances with good double-barrelled muzzle-loaders. There is no game to shoot, but to have a gun raises them in their own estimation, and they like to be prepared for contingencies. Mr. —— had a troublesome place of it. The negro peasantry were good-humoured, he said, but not universally honest. They stole cattle, and would not give evidence against each other. If brought into court, they held a pebble in their mouths, being under the impression that when they were so provided perjury did not count. Their education was only skin-deep, and the schools which the Government provided had not touched their characters at all. Mr. ——'s duties brought him in contact with the unfavourable specimens. I received a far pleasanter impression from a Moravian minister, who called on me with a friend who had lately taken a farm. I was particularly glad to see this gentleman, for of the Moravians everyone had spoken well to me. He was not the least enthusiastic about his poor black sheep, but he said that, if they were not better than the average English labourers, he did not think them worse. They were called idle. They would work well enough if they had fair wages, and if the wages were paid regularly; but what could be expected when women servants had but three shillings a week and 'found themselves,' when the men had but a shilling a day and the pay was kept in arrear, in order that, if they came late to work, or if they came irregularly, it might be kept back or cut down to what the employer chose to give? Under such conditions any man of any colour would prefer to work for himself if he had a garden, or would be idle if he had none. 'Living' costs next to nothing either to them or their families. But the minister said, and his friend confirmed it by his own experience, that these same fellows would work regularly and faithfully for any master whom they person- ally knew and could rely upon, and no Englishman coming to settle there need be afraid of failing for want of labour, if he had sense and energy, and did not prefer to lie down and groan. The blacks, my friends said, were kindly hearted, respect- ful, and well-disposed, but they were children; easily excited, easily tempted, easily misled, and totally unfit for self-government. If we wished to ruin them altogether, we should persevere in the course to which, they were sorry to hear, we were so inclined. The real want in the island was of intelligent Englishmen to employ and direct them, and Englishmen were going away so fast that they feared there would soon be none of them left. This was the opinion of two moderate and excellent men, whose natural and professional prejudices were all on the black man's side.

It was confirmed both in its favourable and unfavourable aspects by another im- partial authority. My first American acquaintances had gone, but their rooms were occupied by another of their countrymen, a specimen of a class of whom more will be heard in Jamaica if the fates are kind. The English in the island cast in their lot with sugar, and if sugar is depressed they lose heart. Americans keep their 'eyes skinned,' as they call it, to look out for other openings. They have discovered, as I said, 'that there are dollars in Jamaica,' and one has come, and has set up a trade in plantains, in which he is making a fortune; and this gentleman has perceived that there were 'dollars in the bamboo,' and for bamboos there was no place in the world like the West Indies. He came to Jamaica, brought machines to clear the fibre, tried to make ropes of it, to make canvas, paper, and I know not what. I think he told me that he had spent a quarter of a million dollars, instead of finding any, before he hit upon a paying use for it. The bamboo fibre has certain elastic incompressible properties in which it is without a rival. He forms it into 'packing' for the boxes of the wheels of railway carriages, where it holds oil like a sponge, never hardens, and never wears out. He sends the packing over the world, and the demand grows as it is tried. He has set up a factory, thirty miles from Mandeville, in the valley of the Black River. He has a large body of the negroes working for him who are said to be so unmanageable. He, like Dr. Nicholls in Dominica, does not find them unmanageable at all. They never leave him; they work for him from year to year as regularly as if they were slaves. They have their small faults, but he does not magnify them into vices. They are attached to him with the old-fashioned affection which good labourers always feel for employers whom they respect, and dismissal is dreaded as the severest of punishments. In the course of time he thought that they might become fit for political privileges. To confer such privileges on them at present would fling Jamaica back into absolute barbarism.

I said I wished that more of his countrymen would come and settle in Jamaica as he had done and a few others already. American energy would be like new blood in the veins of the poor island. He answered that many would probably come if they could be satisfied that there would be no more political experimenting; but they would not risk their capital if there was a chance of a black parliament.

If we choose to make Jamaica into a Hayti, we need not look for Americans down that way.

Let us hope that enthusiasm for constitutions will for once moderate its ardour. The black race has suffered enough at our hands. They have been sacrificed to slavery; are they to be sacrificed again to a dream or a doctrine? There has a new creed risen, while the old creed is failing. It has its priests and its prophets, its formulas and its articles of belief.

Whosoever will be saved, before all things it is necessary that he hold the Radical faith.

And the Radical faith is this: all men are equal, and the voice of one is as the voice of another.

And whereas one man is wise and another foolish, and one is upright and another crooked, yet in this suffrage none is greater or less than another. The vote is equal, the dignity co-eternal.

Truth is one and right is one; yet right is right because the majority so declare it, and justice is justice because the majority so declare it.

And if the majority affirm one thing to-day, that is right; and if the majority affirm the opposite to-morrow, that is right.

Because the will of the majority is the ground of right and there is no other, c. c. c.

This is the Radical faith, which, except every man do keep whole and undefiled, he is a Tory and an enemy of the State, and without doubt shall perish everlastingly.

Once the Radical was a Liberal and went for toleration and freedom of opinion. He has become a believer now. He is right and you are wrong, and if you do not agree with him you are a fool, and you are wicked besides. Voltaire says that atheism and superstition are the two poles of intellectual disease. Superstition he thinks the worse of the two. The atheist is merely mistaken, and can be cured if you show him that he is wrong. The fanatic can never be cured. Yet each alike, if he prevails, will destroy human society. What would Voltaire have expected for poor mankind had he seen both the precious qualities combined in this new Symbolum Fidei?

A creed is not a reasoned judgment based upon experience and insight. It is a child of imagination and passion. Like an organised thing, it has its appointed period and then dies. You cannot argue it out of existence. It works for good; it works for evil; but work it will while the life is in it. Faith, we are told, is not contradictory to reason, but is above reason. Whether reason or faith sees truer, events will prove.

One more observation this American gentleman made to me. He was speaking of the want of spirit and of the despondency of the West Indian whites. 'I never knew, sir,' he said, 'any good come of desponding men. If you intend to strike a mark, you had better believe that you can strike it. No one ever hit anything if he thought that he was most likely to miss it. You must take a cheerful view of things, or you will have no success in this world.'

'Tyne heart tyne a',' the Scotch proverb says. The Anglo-West Indians are tyning heart, and that is the worst feature about them. They can get no help except in themselves, and they can help themselves after all if we allow them fair play. The Americans will not touch them politically, but they will trade with them; they will bring their capital and their skill and knowledge among them, and make the islands richer and more prosperous than ever they were—on one condition: they will risk nothing in such enterprises as long as the shadow hangs over them of a possible government by a black majority. Let it suffice to have created one Ireland without deliberately manufacturing a second.

CHAPTER XVI.

Jamaican hospitality—Cherry Garden—George William Gordon—The Gordon riots—Governor Eyre—A dispute and its consequences—Jamaican country-house society—Modern speculation—A Spanish fable—Port Royal—The commodore—Naval theatricals—The modern sailor.

The surviving representatives of the Jamaican gentry are as hospitable as their fathers and grandfathers used to be. An English visitor who wishes to see the island is not allowed to take his chance at hotels—where, indeed, his chance would be a bad one. A single acquaintance is enough to start with. He is sent on with letters of introduction from one house to another, and is assured of a favourable reception. I was treated as kindly as any stranger would be, and that was as kindly as possible. But friends do not ask us to stay with them that their portraits may be drawn in the traveller's journals; and I mention no one who was thus good to me, unless some general interest attaches either to himself or his residence. Such interest does, however, attach to a spot where, after leaving Mandeville, I passed a few days. The present owner of it was the chief manager of the Kingston branch of the Colonial Bank: a clever accomplished man of business, who understood the financial condition of the West Indies better perhaps than any other man living. He was a botanist besides; he had a fine collection of curious plants which were famous in the island; and was otherwise a gentleman of the highest standing and reputation. His lady was one of the old island aristocracy—high-bred, cultivated, an accomplished artist; a person who would have shone anywhere and in any circle, and was, therefore, contented to be herself, and indifferent whether she shone or not. A visit in such a family was likely to be instructive, and was sure to be agreeable; and on these grounds alone I should have accepted gratefully the opportunity of knowing them better which they kindly made for me by an invitation to stay with them. But their place, which was called Cherry Garden, and which I had seen from the grounds at Government House, had a further importance of its own in having been the home of the unfortunate George William Gordon.

The disturbances with which Mr. Gordon was connected, and for his share in which he was executed, are so recent and so notorious that I need give no detailed account of them, though, of course, I looked into the history again and listened to all that I could hear about it. Though I had taken no part in Mr. Eyre's defence, I was one of those who thought from the first that Mr. Eyre had been unworthily sacrificed to public clamour. Had the agitation in Jamaica spread, and taken the form which it easily might have taken, he would have been blamed as keenly by one half the world if he had done nothing to check it as he was blamed, in fact, by the other for too much energy. Carlyle used to say that it was as if, when a ship had been on fire, and the captain by skill and promptitude had put the fire out, his owner were to say to him, 'Sir, you poured too much water down the hold and damaged the cargo.' The captain would answer, 'Yes, sir, but I have saved your ship.' This was the view which I carried with me to Jamaica, and I have brought it back with me the same in essentials, though qualified by clearer perceptions of the real nature of the situation.

Something of a very similar kind had happened in Natal just before I visited that colony in 1874. I had seen the whites there hardly recovering from a panic in which a common police case had been magnified by fear into the beginning of an insurrection. Langalibalele, a Caffre chief within the British dominions, had been insubordinate. He had been sent for to Maritzberg, and had invented excuses for disobedience to a lawful order. The whites believed at once that there was to be a general Caffre rebellion in which they would all be murdered. They resolved to be beforehand with it. They carried fire and sword through two considerable tribes. At first they thought that they had covered themselves with glory; calmer reflection taught many of them that perhaps they had been too hasty, and that Langalibalele had never intended to rebel at all. The Jamaican disturbance was of a similar kind. Mr. Gordon had given less provocation than the Caffre chief, but the circumstances were analogous, and the actual danger was probably greater. Jamaica had then constitutional, though not what is called responsible, government. The executive power remained with the Crown. There had been differences of opinion between the governor and the Assembly. Gordon, a man of colour, was a prominent member of the opposition. He had called public meetings of the blacks in a distant part of the island, and was endeavouring to bring the pressure of public opinion on the opposition side. Imprudent as such a step might have been among an ignorant and excitable population, where whites and blacks were so unequal in numbers, and where they knew so little of each other, Mr. Gordon was not going beyond what in constitutional theory he was legally entitled to do; nor was his language on the platform, though violent and inflammatory, any more so than what we listen to patiently at home. Under a popular constitution the people are sovereign; the members of the assemblies are popular delegates; and when there is a diversion of opinion any man has a right to call the constituencies to express their sentiments. If stones were thrown at the police and seditious cries were raised, it was no more than might be reasonably expected.

We at home can be calm on such occasions because we know that there is no real danger, and that the law is strong enough to assert itself. In Jamaica a few thousand white people were living in the middle of negroes forty times their number—once their slaves, now raised to be their political equals—each regarding the other on the least provocation with resentment and suspicion. In England the massacre in Hayti is a half-forgotten story. Not one person in a thousand of those who clamoured for the prosecution of Governor Eyre had probably ever heard of it. In Jamaica it is ever present in the minds of the Europeans as a frightful evidence of what the negroes are capable when roused to frenzy. The French planters had done nothing particularly cruel to deserve their animosity, and were as well regarded by their slaves as ever we had been in the English islands. Yet in a fever of political excitement, and as a reward for the decree of the Paris Revolutionary Government, which declared them free, they allowed the liberty which was to have elevated them to the white man's level to turn them into devils; and they massacred the whole of the French inhabitants. It was inevitable that when the volcano in Jamaica began to show symptoms of similar activity the whites residing there should be unable to look on with the calmness which we, from thousands of miles away, unreasonably expected of them. They imagined their houses in flames, and themselves and their families at the mercy of a furious mob. No personal relation between the two races has grown up to take the place of slavery. The white gentry have blacks for labourers, blacks for domestic servants, yet as a rule (though, of course, there are exceptions) they have no interest in each other, no esteem nor confidence: therefore any symptom of agitation is certain to produce a panic, and panic is always violent.

The blacks who attended Gordon's meetings came armed with guns and cutlasses; a party of white volunteers went in consequence to watch them, and to keep order if they showed signs of meaning insurrection. Stones were thrown; the Riot Act was read, more stones followed, and then the volunteers fired, and several persons were killed. Of course there was fury. The black mob then actually did rise. They marched about that particular district destroying plantations and burning houses. That they did so little, and that the flame did not spread, was a proof that there was no premeditation of rebellion, no prepared plan of action, no previous communication between the different parts of the island with a view to any common movement. There was no proof, and there was no reason to suppose, that Gordon had intended an armed outbreak. He would have been a fool if he had, when constitutional agitation and the weight of numbers at his back would have secured him all that he wanted. When inflammable materials are brought together, and sparks are flying, you cannot equitably distribute the blame or the punishment. Eyre was responsible for the safety of the island. He was not a Jamaican. The rule in the colonial service is that a governor remains in any colony only long enough to begin to understand it. He is then removed to another of which he knows nothing. He is therefore absolutely dependent in any difficulty upon local advice. When the riots began every white man in Jamaica was of one opinion, that unless the fire was stamped out promptly they would all be murdered. Being without experience himself, it was very difficult for

Mr. Eyre to disregard so complete a unanimity. I suppose that a perfectly calm and determined man would have seen in the unanimity itself the evidence of alarm and imagination. He ought perhaps to have relied entirely on the police and the regular troops, and to have called in the volunteers. But here again was a difficulty; for the police were black, and the West India regiments were black, and the Sepoy rebellion was fresh in everybody's memory. He had no time to deliberate. He had to act, and to act promptly; and if, relying on his own judgment, he had disregarded what everyone round him insisted upon, and if mischief had afterwards come of it, the censure which would have fallen upon him would have been as severe as it would have been deserved. He assumed that the English colonists were right and that a general rebellion had begun. They all armed. They formed into companies. The disturbed district was placed under martial law, and these extemporised regiments, too few in number to be merciful, saw safety only in striking terror into the poor wretches. It was in Jamaica as it was in Natal afterwards; but we must allow for human nature and not be hasty to blame. If the rising at Morant Bay was but the boiling over of a pot from the orator of an excited patriot, there was deplorable cruelty and violence. But, again, it was all too natural. Men do not bear easily to see their late servants on their way to become their political masters, and they believe the worst of them because they are afraid. A model governor would have rather restrained their ardour than encouraged it; but all that can be said against Mr. Eyre (so far as regarded the general suppression of the insurgents) is that he acted as nine hundred and ninety-nine men out of a thousand would have acted in his place, and more ought not to be expected of average colonial governors.

His treatment of Gordon, the original cause of the disturbance, was more questionable. Gordon had returned to his own house, the house where I was going, within sight of Eyre's windows. It would have been fair, and perhaps right, to arrest him, and right also to bring him to trial, if he had committed any offence for which he could be legally punished. So strong was the feeling against him that, if every white man in Kingston had been empannelled, there would have been a unanimous verdict, and they would not have looked too closely into niceties of legal construction. Unfortunately it was doubtful whether Gordon had done anything which could be construed into a capital crime. He had a right to call public meetings together. He had a right to appeal to political passions, and to indulge as freely as he pleased in the patriotic commonplaces of platforms, provided he did not himself advise or encourage a breach of the peace, and this it could not be easily proved that he had done. He was, however, the leader of the opposition to the Government. The opposition had broken into a riot, and Gordon was guilty of having excited the feelings which led to it. The leader could not be allowed to escape unpunished while his followers were being shot and flogged. The Kingston district where he resided was under the ordinary law. Eyre sent him into the district which was under martial law, tried him by a military court and hanged him.

The Cabinet at home at first thanked their representative for having saved the island. A clamour rose, and they sent out a commission to examine into what had happened. The commission reported unfavourably, and Eyre was dismissed and ruined. In Jamaica I never heard anyone express a doubt on the full propriety of his action. He carried away with him the affection and esteem of the whole of the English colonists, who believe that he saved them from destruction. In my own opinion the fault was not in Mr. Eyre, and was not in the unfortunate Gordon, but in those who had insisted on applying a constitutional form of government to a country where the population is so unfavourably divided. If the numbers of white and black were more nearly equal, the objection would be less, for the natural superiority of the white would then assert itself without difficulty, and there would be no panics. Where the disproportion is so enormous as it is in Jamaica, where intelligence and property are in a miserable minority, and a half-reclaimed race of savages, cannibals not long ago, and capable, as the state of Hayti shows, of reverting to cannibalism again, are living beside them as their political equals, such panics arise from the nature of things, and will themselves cause the catastrophe from the dread of which they spring. Mutual fear and mistrust can lead to nothing in the end but violent collisions. The theory of constitutional government is that the majority shall rule the minority, and as long as the qualities, moral and mental, of the parties are not grossly dissimilar, such an arrangement forms a tolerable modus vivendi. Where in character, in mental force, in energy, in cultivation, there is no equality at all, but an inequality which has existed for thousands of years, and is as plain to-day as it was in the Egypt of the Pharaohs, to expect that the intelligent few will submit to the unintelligent many is to expect what has never been found and what never ought to be found. The whites cannot be trusted to rule the blacks, but for the blacks to rule the whites is a yet grosser anomaly. Were England out of the way, there would be a war of extermination between them. England prohibits it, and holds the balance in forced equality. England, therefore, so long as the West Indies are English, must herself rule, and rule impartially, and so acquit herself of her self-chosen responsibilities. Let the colonies which are occupied by our own race rule themselves as we rule ourselves. The English constituencies have no rights over the constituencies of Canada and Australia, for the Canadians and Australians are as well able to manage their own affairs as we are to manage ours. If they prefer even to elect governors of their own, let them do as they please. The link between us is community of blood and interest, and will not part over details of administration. But in these other colonies which are our own we must accept the facts as they are. Those who will not recognise realities are always beaten in the end.

The train from Porus brought us back to Kingston an hour before sunset. The evening was lovely, even for Jamaica. The sea breeze had fallen. The land breeze had not risen, and the dust lay harmless on road and hedge. Cherry Garden, to which I was bound, was but seven miles distant by the direct road, so I calculated on a delightful drive which would bring me to my destination before dark. So I calculated; but alas! for human expectation. I engaged a 'buggy' at the station, with a decent-looking conductor, who assured me that he knew the way to Cherry Garden as well as to his own door. His horse looked starved and miserable. He insisted that there was not another in Kingston that was more than a match for it. We set out, and for the first two or three miles we went on well enough, conversing amicably upon things in general. But it so happened that it was again market day. The road was thronged as before with women plodding along with their baskets on their heads, a single male on a donkey to each detachment of them, carrying nothing, like an officer with a company of soldiers. Foolish indignation rose in me, and I asked my friend if he was not ashamed of seeing the poor creatures toiling so cruelly, while their lords and masters amused themselves. I appealed to his feelings as a man, as if it was likely that he had got any. The wretch only laughed. 'Ah, massa,' he said, with his tongue in his cheek, 'women do women's work, men do men's work—all right.' 'And what is men's work?' I asked. Instead of answering he went on, 'Look at they women, massa—how they laugh—how happy they be! Nobody more happy than black woman, massa.' I would not let him off. I pricked into him, till he got excited too, and we argued and contradicted each other, till at last the horse, finding he was not attended to, went his own way and that was a wrong one. Between Kingston and our destination there is a deep sandy flat, overgrown with bush and penetrated in all directions with labyrinthine lanes. Into this we had wandered in our quarrels, and neither of us knew where we were. The sand was loose; our miserable beast was above his fetlocks in it, and was visibly dropping under his efforts to drag us along even at a walk. The sun went down. The tropic twilight is short. The evening star shone out in the west, and the crescent moon over our heads. My man said this and said that; every word was a lie, for he had lost his way and would not allow it. We saw a light through some trees. I sent him to inquire. We were directed one way and another way, every way except the right one. We emerged at last upon a hard road of some kind. The stars told me the general direction. We came to cottages where the name of Cherry Garden was known, and we were told that it was two miles off; but alas! again there were two roads to it; a short and good one, and a long and bad one, and they sent us by the last. There was a steep hill to climb, for the house is 800 feet above the sea. The horse could hardly crawl, and my 'nigger' went to work to flog him to let off his own ill humour. I had to stop that by force, and at last, as it grew too dark to see the road under the trees, I got out and walked, leaving him to follow at a foot's pace. The night was lovely. I began to think that we should have to camp out after all, and that it would be no great hardship.

It was like the gloaming of a June night in England, the daylight in the open spots not entirely gone, and mixing softly with the light of moon and planet and the flashing of the fireflies. I plodded on mile after mile, and Cherry Garden still receded to one mile farther. We came to a gate of some consequence. The outline of a large mansion was visible with gardens round it. I concluded that we had arrived, and was feeling for the latch when the forms of a lady and gentleman appeared against the sky who were strolling in the grounds. They directed me still upwards, with the mile which never diminished still to be travelled. Like myself, our weary animal had gathered hopes from the sight of the gate. He had again to drag on as he could. His owner was subdued and silent, and obeyed whatever order I gave him. The trees now closed over us so thick that I could see nothing. Vainly I repented of my unnecessary philanthropy which had been the cause of the mischief; what had I to do with black women, or white either for that matter? I had to feel the way with my feet and a stick. I came to a place where the lane again divided. I tried the nearest turn. I found a trench across it three feet deep, which had been cut by a torrent. This was altogether beyond the capacity of our unfortunate animal, so I took the other boldly, prepared if it proved wrong to bivouac till morning with my 'nigger,' and go on with my argument. Happily there was no need; we came again on a gate which led into a field. There was a drive across it and wire fences. Finally lights began to glimmer and dogs to bark: we were at the real Cherry Garden at last, and found the whole household alarmed for what had become of us. I could not punish my misleader by stinting his fare, for I knew that I had only myself to blame. He was an honest fellow after all. In the disturbance of my mind I left a rather valuable umbrella in his buggy. He discovered it after he had gone, and had grace enough to see that it was returned to me.

My entertainers were much amused at the cause of the misadventure, perhaps unique of its kind; to address homilies to the black people on the treatment of their wives not being the fashion in these parts.

If there are no more Aaron Bangs in Jamaica, there are very charming people; as I found when I turned this new leaf in my West Indian experience. Mr. M——could not have taken more pains with me if I had been his earliest friend. The chief luxury which he allowed himself in his simple life was a good supply of excellent horses. His business took him every day to Kingston, but he left me in charge of his family, and I had 'a good time,' as the Americans say. The house was large, with fine airy rooms, a draught so constantly blowing through it that the candles had to be covered with bell glasses; but the draughts in these countries are the very breath of life. It had been too dark when I arrived to see anything of the surroundings, and the next morning I strolled out to see what the place was like. It lies just at the foot of the Blue Mountains, where the gradual slope from the sea begins to become steep. The plain of Kingston lay stretched before me, with its woods and cornfields and villas, the long straggling town, the ships at anchor in the harbour, the steamers passing in and out with their long trails of smoke, the sand-spit like a thin grey line lying upon the water, as the natural breakwater by which the harbour is formed, and beyond it the broad blue expanse of the Caribbean Sea. The foreground was like an English park, studded over with handsome forest trees and broken by the rains into picturesque ravines. Some acres were planted with oranges of the choicer sorts, as an experiment to show what Jamaica could do, but they were as yet young and had not come into bearing. Round the house were gardens where the treasures of our hot-houses were carelessly and lavishly scattered. Stephanotis trailed along the railing or climbed over the trellis. Oleanders white and pink waved over marble basins, and were sprinkled by the spray from spouting fountains. Crotons stood about in tubs, not small plants as we know them, but large shrubs; great purple or parti-coloured bushes. They have a fancy for crotons in the West Indies; I suppose as a change from the monotony of green. I cannot share it. A red leaf, except in autumn before it falls, is a kind of monster, and I am glad that Nature has made so few of them. In the shade of the trees behind the house was a collection of orchids, the most perfect, I believe, in the island.

KINGSTON AND HARBOUR FROM CHERRY GARDEN.
KINGSTON AND HARBOUR FROM CHERRY GARDEN.

And here Gordon had lived. Here he had been arrested and carried away to his death; his crime being that he had dreamt of regenerating the negro race by baptising them in the Jordan of English Radicalism. He would have brought about nothing but confusion, and have precipitated Jamaica prematurely into the black anarchy into which perhaps it is still destined to fall. But to hang him was an extreme measure, and, in the present state of public opinion, a dangerous one.

One does not associate the sons of darkness with keen perceptions of the beautiful. Yet no mortal ever selected a lovelier spot for a residence than did Gordon in choosing Cherry Garden. How often had his round dark eyes wandered over the scenes at which I was gazing, watched the early rays of the sun slanting upwards to the high peaks of the Blue Mountains, or the last as he sank in gold and crimson behind the hills at Mandeville; watched the great steamers entering or leaving Port Royal, and at night the gleam of the lighthouse from among the palm trees on the spit. Poor fellow! one felt very sorry for him, and sorry for Mr. Eyre, too. The only good that came of it all was the surrender of the constitution and the return to Crown government, and this our wonderful statesmen are beginning to undo.

No one understood better than Mr. M—— the troubles and dangers of the colony, but he was inclined, perhaps by temperament, perhaps by knowledge, to take a cheerful view of things. For the present at least he did not think that there was anything serious to be feared. The finances, of which he had the best means of judging, were in tolerable condition. The debt was considerable, but more than half of it was represented by a railway. If sugar was languishing, the fruit trade with the United States was growing with the liveliest rapidity. Planters and merchants were not making fortunes, but business went on. The shares in the Colonial Bank were not at a high quotation, but the securities were sound, the shareholders got good dividends, and eight and ten per cent. was the interest charged on loans. High interest might be a good sign or a bad one. Anyway Mr. M—— could not see that there was much to be afraid of in Jamaica. There had been bad times before, and they had survived notwithstanding. He was a man of business, and talked himself little about politics. As it had been, so it would be again.

In his absence at his work I found friends in the neighbourhood who were all attention and politeness. One took me to see my acquaintances at the camp again. Another drove me about, showed me the house where Scott had lived, the author of 'Tom Cringle.' One round in particular left a distinct impression. It was through a forest which had once been a flourishing sugar estate. Deep among the trees were the ruins of an aqueduct which had brought water to the mill, now overgrown and crumbling. The time had not been long as we count time in the history of nations, but there had been enough for the arches to fall in, the stream to return to its native bed, the tropical vegetation to spring up in its wild luxuriance and bury in shade the ruins of a past civilisation.

I fell in with interesting persons who talked metaphysics and theology with me, though one would not have expected it in Jamaica. In this strange age of ours the spiritual atmosphere is more confused than at any period during the last eighteen hundred years. Men's hearts are failing them for fear, not knowing any longer where to rest. We look this way and that way, and catch at one another like drowning men. Go where you will, you find the same phenomena. Science grows, and observers are adding daily to our knowledge of the nature and structure of the material universe, but they tell us nothing, and can tell us nothing, of what we most want to know. They cannot tell us what our own nature is. They cannot tell us what God is, or what duty is. We had a belief once, in which, as in a boat, we floated safely on the unknown ocean; but the philosophers and critics have been boring holes in the timbers to examine the texture of the wood, and now it leaks at every one of them. We have to help ourselves in the best way that we can. Some strike out new ideas for themselves, others go back to the seven sages, and lay again for themselves the old eggs, which, after laborious incubation, will be addled as they were addled before. To my metaphysical friends in Jamaica the 'Light of Asia' had been shining amidst German dreams, and the moonlight of the Vedas had been illuminating the pessimism of Schopenhauer. So it is all round. Mr. —— goes to Mount Carmel to listen for communications from Elijah; fashionable countesses to the shrine of Our Lady at Lourdes. 'Are you a Buddhist?' lisps the young lady in Mayfair to the partner with whom she is sitting out at a ball. 'It is so nice,' said a gentleman to me who has been since promoted to high office in an unfortunate colony, 'it is so nice to talk of such things to pretty girls, and it always ends in one way, you know.' Conversations on theology, at least between persons of opposite sex, ought to be interdicted by law for everyone under forty. But there are questions on which old people may be permitted to ask one another what they think, if it only be for mutual comfort in the general vacancy. We are born alone, we pass alone into the great darkness. When the curtain falls is the play over? or is a new act to commence? Are we to start again in a new sphere, carrying with us what we have gained in the discipline of our earthly trials? Are we to become again as we were before we came into this world, when eternity had not yet splintered into time, or the universal being dissolved into individual existences? For myself, I have long ceased to speculate on these subjects, being convinced that they have no bottom which can be reasoned out by the intellect. We are in a world where much can be learnt which affects our own and others' earthly welfare, and we had better leave the rest alone. Yet one listens and cannot choose but sympathise when anxious souls open out to you what is going on within them. A Spanish legend, showing with whom these inquiries began and with what result, is not without its value.

Jupiter, having made the world, proceeded to make animals to live in it. The ass was the earliest created. He looked about him. He looked at himself; and, as the habit of asses is, he asked himself what it all meant; what it was to be an ass, where did he come from, and what he was for? Not being able to discover, he applied to his maker. Jupiter told him that he was made to be the slave of another animal to be called Man. He was to carry men on his back, drag loads for them, and be their drudge. He was to live on thistles and straw, and to be beaten continually with sticks and ropes'-ends. The ass complained. He said that he had done nothing to deserve so hard a fate. He had not asked to be born, and he would rather not have been born. He inquired how long this life, or whatever it was, had to continue. Jupiter said it had to last thirty years. The poor ass was in consternation. If Jupiter would reduce the thirty to ten he undertook to be patient, to be a good servant, and to do his work patiently. Jupiter reflected and consented, and the ass retired grateful and happy.

The dog, who had been born meanwhile, heard what had passed. He, too, went to Jupiter with the same question. He learnt that he also was a slave to men. In the day he was to catch their game for them, but was not to eat it himself. At night he was to be chained by a ring and to lie awake to guard their houses. His food was to be bones and refuse. Like the ass he was to have had thirty years of it, but on petition they were similarly exchanged for ten.

The monkey came next. His function, he was told, was to mimic humanity, to be led about by a string, and grimace and dance for men's amusement. He also remonstrated at the length of time, and obtained the same favour.

Last came the man himself. Conscious of boundless desires and, as he imagined, of boundless capabilities, he did not inquire what he was, or what he was to do. Those questions had been already answered by his vanity. He did not come to ask for anything, but to thank Jupiter for having created so glorious a being and to ascertain for how many ages he might expect to endure. The god replied that thirty years was the term allotted to all personal existences.

'Only thirty years!' he exclaimed. 'Only thirty years for such capacities as mine. Thirty years will be gone like a dream. Extend them! oh, extend them, gracious Jupiter, that I may have leisure to use the intellect which thou hast given me, search into the secrets of nature, do great and glorious actions, and serve and praise thee, O my creator! longer and more worthily.'

The lip of the god curled lightly, and again he acquiesced. 'I have some spare years to dispose of,' he said, 'of which others of my creatures have begged to be relieved. You shall have thirty years of your own. From thirty to fifty you shall have the ass's years, and labour and sweat for your support. From fifty to seventy you shall have the dog's years, and take care of the stuff, and snarl and growl at what younger men are doing. From seventy to ninety you shall have the monkey's years, and smirk and grin and make yourself ridiculous. After that you may depart.'

I was going on to Cuba. The commodore had insisted on my spending my last days with him at Port Royal. He undertook to see me on board the steamer as it passed out of the harbour. I have already described his quarters. The naval station has no colonial character except the climate, and is English entirely. The officers are the servants of the Admiralty, not of the colonial government. Their interests are in their profession. They look to promotion in other parts of the world, and their functions are on the ocean and not on the land. The commodore is captain of the guardship; but he has a commander under him and he resides on shore. Everyone employed in the dockyard, even down to his own household, is rated on the ship's books, consequently they are all men. There is not a woman servant about the place, save his lady's ladies'-maid. His daughters learn to take care of themselves, and are not brought up to find everything done for them. His boys are about the world in active service growing into useful and honourable manhood.

Thus the whole life tastes of the element to which it belongs, and is salt and healthy as the ocean itself. It was not without its entertainments. The officers of the garrison were to give a ball. The young ladies of Kingston are not afraid of the water, cross the harbour in the steam launches, dance till the small hours, return in the dark, drive their eight or ten miles home, and think nothing of it. In that climate, night is pleasanter to be abroad in than day. I could not stay to be present, but I was in the midst of the preparations, and one afternoon there was a prospect of a brilliant addition to the party. A yacht steamed inside the Point—long, narrow, and swift as a torpedo boat. She carried American colours, and we heard that she was the famous vessel of the yet more famous Mr. Vanderbilt, who was on board with his family. Here was an excitement! The commodore was ordered to call the instant that she was anchored. Invitations were prepared—all was eagerness. Alas! she did not anchor at all. She learnt from the pilot that, the small-pox being in Jamaica, if any of her people landed there she would be quarantined in the other islands, and to the disappointment of everyone, even of myself, who would gladly have seen the great millionaire, she turned about and went off again to sea.

I was very happy at the commodore's—low spirits not being allowed in that wholesome element. Decks were washed every morning as if at sea, i.e. every floor was scrubbed and scoured. It was an eternal washing day, lines of linen flying in the brisk sea breeze. The commodore was always busy making work if none had been found for him. He took me one day to see the rock spring where Rodney watered his fleet, as the great admiral describes in one of his letters, and from which Port Royal now draws its supply. The spring itself bursts full and clear out of the limestone rock close to the shore, four or five miles from Kingston. There is a natural basin, slightly improved by art, from which the old conduit pipes carry the stream to the sea. The tug comes daily, fills its tanks, and returns. The commodore has tidied up the place, planted shrubs, and cleared away the bush; but half the water at least, is still allowed to leak away, and turns the hollow below into an unwholesome swamp. It may be a necessity, but it is also a misfortune, that the officers at distant stations hold their appointments for so short a term. By the time that they have learnt what can or ought to be done, they are sent elsewhere, and their successor has to begin over again. The water in this spring, part of which is now worse than wasted and the rest carried laboriously in a vessel to Port Royal to be sold by measure to the people there, might be all conducted thither by pipes at small cost and trouble, were the commodore to remain a few years longer at the Jamaica Station.

He is his own boatman, and we had some fine sails about the lagoon—the breeze always fresh and the surface always smooth. The shallow bays swarm with small fish, and it was a pretty thing to watch the pelicans devouring them. They gather in flocks, sweep and wheel in the air, and when they plunge they strike the water with a violence which one would expect would break their wings. They do not dive, but seize their prey with their long, broad bills, and seem never to miss.

Between the ships and the barracks, there are many single men in Port Royal, for whom amusement has to be found if they are to be kept from drink. A canteen is provided for them, with bowling alley, tennis court, beer in moderation, and a reading room, for such as like it, with reviews and magazines and newspapers They can fish if they want sport, and there are sharks in plenty a cable's length from shore; but the schoolmaster has been abroad, and tastes run in more refined directions. The blacks of Tobago acted 'The Merchant of Venice' before Governor S——. The ships' companies of the gunboats at Port Royal gave a concert while I was there. The officers took no part, and left the men to manage it as they pleased. The commodore brought his party; the garrison, the crews of the other ships, and stray visitors came, and the large room at the canteen was completely full. The taste of the audience was curious. Dibdin was off the boards altogether, and favour was divided between the London popular comic song and the sentimental—no longer with any flavour of salt about it, but the sentimental spoony and sickly. 'She wore a wreath of roses' called out the highest enthusiasm. One of the performers recited a long poem of his own about Mary Stuart, 'the lovely and unfortunate.' Then followed the buffoonery; and this was at least genuine rough and tumble if there was little wit in it. A lad capered about on a tournament horse which flung him every other moment. Various persons pretended to be drunk, and talked and staggered as drunken men do. Then there was a farce, how conceived and by what kind of author I was puzzled to make out. A connoisseur of art is looking for Greek antiques. He has heard that a statue has recently been discovered of 'Ajax quarrelling with his mother-in-law.' What Ajax was quarrelling about or who his mother-in-law might be does not appear. A couple of rogues, each unknown to the other, practise on the connoisseur's credulity. Each promises him the statue; each dresses up a confederate on a pedestal with a modern soldier's helmet and a blanket to represent a Greek hero. The two figures are shown to him. One of them, I forget how, contrived to pass as Ajax; the other had turned into Hercules doing something to the Stymphalides. At last they get tired of standing to be looked at, jump down, and together knock over the connoisseur. Ajax then turns on Hercules, who, of course, is ready for a row. They fight till they are tired, and then make it up over a whisky bottle.

So entirely new an aspect of the British tar took me by surprise, and I speculated whether the inventors and performers of this astonishing drama were an advance on the Ben Bunting type. I was, of course, inclined to say no, but my tendency is to dislike changes, and I allow for it. The commodore said that in certain respects there really was an advance. The seamen fell into few scrapes, and they did not get drunk so often. This was a hardy assertion of the commodore, as a good many of them were drunk at that moment. I could see myself that they were better educated. If Ben Bunting had been asked who Ajax and Hercules were, he would have taken them to be three-deckers which were so named, and his knowledge would have gone no farther. Whether these tars of the new era are better sailors and braver and truer men is another question. They understand their rights much better, if that does any good to them. The officers used to be treated with respect at all times and seasons. This is now qualified. When they are on duty, the men are as respectful as they used to be; when they are off duty, the commodore himself is only old H——.

We returned to the dockyard in a boat under a full moon, the guardship gleaming white in the blue midnight and the phosphorescent water flashing under the oars. The 'Dee,' which was to take me to Havana, was off Port Royal on the following morning. The commodore put me on board in his gig, with the white ensign floating over the stern. I took leave of him with warm thanks for his own and his family's hospitable entertainment of me. The screw went round—we steamed away out of the harbour, and Jamaica and the kind friends whom I had found there faded out of sight. Jamaica was the last of the English West India Islands which I visited. I was to see it again, but I will here set down the impressions which had been left upon me by what I had seen there and seen in the Antilles.

CHAPTER XVII.

Present state of Jamaica—Test of progress—Resources of the island—Political alternatives—Black supremacy and probable consequences—The West Indian problem.

As I was stepping into the boat at Port Royal, a pamphlet was thrust into my hand, which I was entreated to read at my leisure. It was by some discontented white of the island—no rare phenomenon, and the subject of it was the precipitate decline in the value of property there. The writer, unlike the planters, insisted that the people were taxed in proportion to their industry. There were taxes on mules, on carts, on donkeys, all bearing on the small black proprietors, whose ability to cultivate was thus checked, and who were thus deliberately encouraged in idleness. He might have added, although he did not, that while both in Jamaica and Trinidad everyone is clamouring against the beetroot bounty which artificially lowers the price of sugar, the local councils in these two islands try to counteract the effect and artificially raise the price of sugar by an export duty on their own produce—a singular method of doing it which, I presume, admits of explanation. My pamphleteer was persuaded that all the world were fools, and that he and his friends were the only wise ones: again a not uncommon occurrence in pamphleteers. He demanded the suppression of absenteeism; he demanded free trade. In exchange for the customs duties, which were to be abolished, he demanded a land tax—the very mention of which, I had been told by others, drove the black proprietors whom he wished to benefit into madness. He wanted Home Rule. He wanted fifty things besides which I have forgotten, but his grand want of all was a new currency. Mankind, he thought, had been very mad at all periods of their history. The most significant illustration of their madness had been the selection of gold and silver as the medium of exchange. The true base of the currency was the land. The Government of Jamaica was to lend to every freeholder up to the mortgage value of his land in paper notes, at 5 per cent. interest, the current rate being at present 8 per cent. The notes so issued, having the land as their security, would be in no danger of depreciation, and they would flow over the sugar estates like an irrigating stream. On the produce of sugar the fate of the island depended.

On the produce of sugar? And why not on the produce of a fine race of men? The prospects of Jamaica, the prospects of all countries, depend not on sugar or on any form or degree of material wealth, but on the characters of the men and women whom they are breeding and rearing. Where there are men and women of a noble nature, the rest will go well of itself; where these are not, there will be no true prosperity though the sugar hogsheads be raised from thousands into millions. The colonies are interesting only as offering homes where English people can increase and multiply; English of the old type with simple habits, who do not need imported luxuries. There is room even in the West Indies for hundreds of thousands of them if they can be contented to lead human lives, and do not go there to make fortunes which they are to carry home with them. The time may not be far off when men will be sick of making fortunes, sick of being ground to pattern in the commonplace mill-wheel of modern society; sick of a state of things which blights and kills simple and original feeling, which makes us think and speak and act under the tyranny of general opinion, which masquerades as liberty and means only submission to the newspapers. I can conceive some modern men may weary of all this, and retire from it like the old ascetics, not as they did into the wilderness, but behind their own walls and hedges, shutting out the world and its noises, to inquire whether after all they have really immortal souls, and, if they have, what ought to be done about them. The West India Islands, with their inimitable climate and soil and prickly pears ad libitum to make fences with, would be fine places for such recluses. Failing these ideal personages, there is work enough of the common sort to create wholesome prosperity. There are oranges to be grown, and pines and plantains, and coffee and cocoa, and rice and indigo and tobacco, not to speak of the dollars which my American friend found in the bamboos, and of the further dollars which other Americans will find in the untested qualities of thousands of other productions. Here are opportunities for innocent industrious families, where children can be brought up to be manly and simple and true and brave as their fathers were brought up, or as their fathers expressed it 'in the nurture and admonition of the Lord;' while such neighbours as their dark brothers-in-law might have a chance of a rise in life, in the only sense in which a 'rise' can be of real benefit to them. These are the objects which statesmen who have the care and conduct of a nation's welfare ought to set before themselves, and unfortunately they are the last which are remembered in countries which are popularly governed. There is a clamour for education in such countries, but education means to them only the sharpening of the faculties for the competitive race which is called progress. In democracies no one man is his brother's keeper. Each lives and struggles to make his own way and his own position. All that is insisted on is that there shall be a fair stage and that every lad shall learn the use of the weapons which will enable him to fight his own way. Ἀρετὴ

, 'manliness,' the most essential of all acquisitions and the hardest to cultivate, as Aristotle observed long ago, is assumed in democracies as a matter of course. Of ἀρετὴ

a moderate quantity (ὁποσονοῦν

) would do, and in Aristotle's opinion this was the rock on which the Greek republics foundered. Their ἀρετὴ

did not come as a matter of course, and they lost it, and the Macedonians and the Romans ate them up.

From this point of view political problems, and the West Indian among them, present unusual aspects. Looking to the West Indies only, we took possession of those islands when they were of supreme importance in our great wrestle with Spain and France. We were fighting then for the liberties of the human race. The Spaniards had destroyed the original Carib and Indian inhabitants. We induced thousands of our own fellow-countrymen to venture life and fortune in the occupation of our then vital conquests. For two centuries we furnished them with black servants whom we purchased on the African coast and carried over and sold there, making our own profits out of the trade, and the colonists prospered themselves and poured wealth and strength into the empire of which they were then an integral part. A change passed over the spirit of the age. Liberty assumed a new dress. We found slavery to be a crime; we released our bondmen; we broke their chains as we proudly described it to ourselves; we compensated the owners, so far as money could compensate, for the entire dislocation of a state of society which we had ourselves created; and we trusted to the enchantment of liberty to create a better in its place. We had delivered our own souls; we had other colonies to take our emigrants. Other lands under our open trade would supply us with the commodities for which we had hitherto been dependent on the West Indies. They ceased to be of commercial, they ceased to be of political, moment to us, and we left them to their own resources. The modern English idea is that everyone must take care of himself. Individuals or aggregates of individuals have the world before them, to open the oyster or fail to open it according to their capabilities. The State is not to help them; the State is not to interfere with them unless for political or party reasons it happens to be convenient. As we treat ourselves we treat our colonies. Those who have gone thither have gone of their own free will, and must take the consequences of their own actions. We allow them no executional privileges which we do not claim for ourselves. They must stand, if they are to stand, by their own strength. If they cannot stand they must fall. This is our notion of education in 'manliness,' and for immediate purposes answers well enough. Individual enterprise, unendowed but unfettered, built the main buttresses of the British colonial empire. Australians and New Zealanders are English and Scotchmen who have settled at the antipodes where there is more room for them than at home. They are the same people as we are, and they have the same privileges as we have. They are parts of one and the same organic body as branches from the original trunk. The branch does not part from the trunk, but it discharges its own vital functions by its own energy, and we no more desire to interfere than London desires to interfere with Manchester.

So it stands with us where the colonists are of our race, with the same character and the same objects; and, as I said, the system answers. Under no other relations could we continue a united people. But it does not answer—it has failed wherever we have tried it—when the majority of the inhabitants of countries of which for one or other reason we have possessed ourselves, and of which we keep possession, are not united to us by any of these natural bonds, where they have been annexed by violence or otherwise been forced under our flag. It has failed conspicuously in Ireland. We know that it would fail in the East Indies if we were rash enough to venture the experiment. Self-government in connection with the British Empire implies a desire or a willingness in those who are so left to themselves that the connection shall continue. We have been so sanguine as to believe that the privilege of being British subjects is itself sufficient to secure their allegiance; that the liberties which we concede will not be used for purposes which we are unable to tolerate; that, being left to govern themselves, they will govern in harmony with English interests and according to English principles. The privilege is not estimated so highly. They go their own way and not our way, and therefore we must look facts in the face as they are, and not as we wish them to be. If we extend to Ireland the independence which only links us closer to Australia, Ireland will use it to break away from us. If we extend it to Bengal and Madras and Bombay, we shall fling them into anarchy and bring our empire to an end. We cannot for our safety's sake part with Ireland. We do not mean to part with our Asiatic dominions. The reality of the relation in both cases is the superior force of England, and we must rely upon it and need not try to conceal that we do, till by the excellence of our administration we have converted submission into respect and respect into willingness for union. This may be a long process and a difficult one. If we choose to maintain our empire, however, we must pay the price for empire, and it is wiser, better, safer, in all cases to admit the truth and act upon it. Yet Englishmen so love liberty that they struggle against confessing what is disagreeable to them. Many of us would give Ireland, would give India Home Rule, and run the risk of what would happen, and only a probability, which reaches certainty, of the consequences to be expected to follow prevents us from unanimously agreeing. About the West Indies we do not care very earnestly. Nothing seriously alarming can happen there. So much, therefore, for the general policy of leaving them to help themselves out of their difficulties we have adopted completely. The corollary that they must govern themselves also on their own responsibilities we hesitate as yet to admit completely; but we do not recognise that any responsibility for their failing condition rests on us; and the inclination certainly, and perhaps the purpose, is to throw them entirely upon themselves at the earliest moment. Cuba sends representatives to the Cortes at Madrid, Martinique and Guadaloupe to the Assembly at Paris. In the English islands, being unwilling to govern without some semblance of a constitution, we try tentatively varieties of local boards and local councils, admitting the elective principle but not daring to trust it fully; creating hybrid constitutions, so contrived as to provoke ill feeling where none would exist without them, and to make impossible any tolerable government which could actively benefit the people. We cannot intend that arrangements the effects of which are visible so plainly in the sinking fortunes of our own kindred there, are to continue for ever. We suppose that we cannot go back in these cases. It is to be presumed, therefore, that we mean to go forward, and in doing so I venture to think myself that we shall be doing equal injustice both to our own race and to the blacks, and we shall bring the islands into a condition which will be a reproach and scandal to the empire of which they will remain a dishonoured part. The slave trade was an imperial monopoly, extorted by force, guaranteed by treaties, and our white West Indian interest was built up in connection with and in reliance upon it. We had a right to set the slaves free; but the payment of the indemnity was no full acquittance of our obligations for the condition of a society which we had ourselves created. We have no more right to make the emancipated slave his master's master in virtue of his numbers than we have a right to lay under the heel of the Catholics of Ireland the Protestant minority whom we planted there to assist us in controlling them.

It may be said that we have no intention of doing anything of the kind, that no one at present dreams of giving a full colonial constitution to the West Indian Islands. They are allowed such freedom as they are capable of using; they can be allowed more as they are better educated and more fit for it, c. c.

One knows all that, and one knows what it is worth in the half-elected, half-nominated councils. Either the nominated members are introduced merely as a drag upon the wheel, and are instructed to yield in the end to the demands of the representative members, or they are themselves the representatives of the white minority. If the first, the majority rule already; if the second, such constitutions are contrived ingeniously to create the largest amount of irritation, and to make impossible, as long as they last, any form of effective and useful government. Therefore they cannot last, and are not meant to last. A principle once conceded develops with the same certainty with which a seed grows when it is sown. In the English world, as it now stands, there is no middle alternative between self-government and government by the Crown, and the cause of our reluctance to undertake direct charge of the West Indies is because such undertaking carries responsibility along with it. If they are brought so close to us we shall be obliged to exert ourselves, and to rescue them from a condition which would be a reproach to us.

The English of those islands are melting away. That is a fact to which it is idle to try to shut our eyes. Families who have been for generations on the soil are selling their estates everywhere and are going off. Lands once under high cultivation are lapsing into jungle. Professional men of ability and ambition carry their talents to countries where they are more sure of reward. Every year the census renews its warning. The rate may vary; sometimes for a year or two there may seem to be a pause in the movement, but it begins again and is always in the same direction. The white is relatively disappearing, the black is growing; that is the fact with which we have to deal.

We may say if we please, 'Be it so then; we do not want those islands; let the blacks have them, poor devils. They have had wrongs enough in this world; let them take their turn and have a good time now.' This I imagine is the answer which will rise to the lips of most of us, yet it will be an answer which will not be for our honour, nor in the long run for our interest. Our stronger colonies will scarcely attach more value to their connection with us if they hear us declare impatiently that because part of our possessions have ceased to be of money value to us, we will not or we cannot take the trouble to provide them with a decent government, and therefore cast them off. Nor in the long run will it benefit the blacks either. The islands will not be allowed to run wild again, and if we leave them some one else will take them who will be less tender of his coloured brother's sensibilities. We may think that it would not come to that. The islands will still be ours; the English flag will still float over the forts; the government, whatever it be, will be administered in the Queen's name. Were it worth while, one might draw a picture of the position of an English governor, with a black parliament and a black ministry, recommending by advice of his constitutional ministers some measure like the Haytian Land Law.

No Englishman, not even a bankrupt peer, would consent to occupy such a position; the blacks themselves would despise him if he did; and if the governor is to be one of their own race and colour, how long could such a connection endure?

No one I presume would advise that the whites of the island should govern. The relations between the two populations are too embittered, and equality once established by law, the exclusive privilege of colour over colour cannot be restored. While slavery continued the whites ruled effectively and economically; the blacks are now free as they; there are two classes in the community; their interests are opposite as they are now understood, and one cannot be trusted with control over the other. As little can the present order of things continue. The West India Islands, once the pride of our empire, the scene of our most brilliant achievements, are passing away out of our hands; the remnant of our own countrymen, weary of an unavailing struggle, are more and more eager to withdraw from the scene, because they find no sympathy and no encouragement from home, and are forbidden to accept help from America when help is offered them, while under their eyes their quondam slaves are multiplying, thriving, occupying, growing strong, and every day more conscious of the changed order of things. One does not grudge the black man his prosperity, his freedom, his opportunities of advancing himself; one would wish to see him as free and prosperous as the fates and his own exertions can make him, with more and more means of raising himself to the white man's level. But left to himself, and without the white man to lead him, he can never reach it, and if we are not to lose the islands altogether, or if they are not to remain with us to discredit our capacity to rule them, it is left to us only to take the same course which we have taken in the East Indies with such magnificent success, and to govern whites and blacks alike on the Indian system. The circumstances are precisely analogous. We have a population to deal with, the enormous majority of whom are of an inferior race. Inferior, I am obliged to call them, because as yet, and as a body, they have shown no capacity to rise above the condition of their ancestors except under European laws, European education, and European authority, to keep them from making war on one another. They are docile, good-tempered, excellent and faithful servants when they are kindly treated; but their notions of right and wrong are scarcely even elementary; their education, such as it may be, is but skin deep, and the old African superstitions lie undisturbed at the bottom of their souls. Give them independence, and in a few generations they will peel off such civilisation as they have learnt as easily and as willingly as their coats and trousers.

Govern them as we govern India, with the same conscientious care, with the same sense of responsibility, with the same impartiality, the same disinterested attention to the well-being of our subjects in its highest and most honourable sense, and we shall give the world one more evidence that while Englishmen can cover the waste places of it with free communities of their own blood, they can exert an influence no less beneficent as the guides and rulers of those who need their assistance, and whom fate and circumstances have assigned to their care. Our kindred far away will be more than ever proud to form part of a nation which has done more for freedom than any other nation ever did, yet is not a slave to formulas, and can adapt its actions to the demands of each community which belongs to it. The most timid among us may take courage, for it would cost us nothing save the sacrifice of a few official traditions, and an abstinence for the future from doubtful uses of colonial patronage. The blacks will be perfectly happy when they are satisfied that they have nothing to fear for their persons or their properties. To the whites it would be the opening of a new era of hope. Should they be rash enough to murmur, they might then be justly left to the consequences of their own folly.

CHAPTER XVIII.

Passage to Cuba—A Canadian commissioner—Havana—The Moro—The city and harbour—Cuban money—American visitors—The cathedral—Tomb of Columbus—New friends—The late rebellion—Slave emancipation—Spain and progress—A bull fight.

I had gone to the West Indies to see our own colonies, but I could not leave those famous seas which were the scene of our ocean duels with the Spaniards without a visit to the last of the great possessions of Philip II. which remained to his successors. I ought not to say the last, for Puerto Rico is Spanish also, but this small island is insignificant and has no important memories connected with it. Puerto Rico I had no leisure to look at and did not care about, and to see Cuba as it ought to be seen required more time than I could afford; but Havana was so interesting, both from its associations and its present condition, that I could not be within reach of it and pass it by. The body of Columbus lies there for one thing, unless a trick was played when the remains which were said to be his were removed from St. Domingo, and I wished to pay my orisons at his tomb. I wished also to see the race of men who have shared the New World with the Anglo-Saxons, and have given a language and a religion to half the American continent, in the oldest and most celebrated of their Transatlantic cities.

Cuba also had an immediate and present interest. Before the American civil war it was on the point of being absorbed into the United States. The Spanish Cubans had afterwards a civil war of their own, of which only confused accounts had reached us at home. We knew that it had lasted ten years, but who had been the parties and what their objects had been was very much a mystery. No sooner was it over than, without reservation or compensation, the slaves had been emancipated. How a country was prospering which had undergone such a succession of shocks, and how the Spaniards were dealing with the trials which were bearing so hard on our own islands, were inquiries worth making. But beyond these it was the land of romance. Columbus and Las Casas, Cortez and Pizarro, are the demigods and heroes of the New World. Their names will be familiar to the end of time as the founders of a new era, and although the modern Spaniards sink to the level of the modern Greeks, their illustrious men will hold their place for ever in imagination and memory.

Our own Antilles had, as I have said, in their terror of small-pox, placed Jamaica under an interdict. The Spaniards at Cuba were more generous or more careless. Havana is on the north side of the island, facing towards Florida; thus, in going to it from Port Royal, we had to round the westernmost cape, and had four days of sea before us. We slid along the coast of Jamaica in smooth water, the air, while day lasted, intensely hot, but the breeze after nightfall blowing cool from off the mountains. We had a polite captain, polite officers, and agreeable fellow-passengers, two or three Cubans among them, swarthy, dark-eyed, thick-set men—Americanos; Spaniards with a difference—with whom I cultivated a kind of intimacy. In a cabin it was reported that there were again Spanish ladies on their way to the demonic gaieties at Darien, but they did not show.

Among the rest of the party was a Canadian gentleman, a Mr. ——, exceptionally well-informed and intelligent. Their American treaty having been disallowed, the West Indies had proposed to negotiate a similar one with the Canadian Dominion. The authorities at Ottawa had sent Mr. M—— to see if anything could be done, and Mr. M—— was now on his way home, not in the best of humours with our poor relations. 'The Jamaicans did not know what they wanted,' he said. 'They were without spirit to help themselves; they cried out to others to help them, and if all they asked could not be granted they clamoured as if the whole world was combining to hurt them. There was not the least occasion for these passionate appeals to the universe; they could not at this moment perhaps "go ahead" as fast as some countries, but there was no necessity to be always going ahead. They had a fine country, soil and climate all that could be desired, they had all that was required for a quiet and easy life, why could they not be contented and make the best of things?' Unfortunate Jamaicans! The old mother at home acts like an unnatural parent, and will neither help them nor let their Cousin Jonathan help them. They turn for comfort to their big brother in the north, and the big brother being himself robust and healthy, gives them wholesome advice.

Adventures do occasionally happen at sea even in this age of steam engines. Ships catch fire or run into each other, or go on rocks in fogs, or are caught in hurricanes, and Nature can still assume her old terrors if she pleases. Shelley describes a wreck on the coast of Cornwall, and the treacherous waters of the ocean in the English Channel, now wild in fury, now smiling

As on the morn When the exulting elements in scorn Satiated with destroyed destruction lay Sleeping in beauty on their mangled prey, As panthers sleep.

The wildest gale which ever blew on British shores was a mere summer breeze compared to a West Indian tornado. Behind all that beauty there lies the temper and caprice, not of a panther, but of a woman. But no tornadoes fell in our way, nor anything else worth mentioning, not even a buccaneer or a pirate. We saw the islands which these gentry haunted, and the headlands made memorable by their desperate deeds, but they are gone, even to the remembrance of them. What they were and what they did lies buried away in book mausoleums like Egyptian mummies, all as clean forgotten as if they had been honest men, they and all the wild scenes which these green estuaries have witnessed.

Havana figures much in English naval history. Drake tried to take it and failed; Penn and Venables failed. We stormed the forts in 1760, and held them and held the city till the Seven Years' War was over. I had read descriptions of the place, but they had given me no clear conception of what it would be like, certainly none at all of what it was like. Kingston is the best of our West Indian towns, and Kingston has not one fine building in it. Havana is a city of palaces, a city of streets and plazas, of colonnades, and towers, and churches and monasteries. We English have built in those islands as if we were but passing visitors, wanting only tenements to be occupied for a time. The Spaniards built as they built in Castile; built with the same material, the white limestone which they found in the New World as in the Old. The palaces of the nobles in Havana, the residence of the governor, the convents, the cathedral, are a reproduction of Burgos or Valladolid, as if by some Aladdin's lamp a Castilian city had been taken up and set down again unaltered on the shore of the Caribbean Sea. And they carried with them their laws, their habits, their institutions and their creed, their religious orders, their bishops, and their Inquisition. Even now in her day of eclipse, when her genius is clouded by the modern spirit against which she fought so long and so desperately, the sons of Spain still build as they used to build, and the modern squares and market places, the castles and fortresses, which have risen in and round the ancient Havana, are constructed on the old massive model, and on the same lines. However it may be with us, and whatever the eventual fate of Cuba, the Spanish race has taken root there, and is visibly destined to remain. They have poured their own people into it. In Cuba alone there are ten times as many Spaniards as there are English and Scotch in all our West Indies together, and Havana is ten times the size of the largest of our West Indian cities. Refugees have flocked thither from the revolutions in the Peninsula. The Canary Islands overflow into it. You know the people from Teneriffe by their stature; they are the finest surviving specimens of the old conquering breed. The political future is dark; the government is unimaginably corrupt—so corrupt that change is inevitable, though what change it would be idle to prophesy. The Americans looked at the island which lay so temptingly near them, but they were wise in their generation. They reflected that to introduce into an Anglo-Saxon republic so insoluble an element as a million Spanish Roman Catholics alien in blood and creed, with half a million blacks to swell the dusky flood which runs too full among them already, would be to invite an indigestion of serious consequence. A few years since the Cubans born were on the eve of achieving their independence like their brothers in Mexico and South America. Perhaps they will yet succeed. Spanish, at any rate, they are to the bone and marrow, and Spanish they will continue. The magnitude of Havana, and the fullness of life which was going on there, entirely surprised me. I had thought of Cuba as a decrepit state, bankrupt or finance-exhausted by civil wars, and on the edge of social dissolution, and I found Havana at least a grand imposing city—a city which might compare for beauty with any in the world. The sanitary condition is as bad as negligence can make it—so bad that a Spanish gentleman told me that if it were not for the natural purity of the air they would have been all dead like flies long ago. The tideless harbour is foul with the accumulations of three hundred years. The administration is more good-for-nothing than in Spain itself. If, in spite of this, Havana still sits like a queen upon the waters, there are some qualities to be found among her people which belonged to the countrymen and subjects of Ferdinand the Catholic.

The coast line from Cape Tubiron has none of the grand aspects of the Antilles or Jamaica. Instead of mountains and forests you see a series of undulating hills, cultivated with tolerable care, and sprinkled with farmhouses. All the more imposing, therefore, from the absence of marked natural forms, are the walls and towers of the great Moro, the fortress which defends the entrance of the harbour. Ten miles off it was already a striking object. As we ran nearer it rose above us stern, proud, and defiant, upon a rock right above the water, with high frowning bastions, the lighthouse at an angle of it, and the Spanish banner floating proudly from a turret which overlooked the whole. The Moro as a fortification is, I am told, indefensible against modern artillery, presenting too much surface as a target; but it is all the grander to look at. It is a fine specimen of the Vauban period, and is probably equal to any demands which will be made upon it. The harbour is something like Port Royal, a deep lagoon with a narrow entrance and a long natural breakwater between the lagoon and the ocean; but what at Port Royal is a sand-spit eight miles long, is at Havana a rocky peninsula on which the city itself is built. The opening from the sea is half a mile wide. On the city side there are low semicircular batteries which sweep completely the approaches and the passage itself. The Moro rises opposite at the extreme point of the entrance, and next to it, farther in towards the harbour on the same side, on the crest and slopes of a range of hills, stands the old Moro, the original castle which beat off Drake and Oliver's sea-generals, and which was captured by the English in the last century. The lines were probably weaker than they are at present, and less adequately manned. A monument is erected there to the officers and men who fell in the defence.

HAVANA, FROM THE QUARRIES
HAVANA, FROM THE QUARRIES

The city as we steamed by looked singularly beautiful, with its domes and steeples and marble palaces, and glimpses of long boulevards and trees and handsome mansions and cool arcades. Inside we found ourselves in a basin, perhaps of three miles diameter, full of shipping of all sorts and nationalities. The water, which outside is pure as sapphire, has become filthy with the pollutions of a dozen generations. The tide, which even at the springs has but a rise and fall of a couple of feet, is totally ineffective to clear it, and as long as they have the Virgin Mary to pray to, the pious Spaniards will not drive their sewage into the ocean. The hot sun rays stream down into the thick black liquid. Horrible smells are let loose from it when it is set in motion by screw or paddle, and ships bring up at mooring buoys lest their anchors should disturb the compost which lies at the bottom. Yet one forgot the disagreeables in the novelty and striking character of the scene. A hundred boats were plying to and fro among the various vessels, with their white sails and white awnings. Flags of all countries were blowing out at stern or from masthead; among them, of course, the stars and stripes flying jauntily on some splendid schooner which stood there like a cock upon a dunghill that might be his own if he chose to crow for it.

As soon as we had brought up we were boarded by the inevitable hotel touters, custom-house officers, porters, and boatmen. Interpreters offered their services in the confusion of languages. Gradually there emerged out of the general noise two facts of importance. First, that I ought to have had a passport, and if I had not brought one that I was likely to be fined at the discretion of Spanish officials. Secondly, that if I trusted to my own powers of self-defence, I should be the victim of indefinite other extortions. Passport I had none—such things are not required any longer in Spain, and it had not occurred to me that they might still be in demand in a Spanish colony. As to being cheated, no one could or would tell me what I was to pay for anything, for there were American dollars, Spanish dollars, Mexican dollars, and Cuban dollars, all different. And there were multiples of dollars in gold, and single dollars in silver, and last and most important of all there was the Cuban paper dollar, which was 230 per cent. below the Cuban gold dollar. And in this last the smaller transactions of common life were carried on, the practical part of it to a stranger being that when you had to receive you received in paper, and when you had to pay you paid in specie.

I escaped for the time the penalty which would have been inflicted on me about the passport. I had a letter of introduction to the Captain-General of the island, and the Captain-General—so the viceroy is called—was so formidable a person that the officials did not venture to meddle with me. For the rest I was told that as soon as I had chosen my hotel, the agent, who was on board, would see me through all obstructions, and would not allow me to be plundered by anyone but himself. To this

I had to submit. I named an hotel at random; a polite gentleman in a few moments had a boat alongside for me; I had stept into it when the fair damsels bound for Darien, who had been concealed all this time in their cabin, slipped down the ladder and took their places at my side, to the no small entertainment of the friends whom I had left on board and who were watching us from the deck.

At the wharf I was able to shake off my companions, and I soon forgot the misadventure, for I found myself in Old Castile once more, amidst Spanish faces, Spanish voices, Spanish smells, and Spanish scenes. On the very wharf itself was a church grim and stern, and so massive that it would stand, barring earthquakes, for a thousand years. Church, indeed, it was no longer; it had been turned into a custom-house. But this was because it had been desecrated when we were in Havana by having an English service performed in it. They had churches enough without it, and they preferred to leave this one with a mark upon it of the anger of the Almighty. Of churches, indeed, there was no lack; churches thick as public-houses in a Welsh town. Church beyond church, palace beyond palace, the narrow streets where neighbours on either side might shake hands out of the upper stories, the deep colonnades, the private houses with the windows grated towards the street, with glimpses through the street door into the court and garden within, with its cloisters, its palm trees, and its fountains; the massiveness of the stonework, the curious old-fashioned bookstalls, the dirt, the smell, the carriages, the swearing drivers, the black-robed priest gliding along the footway—it was Toledo or Valladolid again with the sign manual on it of Spain herself in friendly and familiar form. Every face that I saw was Spanish. In Kingston or Port of Spain you meet fifty blacks for one European; all the manual work is done by them. In Havana the proportion is reversed, you hardly see a coloured man at all. Boatmen, porters, cab-drivers or cart-drivers, every one of whom are negroes in our islands, are there Spaniards, either Cuban born or emigrants from home. A few black beggars there were—permitted, as objects of charity to pious Catholics and as a sign of their inferiority of race. Of poverty among the whites, real poverty that could be felt, I saw no sign at all.

After driving for about a mile we emerged out of the old town into a large square and thence into a wide Alameda or boulevard with double avenues of trees, statues, fountains, theatres, clubhouses, and all the various equipments of modern luxuriousness and so-called civilised life. Beyond the Alameda was another still larger square, one side of which was a railway station and terminus. In a colonnade at right angles was the hotel to which I had been recommended; spacious, handsome, in style half Parisian half Spanish, like the Fondas in the Puerto del Sol at Madrid.

Spanish was the language generally spoken; but there were interpreters and waiters more or less accomplished in other tongues, especially in English, of which they heard enough, for I found Havana to be the winter resort of our American cousins, who go, generally, to Cuba, as we go to the Riviera, to escape the ice and winds of the eastern and middle States. This particular hotel was a favourite resort, and was full to overflowing with them. It was large, with an interior quadrangular garden, into which looked tiers of windows; and wings had been thrown out with terraced roofs, suites of rooms opening out upon them; each floor being provided with airy sitting rooms and music rooms. Here were to be heard at least a hundred American voices discussing the experiences and plans of their owners. The men lounged in the hall or at the bar, or sat smoking on the rows of leather chairs under the colonnade, or were under the hands of barbers or haircutters in an airy open saloon devoted to these uses. When I retreated upstairs to collect myself, a lady was making the corridors ring close by as she screamed at a piano in the middle of an admiring and criticising crowd. Dear as the Americans are to me, and welcome in most places as is the sound of those same sweet voices, one had not come to Havana for this. It was necessary to escape somewhere, and promptly, from the discord of noises which I hoped might be due to some momentary accident. The mail company's agent, Mr. R——, lived in the hotel. He kindly found me out, initiated me in the mysteries of Cuban paper money, and giving me a tariff of the fares, found me a cab, and sent me out to look about me.

My first object was the cathedral and the tomb of Columbus. In Catholic cities in Europe churches stand always open; the passer-by can enter when he pleases, fall on his knees and say his silent prayers to his Master whom he sees on the altar. In Havana I discovered afterward that, except at special hours, and those as few as might be, the doors were kept locked and could only be opened by a golden key. It was carnival time, however; there were functions going on of various kinds, and I found the cathedral happily accessible. It was a vast building, little ornamented, but the general forms severe and impressive, in the style of the time of Philip II., when Gothic art had gone out in Spain and there had come in the place of it the implacable sternness which expresses the very genius of the Inquisition. A broad flight of stone steps led up to the great door. The afternoon was extremely hot; the curtains were thrown back to admit as much air as possible. There was some function proceeding of a peculiar kind. I know not what it was; something certainly in which the public had no interest, for there was not a stranger present but myself. But the great cathedral officials were busy at work, and liked to be at their ease. On the wall as you entered a box invited contributions, as limosna por el Santo Padre. The service was I know not what. In the middle of the nave stood twelve large chairs arranged in a semicircle; on these chairs sat twelve canons, like a row of mandarins, each with his little white patch like a silver dollar on the crown of his black head. Five or six minor dignitaries, deacons, precentors, or something of that sort, were droning out monotonous recitations like the buzzing of so many humble-bees in the warm summer air. The dean or provost sat in the central biggest chair of all. His face was rosy, and he wiped it from time to time with a red handkerchief; his chin was double or perhaps treble; he had evidently dined, and would or might have slept but for a pile of snuff on his chair arm, with continual refreshments from which he kept his faculties alive. I sat patiently till it was over, and the twelve holy men rose and went their way. I could then stroll about at leisure. The pictures were of the usual paltry kind. On the chancel arch stood the royal arms of Spain, as the lion and the unicorn used to stand in our parish churches till the High Church clergy mistook them for Erastian wild beasts. At the right side of the altar was the monument which I had come in search of; a marble tablet fixed against the wall, and on it a poorly executed figure in high relief, with a ruff about its neck and features which might be meant for anyone and for no one in particular. Somewhere near me there were lying

I believed and could hope the mortal remains of the discoverer of the New World. An inscription said so. There was written:

O Restos y Imagen del grande Colon
Mil siglos durad guardados en la Urna
Y en remembranza de nuestra Nacion.

The court poet, or whoever wrote the lines, was as poor an artist in verse as the sculptor in stone. The image of the grande Colon is certainly not 'guarded in the urn,' since you see it on the wall before your eyes. The urn, if urn there be, with the 'relics' in it, must be under the floor. Columbus and his brother Diego were originally buried to the right and left of the altar in the cathedral of St. Domingo. When St. Domingo was abandoned, a commission was appointed to remove the body of Christophe to Havana. They did remove a body, but St. Domingo insists that it was Diego that was taken away, that Christophe remains where he was, and that if Spain wants him Spain must pay for him. I followed the canons into the sacristy where they were unrobing. I did not venture to address either of themselves, but I asked an acolyte if he could throw any light upon the matter. He assured me that there neither was nor could have been any mistake. They had the right body and were in no doubt about it. In more pious ages disputes of this sort were settled by an appeal to miracles. Rival pretenders for the possession of the same bones came, however, at last to be able to produce authentic proofs of miracles which had been worked at more than one of the pretended shrines; so that it was concluded that saints' relics were like the loaves and fishes, capable of multiplication without losing their identity, and of having the property of being in several places at the same moment. The same thing has been alleged of the Holy Coat of Trèves and of the wood of the true cross. Havana and St. Domingo may perhaps eventually find a similar solution of their disagreement over the resting place of Columbus.

I walked back to my hotel up a narrow shady street like a long arcade. Here were the principal shops; several libraries among them, into which I strayed to gossip and to look over the shelves. That so many persons could get a living by bookselling implied a reading population, but the books themselves did not indicate any present literary productiveness. They were chiefly old, and from the Old World, and belonged probably to persons who had been concerned in the late rebellion and whose property had been confiscated. They were absurdly cheap; I bought a copy of Guzman de Alfarache for a few pence.

I had brought letters of introduction to several distinguished people in Havana; to one especially, Don G——, a member of a noble Peninsular family, once an officer in the Spanish navy, now chairman of a railway company and head of an important commercial house. His elder brother, the Marques de ——, called on me on the evening of the day of my arrival; a distinguished-looking man of forty or thereabouts, with courteous high-bred manners, rapid, prompt, and incisive, with the air of a soldier, which in early life he had been. He had travelled, spoke various languages, and spoke to me in admirable English. Don G——, who might be a year or two younger, came later and stayed an hour and a half with me. Let me acknowledge here, and in as warm language as I can express it, the obligations under which I stand to him, not for the personal attentions only which he showed me during my stay in Havana, but for giving me an opportunity of becoming acquainted with a real specimen of Plato's superior men, who were now and then, so Plato said, to be met with in foreign travel. It is to him that I owe any knowledge which I brought away with me of the present state of Cuba. He had seen much, thought much, read much. He was on a level with the latest phases of philosophical and spiritual speculation, could talk of Darwin and Spencer, of Schopenhauer, of Strauss, and of Renan, aware of what they had done, aware of the inconvenient truths which they had forced into light, but aware also that they had left the most important questions pretty much where they found them. He had taken no part in the political troubles of the late years in Cuba, but he had observed everything. No one knew better the defects of the present system of government; no one was less ready to rush into hasty schemes for violently mending it.

The ten years' rebellion, of which I had heard so much and knew so little, he first made intelligible to me. Cuba had been governed as a province of Spain, and Spain, like other mother countries, had thought more of drawing a revenue out of it for herself than of the interests of the colony. Spanish officials had been avaricious, and Spanish fiscal policy oppressive and ruinous. The resources of the island in metals, in minerals, in agriculture were as yet hardly scratched, yet every attempt to develop them was paralysed by fresh taxation. The rebellion had been an effort of the Cuban Spaniards, precisely analogous to the revolt of our own North American colonies, to shake off the authority of the court of Madrid and to make themselves independent. They had fought desperately and had for several years been masters of half the island. They had counted on help from the United States, and at one time they seemed likely to get it. But the Americans could not see their way to admitting Cuba into the Union, and without such a prospect did not care to quarrel with Spain on their account. Finding that they were to be left to themselves, the insurgents came to terms and Spanish authority was re-established. Families had been divided, sons taking one side and fathers the other, as in our English Wars of the Roses, perhaps for the same reason, to save the family estates whichever side came out victorious. The blacks had been indifferent, the rebellion having no interest for them at all. They had remained by their masters, and they had been rewarded after the peace by complete emancipation. There was not a slave now in Cuba. No indemnity had been granted to their owners, nor had any been asked for, and the business on the plantations had gone on without interruption. Those who had been slaves continued to work at the same locations, receiving wages instead of food and maintenance; all were satisfied at the change, and this remarkable revolution had been carried out with an ease and completeness which found no parallel in any other slave-owning country.

In spite of rebellion, in spite of the breaking up and reconstruction of the social system, in spite of the indifferent administration of justice, in spite of taxation, and the inexplicable appropriation of the revenue, Cuba was still moderately prosperous, and that it could flourish at all after trials so severe was the best evidence of the greatness of its natural wealth. The party of insurrection was dissolved, and would revive again only under the unlikely contingency of encouragement from the United States. There was a party, however, which desired for Cuba a constitution like the Canadian—Home Rule and the management of its own affairs—and as the black element was far outnumbered and under control, such a constitution would not be politically dangerous.

If the Spanish Government does not mend its ways, concessions of this kind may eventually have to be made, though the improvement to be expected from it is doubtful. Official corruption is engrained in the character and habits of the Spanish people. Judges allowed their decisions to be 'influenced' under Philip III. as much as to-day in the colonies of Queen Christina; and when a fault is the habit of a people, it survives political reforms and any number of turnings of the kaleidoscope.

The encouraging feature is the success of emancipation. There is no jealousy, no race animosity, no supercilious contempt of whites for 'niggers.' The Spaniards have inherited a tinge of colour themselves from their African ancestors, and thus they are all friends together. The liberated slave can acquire and own land if he wishes for it, but as a rule he prefers to work for wages. These happy conditions arise in part from the Spanish temperament, but chiefly from the numerical preponderance of the white element, which, as in the United States, is too secure to be uneasy. The black is not encouraged in insubordination by a sense that he could win in a contest of strength, and the aspect of things is far more promising for the future than in our own islands. The Spaniards, however inferior we may think them to ourselves, have filled their colonies with their own people and are reaping the reward of it. We have so contrived that such English as had settled in the West Indies on their own account are leaving them.

Spain, four centuries ago, was the greatest of European nations, the first in art, or second only to Italy, the first in arms, the first in the men whom she produced. She has been swept along in the current of time. She fought against the stream of tendency, and the stream proved too strong for her, great as she was. The modern spirit, which she would not have when it came in the shape of the Reformation, has flowed over her borders as revolution, not to her benefit, for she is unable to assimilate the new ideas. The old Spain of the Inquisition is gone; the Spain of to-day is divided between Liberalism and Catholic belief. She is sick in the process of the change, and neither she nor her colonies stand any longer in the front lines in the race of civilisation; yet the print of her foot is stamped on the New World in characters which will not be effaced, and may be found to be as enduring as our own.

The colony is perhaps in advance of the mother country. The Catholic Church, Don G—— said, has little influence in Cuba; 'she has had no rival,' he explained, 'and so has grown lazy.' I judged the same from my own observations. The churches on Sundays were thinly attended, and men smiled when I asked them about 'confession.' I inquired about famous preachers. I was told that there was no preaching in Havana, famous or otherwise. I might if I was lucky and chose to go there in the early morning, hear a sermon in the church of the Jesuits; that was all. I went; I heard my Jesuit, who was fluent, eloquent, and gesticulating, but he was pouring out his passionate rhetoric to about fifty women with scarcely a man amongst them. It was piteous to look at him. The Catholic Church, whether it be for want of rivals, or merely from force of time, has fallen from its high estate. It can burn no more heretics, for it has lost the art to raise conviction to sufficient intensity. The power to burn was the measure of the real belief, which people had in the Church and its doctrines. The power has departed with the waning of faith; and religion in Havana, as in Madrid, is but 'use and wont;' not 'belief' but opinion, and opinion which is half insincere. Nothing else can take its place. The day is too late for Protestantism, which has developed into wider forms, and in the matter of satisfied and complete religious conviction Protestants are hardly better off than Catholics.

Don G—— had been much in Spain; he was acquainted with many of the descendants of the old aristocracy, who lingered there in faded grandeur. He had studied the history of his own country. He compared the Spain and England of the sixteenth century with the Spain and England of the present; and, like most of us, he knew where the yoke galled his own neck. But economical and political prosperity is no exhaustive measure of human progress. The Rome of Trajan was immeasurably more splendid than the Rome of the Scipios; yet the progress had been downwards nevertheless. If the object of our existence on this planet is the development of character, if the culminating point in any nation's history be that at which it produces its noblest and bravest men, facts do not tend to assure us that the triumphant march of the last hundred years is accomplishing much in that direction. I found myself arguing with Don G—— that if Charles V. and Philip II. were to come back to this world, and to see whither the movement had brought us of which they had worked so hard to suppress the beginning, they would still say that they had done right in trying to strangle it. The Reformation called itself a protest against lies, and the advocates of it imagined that when the lies, or what they called such, were cleared away, the pure metal of Christianity would remain unsullied. The great men who fought against the movement, Charles V. in his cabinet and Erasmus in his closet, had seen that it could not rest there; that it was the cradle of a revolution in which the whole spiritual and political organisation of Europe would be flung into the crucible. Under that organisation human nature had ascended to altitudes of chivalry, of self-sacrifice, which it had never before reached. The sixteenth century was the blossoming time of the Old World, and no such men had appeared since as then came to the front, either in Spain or Italy, or Germany or France or England. The actual leaders of the Reformation had been bred in the system which they destroyed. Puritanism and Calvinism produced men of powerful character, but they were limited and incapable of continuance; and now the liberty which was demanded had become what the instinct of the great Emperor had told him from the first must be the final shape of it, a revolution which would tolerate no inequalities of culture or position, which insisted that no man was better than another, which was to exalt the low and bring down the high till all mankind should stand upon a common level—a level, not of baseness or badness, but a level of good-humoured, smart, vulgar and vulgarising mediocrity, with melodrama for tragedy, farce for comedy, sounding speech for statesmanlike wisdom; and for a creed, when our fathers thought that we had been made a little lower than the angels, the more modest knowledge that we were only a little higher than the apes. This was the aspect in which the world of the nineteenth century would appear to Sir Thomas More or the Duke of Alva. From the Grand Captain to Señor Castelar, from Lord Burghley to Mr. Gladstone, from Leonardo da Vinci or Velasquez to Gustave Doré, from Cervantes and Shakespeare to 'Pickwick' and the 'Innocents at Home;' from the faith which built the cathedrals to evolution and the survival of the fittest; from the carving and architecture of the Middle Ages to the workmanship of the modern contractor; the change in the spiritual department of things had been the same along the whole line. Charles V. after seeing all that has been achieved, the railways, the steam engines, the telegraphs, the Yankee and his United States, which are the embodiment of the highest aspirations of the modern era, after attending a session of the British Association itself, and seeing the bishops holding out their hands to science which had done such great things for them, might fairly claim that it was a doubtful point whether the change had been really for the better.

It may be answered, and answered truly, that the old thing was dead. The Catholic faith, where it was left standing and where it still stands, produces now nothing higher, nothing better than the Protestant. Human systems grow as trees grow. The seed shoots up, the trunk forms, the branches spread; leaves and flowers and fruit come out year after year as if they were able to renew themselves for ever. But that which has a beginning has an end, that which has life must die when the vital force is exhausted. The faith of More, as well as the faith of Ken or Wilson, were elevating and ennobling as long as they were sincerely believed, but the time came when they became clouded with uncertainty; and confused, perplexed, and honestly anxious, humanity struggles on as well as it can, all things considered, respectably enough, in its chrysalis condition, the old wings gone, the new wings that are to be (if we are ever to have another set) as yet imprisoned in their sheath.

The same Sunday morning when I went in search of my sermon, the hotel was alive as bees at swarming time. There was to be a bull fight in honour of the carnival, and such a bull fight as had never been seen in Havana. Placards on the wall announced that a lady from Spain, Gloriana they called her, was to meet and slay a bull in single combat, and everyone must go and see the wonderful sight. I myself, having seen the real thing in Madrid many years ago, felt no more curiosity, and that a woman should be an actress in such a scene did not revive it. To those who went the performance was a disappointment. The bull provided turned out to be a calf of tender years. The spectators insisted that they would have a mature beast of strength and ferocity, and Gloriana when brought to the point declined the adventure.

There was a prettier scene in the evening. In the cool after nightfall the beauty and fashion of Havana turns out to stroll in the illuminated Alameda. As it was now a high festival the band was to play, and the crowd was as dense as on Exhibition nights at South Kensington. The music was equally good, and the women as graceful and well dressed. I sat for an hour or two listening under the statue of poor Queen Isabella. The image of her still stands where it was placed, though revolution has long shaken her from her throne. All is forgotten now except that she was once a Spanish sovereign, and time and distance have deodorised her memory.

CHAPTER XIX.

Hotels in Havana—Sights in the city—Cigar manufactories—West Indian industries—The Captain-General—The Jesuit college—Father Viñez—Clubs in Havana—Spanish aristocracy—Sea lodging house.

There was much to be seen in Havana, and much to think about. I regretted only that I had not been better advised in my choice of an hotel The dining saloon rang with American voices in their shrillest tones. Every table was occupied by groups of them, nor was there a sound in the room of any language but theirs. In the whole company I had not a single acquaintance. I have liked well almost every individual American that I have fallen in with and come to know. They are frank, friendly, open, and absolutely unaffected, and, like my friend at Miss Roy's in Jamaica, they take cheerful views of life, which is the highest of all recommendations. The distinctness and sharpness of utterance is tolerable and even agreeable in conversation with a single person. When a large number of them are together, all talking in a high tone, it tries the nerves and sets the teeth on edge. Nor could I escape from them in any part of the building. The gentlemen were talking politics in the hall, or lounging under the colonnade. One of them, an absolute stranger, who perhaps knew who I was, asked me abruptly for my opinion of Cardinal Newman. The ladies filled the sitting rooms; their pianos and their duets pierced the walls of my bedroom, and only ceased an hour after midnight. At five in the morning the engines began to scream at the adjoining railway station. The church bells woke at the same hour with their superfluous summons to matins which no one attended. Sleep was next to an impossibility under these hard conditions, and I wanted more and not less of it when I had the duties upon me of sightseeing. Sleep or no sleep, however, I determined that I would see what I could as long as I could keep going.

A few hundred yards off was one of the most famous of the Havana cigar manufactories. A courteous message from the manager, Señor Bances, had informed me that he would be happy to show me over it on any morning before the sun was above the roofs of the houses. I found the señor a handsome elderly gentleman, tall and lean, with Castilian dignity of manner, free and frank in all his communications, with no reserve, concealments, or insincerities. I told him that in my experience cigars were not what they had been, that the last good one which I had smoked I had bought twenty years ago from a contrabandista at Madrid. I had come to Havana to see whether I could find another equally good at the fountain head. He said that he was not at all surprised. It was the same story as at Jamaica; the consumption of cigars had increased with extreme rapidity; the area on which the finest tobacco had been grown was limited, and the expense of growing it was very great. Only a small quantity of the best cigars was now made for the market. In general the plants were heavily manured, and the flavour suffered. Leaf of coarse fibre was used for the core of the cigars, with only a fold or two wrapped round it of more delicate quality. He took me into the different rooms where the manufacture was going on. In the first were perhaps a hundred or a hundred and fifty sallow-faced young men engaged in rolling. They were all Cubans or Spaniards with the exception of a single negro; and all, I should think, under thirty. On each of the tables was one of the names with which we have grown familiar in modern cigar shops, Reynas, Regalias, Principes, and I know not how many else. The difference of material could not be great, but there was a real difference in the fineness of the make, and in the quality of the exterior leaf. The workmen were of unequal capacity and were unequally paid. The señor employed in all about 1,400; at least so I understood him.

The black field hands had eighteenpence a day. The rollers were paid by quality and quantity; a good workman doing his best could earn sixty dollars a week, an idle and indifferent one about twelve. They smoked as they rolled, and there was no check upon the consumption, the loss in this way being estimated at 40,000 dollars a year. The pay was high; but there was another side to it—the occupation was dangerous. If there were no boys in the room, there were no old men. Those who undertook it died often in two or three years. Doubtless with precaution the mortality might be diminished; but, like the needle and the scissor grinders in England, the men themselves do not wish it to be diminished. The risk enters into the wages, and they prefer a short life and a merry one.

The cigarettes, of which the varieties are as many as there are of cigars, were made exclusively by Chinese. The second room which we entered was full of them, their curious yellow faces mildly bending over their tobacco heaps. Of these there may have been a hundred. Of the general expenses of the establishment I do not venture to say anything, bewildered as I was in the labyrinthine complication of the currency, but it must certainly be enormous, and this house, the Partagas, was but one of many equally extensive in Havana alone.

The señor was most liberal. He filled my pockets with packets of excellent cigarettes; he gave me a bundle of cigars. I cannot say whether they were equal to what I bought from my contrabandista, for these may have been idealised by a grateful memory, but they were so incomparably better than any which I have been able to get in London that I was tempted to deal with him, and so far I have had no reason to repent. The boxes with which he provided me bettered the sample, and the price, duty at home included, was a third below what I should have paid in London for an article which I would rather leave unconsumed. A broker whom I fell in with insisted to me that the best cigars all went to London, that my preference for what I got from my señor was mere fancy and vanity, and that I could buy better in any shop in Regent Street. I said that he might but I couldn't, and so we left it.

I tell all this, not with the affectation of supposing that tobacco or my own taste about it can have any interest, but as an illustration of what can be done in the West Indies, and to show how immense a form of industry waits to be developed in our own islands, if people with capital and knowledge choose to set about it. Tobacco as good as the best in Cuba has been grown and can be grown in Jamaica, in St. Domingo, and probably in every one of the Antilles. 'There are dollars in those islands,' as my Yankee said, and many a buried treasure will be brought to light there when capitalists can feel assured that they will not be at the mercy of black constitutional governments.

My letter of introduction to the Captain-General was still undelivered, and as I had made use of it on landing I thought it right at least to pay my respects to the great man. The Marques M—— kindly consented to go with me and help me through the interview, being of course acquainted with him. He was at his country house, a mile out of the town. The buildings are all good in Havana. It was what it called itself, not a palace but a handsome country residence in the middle of a large well-kept garden. The viceroyalty has a fair but not extravagant income attached to it. The Captain-General receives about 8,000l. a year besides allowances. Were the balls and dinners expected of him which our poor governors are obliged to entertain their subjects with, he would not be able to make much out of it. The large fortunes which used to be brought back by the fortunate Captains-General who could connive at the slave trade were no longer attainable; those good days are gone. Public opinion therefore permits them to save their incomes. The Spaniards are not a hospitable people, or rather their notion of hospitality differs in form from ours. They are ready to dine with you themselves as often as you will ask them. Nothing in the shape of dinners is looked for from the Captain-General, and when I as a stranger suggested the possibility of such a thing as an invitation happening to me, my companion assured me that I need not be in the least alarmed. We were introduced into a well-proportioned hall, with a few marble busts in it and casts of Greek and Roman statues. Aides-de-camp and general officers were lounging about, with whom we exchanged distant civilities. After waiting for a quarter of an hour we were summoned by an official into an adjoining room and found ourselves in his Excellency's presence. He was a small gentlemanlike-looking man, out of uniform, in plain morning dress with a silk sash. He received us with natural politeness; cordiality was uncalled for, but he was perfectly gracious. He expressed his pleasure at seeing me in the island; he hoped that I should enjoy myself, and on his part would do everything in his power to make my stay agreeable. He spoke of the emancipation of the slaves and of the social state of the island with pardonable satisfaction, enquired about our own West Indies, c., and finally asked me to tell him in what way he could be of service to me. I told him that I had found such kind friends in Havana already, that I could think of little. One thing only he could do if he pleased. I had omitted to bring a passport with me, not knowing that it would be required. My position was irregular and might be inconvenient. I was indebted to my letter of introduction to his Excellency for admission into his dominions. Perhaps he would write a few words which would enable me to remain in them and go out of them when my visit was over. His Excellency said that he would instruct the Gobierno Civil to see to it, an instruction the meaning of which I too sadly understood. I was not to be allowed to escape the fine. A fresh shower followed of polite words, and with these we took ourselves away.

The afternoon was spent more instructively, perhaps more agreeably, in a different scene. The Marques M—— had been a pupil of the Jesuits. He had personal friends in the Jesuit college at Havana, especially one, Father Viñez, whose name is familiar to students of meteorological science, and who has supplemented and corrected the accepted law of storms by careful observation of West Indian hurricanes. The Jesuits were as well spoken of in Havana as the Moravians in Jamaica. Everyone had a good word for them. They alone, as I have said, took the trouble to provide the good people there with a sermon on Sundays. They alone among the Catholic clergy, though they live poorly and have no endowment, exert themselves to provide a tolerable education for the middle and upper classes. The Marques undertook that if we called we should be graciously received, and I was curious and interested. Their college had been an enormous monastery. Wherever the Spaniards went they took an army of monks with them of all the orders. The monks contrived always to house themselves handsomely. While soldiers fought and settlers planted, the monks' duty was to pray. In process of time it came to be doubted whether the monks' prayers were worth what they cost, or whether, in fact, they had ever had much effect of any kind. They have been suppressed in Spain; they have been clipped short in all the Spanish dominions, and in Havana there are now left only a handful of Dominicans, a few nuns, and these Jesuits, who have taken possession of the largest of the convents, much as a soldier-crab becomes the vigorous tenant of the shell of some lazy sea-snail. They have a college there where there are four hundred lads and young men who pay for their education; some hundreds more are taken out of charity. The Jesuits conduct the whole, and do it all unaided, on their own resources. And this is far from all that they do. They keep on a level with the age; they are men of learning; they are men of science; they are the Royal Society of Cuba. They have an observatory in the college, and the Father Viñez of whom I have spoken is in charge of it. Father Viñez was our particular object. The porter's lodge opened into a courtyard like the quadrangle of a college at Oxford. From the courtyard we turned into a narrow staircase, up which we climbed till we reached the roof, on and under which the Father had his lodgings and his observing machinery. We entered a small room, plainly furnished with a table and a few uncushioned chairs; tables and chairs, all save the Father's, littered with books and papers. Cases stood round the wall, containing self-registering instruments of the most advanced modern type, each with its paper barrel unrolling slowly under clockwork, while a pencil noted upon it the temperature of the air, the atmospheric pressure, the degree of moisture, the ozone, the electricity. In the middle, surrounded by his tools and his ticking clocks, sat the Father, middle-aged, lean and dry, with shrivelled skin and brown threadbare frock. He received my companion with a warm affectionate smile. The Marques told him that I was an Englishman who was curious about the work in which he was engaged, and he spoke to me at once with the politeness of a man of sense. After a few questions asked and answered, he took us out to a shed among the roof-tiles, where he kept his large telescope, his equatorial, and his transit instruments—not on the great scale of State-supported observatories, but with everything which was really essential. He had a laboratory, too, and a workshop, with all the recent appliances. He was a practical optician and mechanic. He managed and repaired his own machinery, observed, made his notes, and wrote his reports to the societies with which he was in correspondence, all by himself. The outfit of such an establishment, even on a moderate scale, is expensive. I said I supposed that the Government gave him a grant. 'So far from it,' he said, 'that we have to pay a duty on every instrument which we import.' 'Who, then, pays for it all?' I asked. 'The order,' he answered, quite simply.

The house, I believe, was a gift, though it cost the State nothing, having been simply seized when the monks were expelled. The order now maintains it, and more than repays the Government for their single act of generosity. At my companion's suggestion Father Viñez gave me a copy of his book on hurricanes. It contains a record of laborious journeys which he made to the scene of the devastations of the last ten years. The scientific value of the Father's work is recognised by the highest authorities, though I cannot venture even to attempt to explain what he has done. He then conducted us over the building, and showed us the libraries, dormitories, playgrounds, and the other arrangements which were made for the students. Of these we saw none, they were all out, but the long tables in the refectory were laid for afternoon tea. There was a cup of milk for each lad, with a plate of honey and a roll of bread; and supper would follow in the evening. The sleeping gallery was divided into cells, open at the top for ventilation, with bed, table, chest of drawers, and washing apparatus—all scrupulously clean. So far as I could judge, the Fathers cared more for the boys' comfort than for their own. Through an open door our conductor faintly indicated the apartment which belonged to himself. Four bare walls, a bare tiled floor, a plain pallet, with a crucifix above the pillow, was all that it contained. There was no parade of ecclesiasticism. The libraries were well furnished, but the books were chiefly secular and scientific. The chapel was unornamented; there were a few pictures, but they were simple and inoffensive. Everything was good of its kind, down to the gymnastic courts and swimming bath. The holiness was kept in the back ground. It was in the spirit and not in the body. The cost of the whole establishment was defrayed out of the payments of the richer students managed economically for the benefit of the rest, with complete indifference on the part of the Fathers to indulgence and pleasures of their own. As we took leave the Marques kissed his old master's brown hand. I rather envied him the privilege.

Something I saw of Havana society in the received sense of the word. There are many clubs there, and high play in most of them, for the Cubans are given to the roulette tables. The Union club which is the most distinguished among them, invites occasional strangers staying in the city to temporary membership as we do at the Athenæum. Here you meet Spanish grandes, who have come to Cuba to be out of reach of revolution, proud as ever and not as poor as you might expect; and when you ask who they are you hear the great familiar names of Spanish history. I was introduced to the president—young, handsome, and accomplished. I was startled to learn that he was the head of the old house of Sandoval. The house of Columbus ought to be there also, for there is still a Christophe Colon, the direct linear representative of the discoverer, disguised under the title of the Duque de Veragua. A perpetual pension of 20,000 dollars a year was granted to the great Christophe and his heirs for ever as a charge on the Cuban revenue. It has been paid to the family through all changes of dynasty and forms of government, and is paid to them still. But the Duque resides in Spain, and the present occupation of him, I was informed, is the breeding and raising bulls for the Plaza de Toros at Seville.

Thus, every way, my stay was made agreeable to me. There were breakfasts and dinners and introductions. Don G—— and his brother were not fine gentlemen only, but were men of business and deeply engaged in the active life of the place. The American consul was a conspicuous figure at these entertainments. America may not find it her interest to annex these islands, but since she ordered the French out of Mexico, and the French obeyed, she is universally felt on that side of the Atlantic to be the supreme arbiter of all their fates. Her consuls are thus persons of consequence. The Cubans like the Americans well. The commercial treaty which was offered to our islands by the United States would have been accepted eagerly by the Spaniards. To them, the Americans have, as yet, not been equally liberal, but an arrangement will soon be completed. They say that they have hills of solid iron in the island and mountains of copper with fifty per cent. of virgin ore in them waiting for the Americans to develop. The present administration would swallow up in taxation the profits of the most promising enterprise that ever was undertaken, but the metals are there, and will come one day into working. The consul was a swift peremptory man who knew his own mind at any rate. Between his 'Yes, sir,' and his 'No, sir,' you were at no loss for his meaning. He told me a story of a 'nigger' officer with whom he had once got into conversation at Hayti. He had inquired why they let so fine an island run to waste? Why did they not cultivate it? The dusky soldier laid his hand upon his breast and waved his hand. 'Ah,' he said, 'that might do for English or Germans or Americans; we of the Latin race have higher things to occupy us.'

I liked the consul well. I could not say as much for his countrymen and countrywomen at my hotel. Individually I dare say they would have been charming; collectively they drove me to distraction. Space and time had no existence for them; they and their voices were heard in all places and at all hours. The midnight bravuras at the pianos mixed wildly in my broken dreams. The Marques M—— wished to take me with him to his country seat and show me his sugar plantations. Nothing could have been more delightful, but with want of sleep and the constant racket I found myself becoming unwell. In youth and strength one can defy the foul fiend and bid him do his worst; in age one finds it wiser to get out of the way.

On the sea, seven miles from Havana, and connected with it by a convenient railway, at a place called Vedado, I found a lodging house kept by a Frenchman (the best cook in Cuba) with a German wife. The situation was so attractive, and the owners of it so attentive, that quiet people went often into 'retreat' there. There were delicious rooms, airy and solitary as I could wish. The sea washed the coral rock under the windows. There were walks wild as if there was no city within a thousand miles—up the banks of lonely rivers, over open moors, or among inclosures where there were large farming establishments with cattle and horses and extensive stables and sheds. There was a village and a harbour where fishing people kept their boats and went out daily with their nets and lines—blacks and whites living and working side by side. I could go where I pleased without fear of interference or question. Only I was warned to be careful of the dogs, large and dangerous, descendants of the famous Cuban bloodhounds, which are kept everywhere to guard the yards and houses. These beasts were really dangerous, and had to be avoided. The shore was of inexhaustible interest. It was a level shelf of coral rock extending for many miles and littered over with shells and coral branches which had been flung up by the surf. I had hoped for bathing. In the open water it is not to be thought of on account of the sharks, but baths have been cut in the rock all along that part of the coast at intervals of half a mile; deep square basins with tunnels connecting them with the sea, up which the waves run clear and foaming. They are within inclosures, roofed over to keep out the sun, and with attendants regularly present. Art and nature combined never made more charming pools; the water clear as sapphire, aerated by the constant inrush of the foaming breakers, and so warm that you could lie in it without a chill for hours. Alas! that I could but look at them and execrate the precious Government which forbade me their use. So severe a tax is laid on these bathing establishments that the owners can only afford to keep them open during the three hottest months in the year, when the demand is greatest.

In the evenings people from Havana would occasionally come down to dine as we go to Greenwich, being attracted partly by the air and partly by my host's reputation.

There was a long verandah under which tables were laid out, and there were few nights on which one or more parties were not to be seen there. Thus I encountered several curious specimens of Cuban humanity, and on one of my runs up to Havana I met again the cigar broker who had so roughly challenged my judgment. He was an original and rather diverting man; I should think a Jew. Whatever he was he fell upon me again and asked me scornfully whether I supposed that the cigars which I had bought of Señor Bances were anything out of the way. I said that they suited my taste and that was enough. 'Ah,' he replied, 'Cada loco con su tema. Every fool had his opinion.' 'I am the loco (idiot), then,' said I, 'but that again is matter of opinion.' He spoke of Cuba and professed to know all about it. 'Can you tell me, then,' said I, 'why the Cubans hate the Spaniards?' 'Why do the Irish hate the English?' he answered. I said it was not an analogous case. Cubans and Spaniards were of the same breed and of the same creed. 'That is nothing,' he replied; 'the Americans will have both Cuba and Ireland before long.' I said I thought the Americans were too wise to meddle with either. If they did, however, I imagined that on our own side of the Atlantic we should have something to say on the subject before Ireland was taken from us. He laughed good-humouredly. 'Is it possible, sir,' he said, 'that you live in England and are so absolutely ignorant?' I laughed too. He was a strange creature, and would have made an excellent character in a novel.

Don G—— or his brother came down occasionally to see how I was getting on and to talk philosophy and history. Other gentlemen came, and the favourite subject of conversation was Spanish administration. One of them told me this story as an illustration of it. His father was the chief partner in a bank; a clerk absconded, taking 50,000 dollars with him; he had been himself sent in pursuit of the man, overtook him with the money still in his possession, and recovered it. With this he ought to have been contented, but he tried to have the offender punished. The clerk replied to the criminal charge by a counter-charge against the house. It was absurd in itself, but he found that a suit would grow out of it which would swallow more than the 50,000 dollars, and finally he bribed the judge to allow him to drop the prosecution. Cosas de España; it lies in the breed. Guzman de Alfarache was robbed of his baggage by a friend. The facts were clear, the thief was caught with Guzman's clothes on his back; but he had influential friends—he was acquitted. He prosecuted Guzman for a false accusation, got a judgment and ruined him.

The question was, whether if the Cubans could make themselves independent there would be much improvement. The want in Cuba just now, as in a good many other places, is the want of some practical religion which insists on moral duty. A learned English judge was trying a case one day, when there seemed some doubt about the religious condition of one of the witnesses. The clerk of the court retired with him to ascertain what it really was, and returned radiant almost immediately, saying, 'All right, my lord. Knows he'll be damned—competent witness—knows he'll be damned.' That is really the whole of the matter. If a man is convinced that if he does wrong he will infallibly be punished for it he has then 'a saving faith.' This, unfortunately, is precisely the conviction which modern forms of religion produce hardly anywhere. The Cubans are Catholics, and hear mass and go to confession; but confession and the mass between them are enough for the consciences of most of them, and those who think are under the influence of the modern spirit, to which all things are doubtful. Some find comfort in Mr. Herbert Spencer. Some regard Christianity as a myth or poem, which had passed in unconscious good faith into the mind of mankind, and there might have remained undisturbed as a beneficent superstition had not Protestantism sprung up and insisted on flinging away everything which was not literal and historical fact. Historical fact had really no more to do with it than with the stories of Prometheus or the siege of Troy. The end was that no bottom of fact could be found, and we were all set drifting.

Notably too I observed among serious people there, what I have observed in other places, the visible relief with which they begin to look forward to extinction after death. When the authority is shaken on which the belief in a future life rests, the question inevitably recurs. Men used to pretend that the idea of annihilation was horrible to them; now they regard the probability of it with calmness, if not with actual satisfaction. One very interesting Cuban gentleman said to me that life would be very tolerable if one was certain that death would be the end of it. The theological alternatives were equally unattractive; Tartarus was an eternity of misery, and the Elysian Fields an eternity of ennui.

There is affectation in the talk of men, and one never knows from what they say exactly what is in their mind. I have often thought that the real character of a people shows itself nowhere with more unconscious completeness than in their cemeteries. Philosophise as we may, few of us are deliberately insincere in the presence of death; and in the arrangements which we make for the reception of those who have been dear to us, and in the lines which we inscribe upon their monuments, we show what we are in ourselves perhaps more than what they were whom we commemorate. The parish churchyard is an emblem and epitome of English country life; London reflects itself in Brompton and Kensal Green, and Paris in Père la Chaise. One day as I was walking I found myself at the gate of the great suburban cemetery of Havana. It was enclosed within high walls; the gateway was a vast arch of brown marble, beautiful and elaborately carved. Within there was a garden simply and gracefully laid out with trees and shrubs and flowers in borders. The whole space inclosed may have been ten acres, of which half was assigned to those who were contented with a mere mound of earth to mark where they lay; the rest was divided into family vaults covered with large white marble slabs, separate headstones marking individuals for whom a particular record was required, and each group bearing the name of the family the members of which were sleeping there. The peculiarity of the place was the absence of inscriptions. There was a name and date, with E.P.D.—'en paz descansa'[15]—or E.G.E.—'en gracia está'[16]—and that seemed all that was needed. The virtues of the departed and the grief of the survivors were taken for granted in all but two instances. There may have been more, but I could find only these.

One was in Latin:

AD COELITES EVOCATÆ UXORI EXIMÆ IGNATIUS.

Ignatius to his admirable wife who has been called up to heaven.

The other was in Spanish verse, and struck me as a graceful imitation of the old manner of Cervantes and Lope de Vega. The design on the monument was of a girl hanging an immortelle upon a cross. The tomb was of a Caridad del Monte, and the lines were:

Bendita Caridad, las que piadosa
Su mano vierte en la funérea losa
Son flores recogidas en el suelo,
Mas con su olor perfumaián el cielo.

It is dangerous for anyone to whom a language is only moderately familiar to attempt an appreciation of elegiac poetry, the effect of which, like the fragrance of a violet, must rather be perceived than accounted for. He may imagine what is not there, for a single word ill placed or ill chosen may spoil the charm, and of this a foreigner can never entirely judge. He may know what each word means, but he cannot know the associations of it. Here, however, is a translation in which the sense is preserved, though the aroma is gone.

The flowers which thou, oh Blessed Charity,
With pious hand hast twined in funeral wreath,
Although on earthly soil they gathered be,
Will sweeten heaven with their perfumed breath.

The flowers, I suppose, were the actions of Caridad's own innocent life, which she was offering on the cross of Christ; but one never can be sure that one has caught the exact sentiment of emotional verse in a foreign language. The beauty lies in an undefinable sweetness which rises from the melody of the words, and in a translation disappears altogether. Who or what Caridad del Monte was, whether a young girl whom somebody had loved, or an allegoric and emblematic figure, I had no one to tell me.

I must not omit one acquaintance which I was fortunate enough to make while staying at my seaside lodging. There appeared there one day, driven out of Havana like myself by the noise, an American ecclesiastic with a friend who addressed him as 'My lord.' By the ring and purple, as well as by the title, I perceived that he was a bishop. His friend was his chaplain, and from their voices I gathered that they were both by extraction Irish. The bishop had what is called a 'clergy-man's throat,' and had come from the States in search of a warmer climate. They kept entirely to themselves, but from the laughter and good-humour they were evidently excellent company for one another, and wanted no other. I rather wished than hoped that accident might introduce me to them. Even in Cuba the weather is uncertain. One day there came a high wind from the sea; the waves roared superbly upon the rocks, flying over them in rolling cataracts. I never saw foam so purely white or waves so transparent. As a spectacle it was beautiful, and the shore became a museum of coralline curiosities. Indoors the effect was less agreeable. Windows rattled and shutters broke from their fastenings and flew to and fro. The weathercock on the house-top creaked as he was whirled about, and the verandahs had to be closed, and the noise was like a prolonged thunder peal. The second day the wind became a cyclone, and chilly as if it came from the pole. None of us could stir out. The bishop suffered even more than I did; he walked up and down on the sheltered side of the house wrapped in a huge episcopalian cloak. I think he saw that I was sorry for him, as I really was. He spoke to me; he said he had felt the cold less in America when the thermometer marked 25° below zero. It was not much, but the silence was broken. Common suffering made a kind of link between us. After this he dropped an occasional gracious word as he passed, and one morning he came and sat by me and began to talk on subjects of extreme interest. Chiefly he insisted on the rights of conscience and the tenderness for liberty of thought which had always been shown by the Church of Rome. He had been led to speak of it by the education question which has now become a burning one in the American Union. The Church, he said, never had interfered, and never could or would interfere, with any man's conscientious scruples. Its own scruples, therefore, ought to be respected. The American State schools were irreligious, and Catholic parents were unwilling to allow their children to attend them. They had established schools of their own, and they supported them by subscriptions among themselves. In these schools the boys and girls learnt everything which they could learn in the State schools, and they learnt to be virtuous besides. They were thus discharging to the full every duty which the State could claim of them, and the State had no right to tax them in addition for the maintenance of institutions of which they made no use, and of the principles of which they disapproved. There were now eight millions of Catholics in the Union. In more than one state they had an actual majority; and they intended to insist that as long as their children came up to the present educational standard, they should no longer be compelled to pay a second education tax to the Government. The struggle, he admitted, would be a severe one, but the Catholics had justice on their side, and would fight on till they won.

In democracies the majority is to prevail, and if the control of education falls within the province of each separate state government, it is not easy to see on what ground the Americans will be able to resist, or how there can be a struggle at all where the Catholic vote is really the largest. The presence of the Catholic Church in a democracy is the real anomaly. The principle of the Church is authority resting on a divine commission; the principle of democracy is the will of the people; and the Church in the long run will have as hard a battle to fight with the divine right of the majority of numbers as she had with the divine right of the Hohenstauffens and the Plantagenets. She is adroit in adapting herself to circumstances, and, like her emblem the fish, she changes her colour with that of the element in which she swims. No doubt she has a strong position in this demand and will know how to use it.

But I was surprised to hear even a Catholic bishop insist that his Church had always paid so much respect to the rights of conscience. I had been taught to believe that in the days of its power the Church had not been particularly tender towards differences of opinion. Fire and sword had been used freely enough as long as fire and sword were available. I hinted my astonishment. The bishop said the Church had been slandered; the Church had never in a single instance punished any man merely for conscientious error. Protestants had falsified history. Protestants read their histories, Catholics read theirs, and the Catholic version was the true one. The separate governments of Europe had no doubt been cruel. In France, Spain, the Low Countries, even in England, heretics had been harshly dealt with, but it was the governments that had burnt and massacred all those people, not the Church. The governments were afraid of heresy because it led to revolution. The Church had never shed any blood at all; the Church could not, for she was forbidden to do so by her own canons. If she found a man obstinate in unbelief, she cut him off from the communion and handed him over to the secular arm. If the secular arm thought fit to kill him, the Church's hands were clear of it.

PORT AU PRINCE, HAYTI.

PORT AU PRINCE, HAYTI.

So Pilate washed his hands; so the judge might say he never hanged a murderer; the execution was the work of the hangman. The bishop defied me to produce an instance in which in Rome, when the temporal power was with the pope and the civil magistrates were churchmen, there had ever been an execution for heresy. I mentioned Giordano Bruno, whom the bishop had forgotten; but we agreed not to quarrel, and I could not admire sufficiently the hardihood and the ingenuity of his argument. The English bishops and abbots passed through parliament the Act de hæretico comburendo, but they were acting as politicians, not as churchmen. The Spanish Inquisition burnt freely and successfully. The inquisitors were archbishops and bishops, but the Holy Office was a function of the State. When Gregory XIII. struck his medal in commemoration of the massacre of St. Bartholomew he was then only the secular ruler of Rome, and therefore fallible and subject to sin like other mortals. The Church has many parts to play; her stage wardrobe is well furnished, and her actors so well instructed in their parts that they believe themselves in all that they say. The bishop was speaking no more than his exact conviction. He told me that in the Middle Ages secular princes were bound by their coronation oath to accept the pope as the arbiter of all quarrels between them. I asked where this oath was, or what were the terms of it? The words, he said, were unimportant. The fact was certain, and down to the fatal schism of the sixteenth century the pope had always been allowed to arbitrate, and quarrels had been prevented. I could but listen and wonder. He admitted that he had read one set of books and I another, as it was clear that he must have done.

In the midst of our differences we found we had many points of agreement. We agreed that the breaking down of Church authority at the Reformation had been a fatal disaster; that without a sense of responsibility to a supernatural power, human beings would sink into ingenious apes, that human society would become no more than a congregation of apes, and that with differences of opinion and belief, that sense was becoming more and more obscured. So long as all serious men held the same convictions, and those convictions were embodied in the law, religion could speak with authority. The authority being denied or shaken, the fact itself became uncertain. The notion that everybody had a right to think as he pleased was felt to be absurd in common things. In every practical art or science the ignorant submitted to be guided by those who were better instructed than themselves. Why should they be left to their private judgment on subjects where to go wrong was the more dangerous. All this was plain sailing. The corollary that if it is to retain its influence the Church must not teach doctrines which outrage the common sense of mankind as Luther led half Europe to believe that the Church was doing in the sixteenth century, we agreed that we would not dispute about. But I was interested to see that the leopard had not changed its spots, that it merely readjusted its attitudes to suit the modern taste, and that if it ever recovered its power it would claw and scratch in the old way. Rome, like Pilate, may protest its innocence of the blood which was spilt in its name and in its interests. Did that tender and merciful court ever suggest to those prelates who passed the Act in England for the burning of heretics that they were transgressing the sacred rights of conscience? Did it reprove the Inquisition or send a mild remonstrance to Philip II.? The eyes of those who are willing to be blinded will see only what they desire to see.

FOOTNOTES:

[15]

He rests in peace.

[16]

He is now in grace.

CHAPTER XX.

Return to Havana—The Spaniards in Cuba—Prospects—American influence—Future of the West Indies—English rumours—Leave Cuba—The harbour at night—The Bahama Channel—Hayti—Port au Prince—The black republic—West Indian history.

The air and quiet of Vedado (so my retreat was called) soon set me up again, and I was able to face once more my hotel and its Americans. I did not attempt to travel in Cuba, nor was it necessary for my purpose. I stayed a few days longer at Havana. I went to operas and churches; I sailed about the harbour in boats, the boatmen, all of them, not negroes, as in the Antilles, but emigrants from the old country, chiefly Gallicians. I met people of all sorts, among the rest a Spanish officer—a major of engineers—who, if he lives, may come to something. Major D—— took me over the fortifications, showed me the interior lines of the Moro, and their latest specimens of modern artillery. The garrison are, of course, Spanish regiments made of home-bred Castilians, as I could not fail to recognise when I heard any of them speak. There are certain words of common use in Spain powerful as the magic formulas of enchanters over the souls of men. You hear them everywhere in the Peninsula; at cafe's, at tables d'hôte, and in private conversation. They are a part of the national intellectual equipment. Either from prudery or because they are superior to old-world superstitions, the Cubans have washed these expressions out of their language; but the national characteristics are preserved in the army, and the spell does not lose its efficacy because the islanders disbelieve in it. I have known a closed post office in Madrid, where the clerk was deaf to polite entreaty, blown open by an oath as by a bomb shell. A squad of recruits in the Moro, who were lying in the shade under a tree, neglected to rise as an officer went by. 'Saludad, C——o!' he thundered out, and they bounded to their feet as if electrified.

On the whole Havana was something to have seen. It is the focus and epitome of Spanish dominion in those seas, and I was forced to conclude that it was well for Cuba that the English attempts to take possession of it had failed. Be the faults of their administration as heavy as they are alleged to be, the Spaniards have done more to Europeanise their islands than we have done with ours. They have made Cuba Spanish—Trinidad, Dominica, St. Lucia, Grenada have never been English at all, and Jamaica and Barbadoes are ceasing to be English. Cuba is a second home to the Spaniards, a permanent addition to their soil. We are as birds of passage, temporary residents for transient purposes, with no home in our islands at all. Once we thought them worth fighting for, and as long as it was a question of ships and cannon we made ourselves supreme rulers of the Caribbean Sea; yet the French and Spaniards will probably outlive us there. They will remain perhaps as satellites of the United States, or in some other confederacy, or in recovered strength of their own; we, in a generation or two, if the causes now in operation continue to work as they are now working, shall have disappeared from the scene. In Cuba there is a great Spanish population; Martinique and Guadaloupe are parts of France; to us it seems a matter of indifference whether we keep our islands or abandon them, and we leave the remnants of our once precious settlements to float or drown as they can. Australia and Canada take care of themselves; we expect our West Indies to do the same, careless of the difference of circumstance. We no longer talk of cutting our colonies adrift; the tone of public opinion is changed, and no one dares to advocate openly the desertion of the least important of them. But the neglect and indifference continue. We will not govern them effectively ourselves: our policy, so far as we have any policy, is to extend among them the principles of self-government, and self-government can only precipitate our extinction there as completely as we know that it would do in India if we were wild enough to venture the plunge. There is no enchantment in self-government which will make people love each other when they are indifferent or estranged. It can only force them into sharper collision.

The opinion in Cuba was, and is, that America is the residuary legatee of all the islands, Spanish and English equally, and that she will be forced to take charge of them in the end whether she likes it or not. Spain governs unjustly and corruptly; the Cubans will not rest till they are free from her, and if once independent they will throw themselves on American protection.

We will not govern our islands at all, but leave them to drift. Jamaica and the Antilles, given over to the negro majorities, can only become like Hayti and St. Domingo; and the nature of things will hardly permit so fair a part of the earth which has been once civilised and under white control to fall back into barbarism.

To England the loss of the West Indies would not itself be serious; but in the life of nations discreditable failures are not measured by their immediate material consequences. To allow a group of colonies to slide out of our hands because we could not or would not provide them with a tolerable government would be nothing less than a public disgrace. It would be an intimation to all the world that we were unable to maintain any longer the position which our fathers had made for us; and when the unravelling of the knitted fabric of the Empire has once begun the process will be a rapid one.

'But what would you do?' I am asked impatiently. 'We send out peers or gentlemen against whose character no direct objection can be raised; we assist them with local councils partly chosen by the people themselves. We send out bishops, we send out missionaries, we open schools. What can we do more? We cannot alter the climate, we cannot make planters prosper when sugar will not pay, we cannot convert black men into whites, we cannot force the blacks to work for the whites when they do not wish to work for them. "Governing," as you call it, will not change the natural conditions of things. You can suggest no remedy, and mere fault-finding is foolish and mischievous.'

I might answer a good many things. Government cannot do everything, but it can do something, and there is a difference between governors against whom there is nothing to object and men of special and marked capacity. There is a difference between governors whose hands are tied by local councils and whose feet are tied by instructions from home, and a governor with a free hand and a wise head left to take his own measures on the spot. I presume that no one can seriously expect that an orderly organised nation can be made out of the blacks, when, in spite of your schools and missionaries, sixty per cent. of the children now born among them are illegitimate. You can do for the West Indies, I repeat over and over again, what you do for the East; you can establish a firm authoritative government which will protect the blacks in their civil rights and protect the whites in theirs. You cannot alter the climate, it is true, or make the soil more fertile. Already it is fertile as any in the earth, and the climate is admirable for the purposes for which it is needed. But you can restore confidence in the stability of your tenure, you can give courage to the whites who are on the spot to remain there, and you can tempt capital and enterprise to venture there which now seek investments elsewhere. By keeping the rule in your own hands you will restore the white population to their legitimate influence; the blacks will again look up to them and respect them as they ought to do. This you can do, and it will cost you nothing save a little more pains in the selection of the persons whom you are to trust with powers analogous to those which you grant to your provincial governors in the Indian peninsula.

A preliminary condition of this, as of all other real improvements, is one, however, which will hardly be fulfilled. Before a beginning can be made, a conviction is wanted that life has other objects besides present interest and convenience; and very few of us indeed have at the bottom of our hearts any such conviction at all. We can talk about it in fine language—no age ever talked more or better—but we don't believe in it; we believe only in professing to believe, which soothes our vanity and does not interfere with our actions. From fine words no harvests grow. The negroes are well disposed to follow and obey any white who will be kind and just to them, and in such following and obedience their only hope of improvement lies. The problem is to create a state of things under which Englishmen of vigour and character will make their homes among them. Annexation to the United States would lead probably to their extermination at no very distant time. The Antilles are small, and the fate of the negroes there might be no better than the fate of the Caribs. The Americans are not a people who can be trifled with; no one knows it better than the negroes. They fear them. They prefer infinitely the mild rule of England, and under such a government as we might provide if we cared to try, the whole of our islands might become like the Moravian settlement in Jamaica, and the black nature, which has rather degenerated than improved in these late days of licence, might be put again in the way of regeneration. The process would be slow—your seedlings in a plantation hang stationary year after year, but they do move at last. We cannot disown our responsibility for these poor adopted brothers of ours. We send missionaries into

Africa to convert them to a better form of religion; why should the attempt seem chimerical to convert them practically to a higher purpose in our own colonies?

The reader will be weary of a sermon the points of which have been reiterated so often. I might say that he requires to have the lesson impressed upon him—that it is for his good that I insist upon it, and not for my own. But this is the common language of all preachers, and it is not found to make the hearers more attentive. I will not promise to say no more upon the subject, for it was forced upon me at every moment and point of my journey. I am arriving near the end, however, and if he has followed so far, he will perhaps go on with me to the conclusion. I had three weeks to give to Havana; they were fast running out, and it was time for me to be going. Strange stories, too, came from England, which made me uneasy till I knew how they were set in circulation. One day Mr. Gladstone was said to have gone mad, and the Queen the next. The Russians were about to annex Afghanistan. Our troops had been cut to pieces in Burmah. Something was going wrong with us every day in one corner of the world or another. I found at last that the telegraphic intelligence was supplied to the Cuban newspapers from New York, that the telegraph clerks there were generally Irish, and their facts were the creation of their wishes. I was to return to Jamaica in the same vessel which had brought me from it. She had been down to the isthmus, and was to call at Havana on her way back. The captain's most English face was a welcome sight to me when he appeared one evening at dinner. He had come to tell me that he was to sail early on the following morning, and I arranged to go on board with him the same night. The Captain-General had not forgotten to instruct the Gobierno Civil to grant me an exeat regno. I do not know that I gained much by his intercession, for without it I should hardly have been detained indefinitely, and as it was I had to pay more dollars than I liked to part with. The necessary documents, however, had been sent through the British consul, and I was free to leave when I pleased. I paid my bill at the hotel, which was not after all an extravagant one, cleared my pocket-book of the remainder of the soiled and tattered paper which is called money, and does duty for it down to a half-penny, and with my distinguished friend Don G——, the real acquisition which I had made in coming to his country, and who would not leave me till I was in the boat, I drove away to the wharf.

It was a still, lovely, starlight night. The moon had risen over the hills, and was shining brightly on the roofs and towers of the city, and on the masts and spars of the vessels which were riding in the harbour. There was not a ripple on the water, and stars and city, towers and ships, stood inverted on the surface pointing downward as into a second infinity. The charm was unfortunately interfered with by odours worse than Coleridge found at Cologne and cursed in rhyme. The drains of Havana, like orange blossom, give off their most fragrant vapours in the dark hours. I could well believe Don G——'s saying, that but for the natural healthiness of the place, they would all die of it like poisoned flies. We had to cut our adieus short, for the mouth of some horrid sewer was close to us. In the boat I did not escape; the water smelt horribly as it was stirred by the oars, charged as it was with three centuries of pollution, and the phosphorescent light shone with a sickly, sulphur-like brilliance. One could have fancied that one was in Charon's boat and was crossing Acheron. When I reached the steamer I watched from the deck the same ghost-like phenomenon which is described by Tom Cringle. A fathom deep, in the ship's shadow, some shark or other monster sailed slowly by in an envelope of spectral lustre. When he stopped his figure disappeared, when he moved on again it was like the movement of a streak of blue flame. Such a creature did not seem as if it could belong to our familiar sunlit ocean.

The state of the harbour is not creditable to the Spanish Government, and I suppose will not be improved till there is some change of dynasty. All that can be said for it is that it is not the worst in these seas. Our ship had just come from the Canal, and had brought the latest news from thence.

But the miscalculations of the work to be done and of the expense of doing it are now notorious to all the world. The alternatives are to abandon an enterprise so splendid in conception, so disastrous in the execution, or to raise and spend fresh tens of millions to follow those that are gone with no certain prospect of success after all. The saddest part of the story will be soonest forgotten—the frightful consumption of human life in those damp and pestilential jungles. M. Lesseps having made his name immortal at Suez, aspired at eclipsing his first achievement, by a second yet more splendidly ambitious, at a time of life when common men are content to retire upon their laurels. He deserves and will receive an unstinted admiration for his energy and his enthusiasm. But his countrymen who have so zealously supported him will be rewarded with no dividend upon their shares, even if the two oceans are eventually united, and no final success can be looked for in the bold projector's life time.

At dawn we swept out under the Moro, and away once more into the free fresh open sea. We had come down on the south side of the island, we returned by the north up the old Bahama Channel where Drake died on his way home from his last unsuccessful expedition—Lope de Vega singing a pæan over the end of the great 'dragon.' Fresh passengers brought fresh talk. There was a clever young Jamaican on board returning from a holiday; he had the spirits of youth about him, and would have pleased my American who never knew good come of despondency. He had hopes for his country, but they rested, like those of every sensible man that I met, on an inability to believe that there would be further advances in the direction of political liberty. A revised constitution, he said, could issue only in fresh Gordon riots and fresh calamities. He had been travelling in the Southern States. He had seen the state of Mississippi deserted by the whites, and falling back into a black wilderness. He had seen South Carolina, which had narrowly escaped ruin under a black and carpet-bagger legislature, and had recovered itself under the steady determination of the Americans that the civil war was not to mean the domination of negro over white. The danger was greater in the English islands than in either of these states, from the enormous disproportion of numbers. The experiment could be ventured only under a high census and a restricted franchise. But the experience of all countries showed that these limited franchises were invidious and could not be maintained, the end was involved in the beginning, and he trusted that prudent counsels would prevail. We had gone too far already.

On board also there was a traveller from a Manchester house of business, who gave me a more flourishing account than I expected of the state of our trade, not so much with the English islands as with the Spaniards in Cuba and on the mainland. His own house, he said, had a large business with Havana; twenty firms in the north of England were competing there, and all were doing well. The Spanish Americans on the west side of the continent were good customers, with the exception of the Mexicans, who were energetic and industrious, and manufactured for their own consumption. These modern Aztecs were skilful workmen, nimble-fingered and inventive. Wages were low, but they were contented with them. Mexico, I was surprised to hear from him, was rising fast into prosperity. Whether human life was any safer then than it was a few years ago, he did not tell me.

Amidst talk and chess and occasional whist after nightfall when reading became difficult, we ran along with smooth seas, land sometimes in sight, with shoals on either side of us.

We were to have one more glimpse of Hayti; we were to touch at Port au Prince, the seat of government of the successors of Toussaint. If beauty of situation could mould human character, the inhabitants of Port au Prince might claim to be the first of mankind. St. Domingo or Española, of which Hayti is the largest division, was the earliest island discovered by Columbus and the finest in the Caribbean Ocean. It remained Spanish, as I have already said, for 200 years, when Hayti was taken by the French buccaneers, and made over by them to Louis XIV. The French kept it till the Revolution. They built towns; they laid out farms and sugar fields; they planted coffee all over the island, where it now grows wild.' Vast herds of cattle roamed over the mountains; splendid houses rose over the rich savannahs. The French Church put out its strength; there were churches and priests in every parish; there were monasteries and nunneries for the religious orders. So firm was the hold that they had gained that Hayti, like Cuba, seemed to have been made a part of the old world, and as civilised as France itself. But French civilisation became itself electric. The Revolution came, and the reign of Liberty. The blacks took arms; they surprised the plantations; they made a clean sweep of the whole French population. Yellow fever swept away the armies which were sent to avenge the massacre, and France being engaged in annexing Europe had no leisure to despatch more. The island being thus derelict, Spain and England both tried their hand to recover it, but failed from the same cause, and a black nation, with a republican constitution and a population perhaps of about a million and a half of pure-blood negroes, has since been in unchallenged possession, and has arrived at the condition which has been described to us by Sir Spenser St. John. Republics which begin with murder and plunder do not come to much good in this world. Hayti has passed through many revolutions, and is no nearer than at first to stability. The present president, M. Salomon, who was long a refugee in Jamaica, came into power a few years back by a turn of the wheel. He was described to me as a peremptory gentleman who made quick work with his political opponents. His term of office having nearly expired, he had re-elected himself shortly before for another seven years and was prepared to maintain his right by any measures which he might think expedient. He had a few regiments of soldiers, who, I was told, were devoted to him, and a fleet consisting of two gunboats commanded by an American officer, to whom he chiefly owed his security.

We had steamed along the Hayti coast all one afternoon, underneath a high range of hills which used to be the hunting ground of the buccaneers. We had passed their famous Tortugas[17] without seeing them. Towards evening we entered the long channel between Gonaive island and the mainland, going slowly that we might not arrive at Port au Prince before daylight. It was six in the morning when the anchor rattled down, and I went on deck to look about me. We were at the head of a fiord rather broader than those in Norway, but very like them—wooded mountains rising on either side of us, an open valley in front, and on the rich level soil washed down by the rains and deposited along the shore, the old French and now President Salomon's capital. Palms and oranges and other trees were growing everywhere among the houses giving the impression of graceful civilisation. Directly before us were three or four wooded islets which form a natural breakwater, and above them were seen the masts of the vessels which were lying in the harbour behind. Close to where we were brought up lay the 'Canada,' an English frigate, and about a quarter of a mile from her an American frigate of about the same size, with the stars and stripes conspicuously flying. We have had some differences of late with the Hayti authorities, and the satisfaction which we asked for having been refused or delayed, a man-of-war had been sent to ask redress in more peremptory terms. The town lay under her guns; the president's ships, which she might perhaps have seized as a security, had been taken out of sight into shallow water, where she could not follow them. The Americans have no particular rights in Hayti, and are as little liked as we are, but they are feared, and they do not allow any business of a serious kind to go on in those waters without knowing what it is about. Perhaps the president's admiral of the station being an American may have had something to do with their presence. Anyway, there the two ships were lying when I came up from below, their hulks and spars outlined picturesquely against the steep wooded shores. The air was hot and steamy; fishing vessels with white sails were drifting slowly about the glassy water. Except for the heat and a black officer of the customs in uniform, and his boat and black crew alongside, I could have believed myself off Mölde or some similar Norwegian town, so like everything seemed, even to the colour of the houses.

We were to stay some hours. After breakfast we landed. I had seen Jacmel, and therefore thought myself prepared for the worst which I should find. Jacmel was an outlying symptom; Port au Prince was the central ulcer. Long before we came to shore there came off whiffs, not of drains as at Havana, but of active dirt fermenting in the sunlight. Calling our handkerchiefs to our help and looking to our feet carefully, we stepped up upon the quay and walked forward as judiciously as we could. With the help of stones we crossed a shallow ditch, where rotten fish, vegetables, and other articles were lying about promiscuously, and we came on what did duty for a grand parade.

We were in a Paris of the gutter, with boulevards and places, fiacres and crimson parasols. The boulevards were littered with the refuse of the houses and were foul as pigsties, and the ladies under the parasols were picking their way along them in Parisian boots and silk dresses. I saw a fiacre broken down in a black pool out of which a blacker ladyship was scrambling. Fever breeds so prodigally in that pestilential squalor that 40,000 people were estimated to have died of it in a single year.

There were shops and stores and streets, men and women in tawdry European costume, and officers on horseback with a tatter of lace and gilding. We passed up the principal avenue, which opened on the market place. Above the market was the cathedral, more hideous than even the Mormon temple at Salt Lake. It was full of ladies; the rank, beauty, and fashion of Port au Prince were at their morning mass, for they are Catholics with African beliefs underneath. They have a French clergy, an archbishop and bishop, paid miserably but still subsisting; subsisting not as objects of reverence at all, as they are at Dominica, but as the humble servants and ministers of black society. We English are in bad favour just now; no wonder, with the guns of the 'Canada' pointed at the city; but the chief complaint is on account of Sir Spenser St. John's book, which they cry out against with a degree of anger which is the surest evidence of its truth. It would be unfair even to hint at the names or stations of various persons who gave me information about the condition of the place and people. Enough that those who knew well what they were speaking about assured me that Hayti was the most ridiculous caricature of civilisation in the whole world. Doubtless the whites there are not disinterested witnesses; for they are treated as they once treated the blacks. They can own no freehold property, and exist only on tolerance. They are called 'white trash.' Black dukes and marquises drive over them in the street and swear at them, and they consider it an invasion of the natural order of things. If this was the worst, or even if the dirt and the disease was the worst, it might be borne with, for the whites might go away if they pleased, and they pay the penalty themselves for choosing to be there. But this is not the worst. Immorality is so universal that it almost ceases to be a fault, for a fault implies an exception, and in Hayti it is the rule. Young people make experiment of one another before they will enter into any closer connection. So far they are no worse than in our own English islands, where the custom is equally general; but behind the immorality, behind the religiosity, there lies active and alive the horrible revival of the West African superstitions; the serpent worship, and the child sacrifice, and the cannibalism. There is no room to doubt it. A missionary assured me that an instance of it occurred only a year ago within his own personal knowledge. The facts are notorious; a full account was published in one of the local newspapers, and the only result was that the president imprisoned the editor for exposing his country. A few years ago persons guilty of these infamies were tried and punished; now they are left alone, because to prosecute and convict them would be to acknowledge the truth of the indictment.

In this, as in all other communities, there is a better side as well as a worse. The better part is ashamed of the condition into which the country has fallen; rational and well-disposed Haytians would welcome back the French but for an impression, whether well founded or ill I know not, that the Americans would not suffer any European nation to reacquire or recover any new territory on their side of the Atlantic. They make the most they can of their French connection. They send their children to Paris to be educated, and many of them go thither themselves. There is money among them, though industry there is none. The Hayti coffee which bears so high a reputation is simply gathered under the bushes which the French planters left behind them, and is half as excellent as it ought to be because it is so carelessly cleaned. Yet so rich is the island in these and other natural productions that they cannot entirely ruin it. They have a revenue from their customs of 5,000,000 dollars to be the prey of political schemers. They have a constitution, of course, with a legislature—two houses of a legislature—universal suffrage, c., but it does not save them from revolutions, which recurred every two or three years till the time of the present president. He being of stronger metal than the rest, takes care that the votes are given as he pleases, shoots down recusants, and knows how to make himself feared. He is a giant, they say—I did not see him—six feet some inches in height and broad in proportion. When in Jamaica he was a friend of Gordon, and the intimacy between them is worth noting, as throwing light on Gordon's political aspirations.

I stayed no longer than the ship's business detained the captain, and I breathed more freely when I had left that miserable cross-birth of ferocity and philanthropic sentiment. No one can foretell the future fate of the black republic, but the present order of things cannot last in an island so close under the American shores. If the Americans forbid any other power to interfere, they will have to interfere themselves. If they find Mormonism an intolerable blot upon their escutcheon, they will have to put a stop in some way or other to cannibalism and devil-worship. Meanwhile, the ninety years of negro self-government have had their use in showing what it really means, and if English statesmen, either to save themselves trouble or to please the prevailing uninstructed sentiment, insist on extending it, they will be found when the accounts are made up to have been no better friends to the unlucky negro than their slave-trading forefathers.

From the head of the bay on which Port au Prince stands there reaches out on the west the long arm or peninsula which is so peculiar a feature in the geography of the island. The arm bone is a continuous ridge of mountains rising to a height of 8,000 feet and stretching for 160 miles. At the back towards the ocean is Jacmel, on the other side is the bight of Leogane, over which and along the land our course lay after leaving President Salomon's city. The day was unusually hot, and we sat under an awning on deck watching the changes in the landscape as ravines opened and closed again, and tall peaks changed their shapes and angles. Clouds came down upon the mountain tops and passed off again, whole galleries of pictures swept by, and nature never made more lovely ones. The peculiarity of tropical mountain scenery is that the high summits are clothed with trees. The outlines are thus softened and rounded, save where the rock is broken into precipices. Along the sea and for several miles inland are the Basses Terres as they used to be called, level alluvial plains, cut and watered at intervals by rivers, once covered with thriving plantations and now a jungle. There are no wild beasts there save an occasional man, few snakes, and those not dangerous. The acres of richest soil which are waiting there till reasonable beings can return and cultivate them, must be hundreds of thousands. In the valleys and on the slopes there are all gradations of climate, abundant water, grass lands that might be black with cattle, or on the loftier ranges white with sheep.

It is strange to think how chequered a history these islands have had, how far they are even yet from any condition which promises permanence. Not one of them has arrived at any stable independence. Spaniards, English and French, Dutch and Danes scrambled for them, fought for them, occupied them more or less with their own people, but it was not to found new nations, but to get gold or get something which could be changed for gold. Only occasionally, and as it were by accident, they became the theatre of any grander game. The war of the Reformation was carried thither, and heroic deeds were done there, but it was by adventurers who were in search of plunder for themselves. France and England fought among the Antilles, and their names are connected with many a gallant action; but they fought for the sovereignty of the seas, not for the rights and liberties of the French or English inhabitants of the islands. Instead of occupying them with free inhabitants, the European nations filled them with slave gangs. They were valued only for the wealth which they yielded, and society there has never assumed any particularly noble aspect. There has been splendour and luxurious living, and there have been crimes and horrors, and revolts and massacres. There has been romance, but it has been the romance of pirates and outlaws. The natural graces of human life do not show themselves under such conditions. There has been no saint in the West Indies since Las Casas, no hero, unless philonegro enthusiasm can make one out of Toussaint. There are no people there in the true sense of the word, with a character and purpose of their own, unless to some extent in Cuba, and therefore when the wind has changed and the wealth for which the islands were alone desired is no longer to be made among them, and slavery is no longer possible and would not pay if it were, there is nothing to fall back upon. The palaces of the English planters and merchants fall to decay; their wines and their furniture, their books and their pictures, are sold or dispersed. Their existence is a struggle to keep afloat, and one by one they go under in the waves.

The blacks as long as they were slaves were docile and partially civilised. They have behaved on the whole well in our islands since their emancipation, for though they were personally free the whites were still their rulers, and they looked up to them with respect. They have acquired land and notions of property, some of them can read, many of them are tolerable workmen and some excellent, but in character the movement is backwards, not forwards. Even in Hayti, after the first outburst of ferocity, a tolerable government was possible for a generation or two. Orderly habits are not immediately lost, but the effect of leaving the negro nature to itself is apparent at last. In the English islands they are innocently happy in the unconsciousness of the obligations of morality. They eat, drink, sleep, and smoke, and do the least in the way of work that they can. They have no ideas of duty, and therefore are not made uneasy by neglecting it. One or other of them occasionally rises in the legal or other profession, but there is no sign, not the slightest, that the generality of the race are improving either in intelligence or moral habits; all the evidence is the other way. No Uncle Tom, no Aunt Chloe need be looked for in a negro's cabin in the West Indies. If such specimens of black humanity are to be found anywhere, it will be where they have continued under the old influences as servants in white men's houses. The generality are mere good-natured animals, who in service had learnt certain accomplishments, and had developed certain qualities of a higher kind. Left to themselves they fall back upon the superstitions and habits of their ancestors. The key to the character of any people is to be found in the local customs which have spontaneously grown or are growing among them. The customs of Dahomey have not yet shown themselves in the English West Indies and never can while the English authority is maintained; but no custom of any kind will be found in a negro hut or village from which his most sanguine friend can derive a hope that he is on the way to mending himself.

Roses do not grow on thorn trees, nor figs on thistles. A healthy human civilisation was not perhaps to be looked for in countries which have been alternately the prey of avarice, ambition, and sentimentalism. We visit foreign countries to see varieties of life and character, to learn languages that we may gain an insight into various literatures, to see manners unlike our own springing naturally out of different soils and climates, to see beautiful works of art, to see places associated with great men and great actions, and subsidiary to these, to see lakes and mountains, and strange skies and seas. But the localities of great events and the homes of the actors in them are only saddening when the spiritual results are disappointing, and scenery loses its charm unless the grace of humanity is in the heart of it. To the man of science the West Indies may be delightful and instructive. Rocks and trees and flowers remain as they always were, and Nature is constant to herself. But the traveller whose heart is with his kind, and who cares only to see his brother mortals making their corner of this planet into an orderly and rational home, had better choose some other object for his pilgrimage.

FOOTNOTES:

[17]

Tortoise Islands; the buccaneers' head quarters.

CHAPTER XXI.

Return to Jamaica—Cherry Garden again—Black servants—Social conditions—Sir Henry Norman—King's House once more—Negro suffrage—The will of the people—The Irish python—Conditions of colonial union—Oratory and statesmanship.

I had to return to Jamaica from Cuba to meet the mail to England. My second stay could be but brief. For the short time that was allowed me I went back to my hospitable friends at Cherry Garden, which is an oasis in the wilderness. In the heads of the family there was cultivation and simplicity and sense. There was a home life with its quiet occupations and enjoyments—serious when seriousness was needed, light and bright in the ordinary routine of existence. The black domestics, far unlike the children of liberty whom I had left at Port au Prince, had caught their tone from their master and mistress, and were low-voiced, humorous, and pleasant to talk with. So perfect were they in their several capacities, that, like the girls at Government House at Dominica, I would have liked to pack them in my portmanteau and carry them home. The black butler received me on my arrival as an old friend. He brought me a pair of boots which I had left behind me on my first visit; he told me 'the female' had found them. The lady of the house took me out for a drive with her. The coachman half-upset us into a ditch, and we narrowly escaped being pitched into a ravine. The dusky creature insisted pathetically that it was not his fault, nor the horse's fault. His ebony wife had left him for a week's visit to a friend, and his wits had gone after her. Of course he was forgiven. Cherry Garden was a genuine homestead, a very menagerie of domestic animals of all sorts and breeds. Horses loitered under the shade of the mangoes; cows, asses, dogs, turkeys, cocks and hens, geese, guinea fowl and pea fowl lounged and strutted about the paddocks. In the grey of the morning they held their concerts; the asses brayed, the dogs barked, the turkeys gobbled, and the pea fowl screamed. It was enough to waken the seven sleepers, but the noises seemed so home-like and natural that they mixed pleasantly in one's dreams. One morning, after they had been holding a special jubilee, the butler apologised for them when he came to call me, and laughed as at the best of jokes when I said they did not mean any harm. The great feature of the day was five cats, with blue eyes and spotlessly white, who walked in regularly at breakfast, ranged themselves on their tails round their mistress's chair, and ate their porridge and milk like reasonable creatures. Within and without all was orderly. The gardens were in perfect condition; fields were being inclosed and planted; the work of the place went on of itself, with the eye of the mistress on it, and her voice, if necessary, heard in command; but black and white were all friends together. What could man ask for, more than to live all his days in such a climate and with such surroundings? Why should a realised ideal like this pass away? Why may it not extend itself till it has transformed the features of all our West Indian possessions? Thousand of English families might be living in similar scenes, happy in themselves and spreading round them a happy, wholesome English atmosphere. Why not indeed? Only because we are enchanted. Because in Jamaica and Barbadoes the white planters had a constitution granted them two hundred years ago, therefore their emancipated slaves must now have a constitution also. Wonderful logic of formulas, powerful as a witches' cauldron for mischief as long as it is believed in. The colonies and the Empire! If the colonies were part indeed of the Empire, if they were taken into partnership as the Americans take theirs, and were members of an organised body, if an injury to each single limb would be felt as an injury to the whole, we should not be playing with their vital interests to catch votes at home. Alas! at home we are split in two, and party is more than the nation, and famous statesmen, thinly disguising their motives under a mask of policy, condemn to-day what they approved of yesterday, and catch at power by projects which they would be the first to denounce if suggested by their adversaries. Till this tyranny be overpast, to bring into one the scattered portions of the Empire is the idlest of dreams, and the most that is to be hoped for is to arrest any active mischief. Happy Americans, who have a Supreme Court with a code of fundamental laws to control the vagaries of politicians and check the passions of fluctuating electoral majorities! What the Supreme Court is to them, the Crown ought to be for us; but the Crown is powerless and must remain powerless, and therefore we are as we are, and our national existence is made the shuttlecock of party contention.

Time passed so pleasantly with me in these concluding days that I could have wished it to be the nothing which metaphysicians say that it is, and that when one was happy it would leave one alone. We wandered in the shade in the mornings, we made expeditions in the evenings, called at friends' houses, and listened to the gossip of the island. It turned usually on the one absorbing subject—black servants and the difficulty of dealing with them. An American lady from Pennsylvania declared emphatically as her opinion that emancipation had been a piece of folly, and that things would never mend till they were slaves again.

One of my own chief hopes in going originally to Jamaica had been to see and learn the views of the distinguished Governor there. Sir Henry Norman had been one of the most eminent of the soldier civilians in India. He had brought with him a brilliant reputation; he had won the confidence in the West Indies of all classes and all colours. He, if anyone, would understand the problem, and from the high vantage ground of experience would know what could or could not be done to restore the influence of England and the prosperity of the colonies. Unfortunately, Sir Henry had been called to London, as I mentioned before, on a question of the conduct of some official, and I was afraid that I should miss him altogether. He returned, however, the day before I was to sail. He was kind enough to ask me to spend an evening with him, and I was again on my last night a guest at King's House.

A dinner party offers small opportunity for serious conversation, nor, indeed, could I expect a great person in Sir Henry's position to enter upon subjects of consequence with a stranger like myself. I could see, however, that I had nothing to correct in the impression of his character which his reputation had led me to form about him, and I wished more than ever that the system of government of which he had been so admirable a servant in India could be applied to his present position, and that he or such as he could have the administration of it. We had common friends in the Indian service to talk about; one especially, Reynell Taylor, now dead, who had been the earliest of my boy companions. Taylor had been one of the handful of English who held the Punjaub in the first revolt of the Sikhs. With a woman's modesty he had the spirit of a knight-errant. Sir Henry described him as the 'very soul of chivalry,' and seemed himself to be a man of the same pure and noble nature, perhaps liable, from the generosity of his temperament, to believe more than I could do in modern notions and in modern political heroes, but certainly not inclining of his own will to recommend any rash innovations. I perceived that like myself he felt no regret that so much of the soil of Jamaica was passing to peasant black proprietors. He thought well of their natural disposition; he believed them capable of improvement. He thought that the possession of land of their own would bring them into voluntary industry, and lead them gradually to the adoption of civilised habits. He spoke with reserve, and perhaps I may not have understood him fully, but he did not seem to me to think much of their political capacity. The local boards which have been established as an education for higher functions have not been a success. They had been described to me in all parts of the island as inflammable centres of peculation and mismanagement. Sir Henry said nothing from which I could gather his own opinion. I inferred, however (he will pardon me if I misrepresent him), that he had no great belief in a federation of the islands, in 'responsible government,' and such like, as within the bounds of present possibilities. Nor did he think that responsible statesmen at home had any such arrangement in view.

That such an arrangement was in contemplation a few years ago, I knew from competent authority. Perhaps the unexpected interest which the English people have lately shown in the colonies has modified opinion in those high circles, and has taught politicians that they must advance more cautiously. But the wind still sits in the old quarter. Three years ago, the self-suppressed constitution in Jamaica was partially re-established. A franchise was conceded both there and in Barbadoes which gave every black householder a vote. Even in poor Dominica, an extended suffrage was hung out as a remedy for its wretchedness. If nothing further is intended, these concessions have been gratuitously mischievous. It has roused the hopes of political agitators, not in Jamaica only, but all over the Antilles. It has taught the people, who have no grievances at all, who in their present state are better protected than any peasantry in the world except the Irish, to look to political changes as a road to an impossible millennium. It has rekindled hopes which had been long extinguished, that, like their brothers in Hayti, they were on the way to have the islands to themselves. It has alienated the English colonists, filled them with the worst apprehensions, and taught them to look wistfully from their own country to a union with America. A few elected members in a council where they may be counterbalanced by an equal number of official members seems a small thing in itself. So long as the equality was maintained, my Yankee friend was still willing to risk his capital in Jamaican enterprises. But the principle has been allowed. The existing arrangement is a half-measure which satisfies none and irritates all, and collisions between the representatives of the people and the nominees of the Government are only avoided by leaving a sufficient number of official seats unfilled. To have re-entered upon a road where you cannot stand still, where retreat is impossible, and where to go forward can only be recommended on the hypothesis that to give a man a vote will itself qualify him for the use of it, has been one of the minor achievements of the last Government of Mr. Gladstone, and is likely to be as successful as his larger exploits nearer home have as yet proved to be. A supreme court, were we happy enough to possess such a thing, would forbid these venturous experiments of sanguine statesmen who may happen, for a moment, to command a trifling majority in the House of Commons.

I could not say what I felt completely to Sir Henry, who, perhaps, had been in personal relations with Mr. Gladstone's Government. Perhaps, too, he was one of those numerous persons of tried ability and intelligence who have only a faint belief that the connection between Great Britain and the colonies can be of long continuance. The public may amuse themselves with the vision of an imperial union; practical statesmen who are aware of the tendencies of self-governed communities to follow lines of their own in which the mother country cannot support them may believe that they know it to be impossible.

As to the West Indies there are but two genuine alternatives: one to leave them to themselves to shape their own destinies, as we leave Australia; the other to govern them as if they were a part of Great Britain with the same scrupulous care of the people and their interests with which we govern Bengal, Madras, and Bombay. England is responsible for the social condition of those islands. She filled them with negroes when it was her interest to maintain slavery, she emancipated those negroes when popular opinion at home demanded that slavery should end. It appears to me that England ought to bear the consequences of her own actions, and assume to herself the responsibilities of a state of things which she has herself created. We are partly unwilling to take the trouble, partly we cling to the popular belief that to trust all countries with the care of their own concerns is the way to raise the character of the inhabitants and to make them happy and contented. We dimly perceive that the population of the West Indies is not a natural growth of internal tendencies and circumstances, and we therefore hesitate before we plunge completely and entirely into the downward course; but we play with it, we drift towards it, we advance as far as we dare, giving them the evils of both systems and the advantages of neither. At the same moment we extend the suffrage to the blacks with one hand, while with the other we refuse to our own people the benefit of a treaty which would have rescued them from imminent ruin and brought them into relations with their powerful kindred close at hand—relations which might save them from the most dangerous consequences of a negro political supremacy—and the result is that the English in those islands are melting away and will soon be crowded out, or will have departed of themselves in disgust. A policy so far-reaching, and affecting so seriously the condition of the oldest of our colonial possessions, ought not to have been adopted on their own authority, by doctrinaire statesmen in a cabinet, without fully and frankly consulting the English nation; and no further step ought to be taken in that direction until the nation has had the circumstances of the islands laid before it, and has pronounced one way or the other its own sovereign pleasure. Does or does not England desire that her own people shall be enabled to live and thrive in the West Indies? If she decides that her hands are too full, that she is over-empired and cannot attend to them—caditquæstio—there is no more to be said. But if this is her resolution the hands of the West Indians ought to be untied. They ought to be allowed to make their sugar treaties, to make any treaties, to enter into the closest relations with America which the Americans will accept, as the only chance which will be left them.

Such abandonment, however, will bring us no honour. It will not further that federation of the British Empire which so many of us now profess to desire. If we wish Australia and Canada to draw into closer union with us, it will not be by showing that we are unable to manage a group of colonies which are almost at our doors. Englishmen all round the globe have rejoiced together in this year which is passing by us over the greatness of their inheritance, and have celebrated with enthusiasm the half-century during which our lady-mistress has reigned over the English world. Unity and federation are on our lips, and we have our leagues and our institutes, and in the eagerness of our wishes we dream that we see the fulfilment of them. Neither the kingdom of heaven nor any other kingdom 'comes with observation.' It comes not with after-dinner speeches however eloquent, or with flowing sentiments however for the moment sincere. The spirit which made the Empire can alone hold it together. The American Union was not saved by oratory. It was saved by the determination of the bravest of the people; it was cemented by the blood which dyed the slopes of Gettysburg. The union of the British Empire, if it is to be more than a dream, can continue only while the attracting force of the primary commands the willing attendance of the distant satellites. Let the magnet lose its power, let the confidence of the colonies in the strength and resolution of their central orb be once shaken, and the centrifugal force will sweep them away into orbits of their own.

The race of men who now inhabit this island of ours show no signs of degeneracy. The bow of Ulysses is sound as ever; moths and worms have not injured either cord or horn; but it is unstrung, and the arrows which are shot from it drop feebly to the ground. The Irish python rises again out of its swamp, and Phœbus Apollo launches no shaft against the scaly sides of it. Phœbus Apollo attempts the milder methods of concession and persuasion. 'Python,' he says, 'in days when I was ignorant and unjust I struck you down and bound you. I left officers and men with you of my own race to watch you, to teach you, to rule you; to force you, if your own nature could not be changed, to leave your venomous ways. You have refused to be taught, you twist in your chains, you bite and tear, and when you can you steal and murder. I see that I was wrong from the first. Every creature has a right to live according to its own disposition. I was a tyrant, and you did well to resist; I ask you to forgive and forget. I set you free; I hand you over my own representatives as a pledge of my goodwill, that you may devour them at your leisure. They have been the instruments of my oppression; consume them, destroy them, do what you will with them; and henceforward I hope that we shall live together as friends, and that you will show yourself worthy of my generosity and of the freedom which you have so gloriously won.'

A sun-god who thus addressed a disobedient satellite might have the eloquence of a Demosthenes and the finest of the fine intentions which pave the road to the wrong place, but he would not be a divinity who would command the willing confidence of a high-spirited kindred. Great Britain will make the tie which holds the colonies to her a real one when she shows them and shows the world that she is still equal to her great place, that her arm is not shortened and her heart has not grown faint.

Men speak of the sacredness of liberty. They talk as if the will of everyone ought to be his only guide, that allegiance is due only to majorities, that allegiance of any other kind is base and a relic of servitude. The Americans are the freest people in the world; but in their freedom they have to obey the fundamental laws of the Union. Again and again in the West Indies Mr. Motley's words came back to me. To be taken into the American Union is to be adopted into a partnership. To belong as a Crown colony to the British Empire, as things stand, is no partnership at all. It is to belong to a power which sacrifices, as it has always sacrificed, the interest of its dependencies to its own. The blood runs freely through every vein and artery of the American body corporate. Every single citizen feels his share in the life of his nation. Great Britain leaves her Crown colonies to take care of themselves, refuses what they ask, and forces on them what they had rather be without. If I were a West Indian I should feel that under the stars and stripes I should be safer than I was at present from political experimenting. I should have a market in which to sell my produce where I should be treated as a friend; I should have a power behind me and protecting me, and I should have a future to which I could look forward with confidence. America would restore me to home and life; Great Britain allows me to sink, contenting herself with advising me to be patient. Why should I continue loyal when my loyalty was so contemptuously valued?

But I will not believe that it will come to this. An Englishman may be heavily tempted, but in evil fortune as in good his heart is in the old place. The administration of our affairs is taken for the present from prudent statesmen, and is made over to those who know how best to flatter the people with fine-sounding sentiments and idle adulation. All sovereigns have been undone by flatterers. The people are sovereign now, and, being new to power, listen to those who feed their vanity. The popular orator has been the ruin of every country which has trusted to him. He never speaks an unwelcome truth, for his existence depends on pleasing, and he cares only to tickle the ears of his audience. His element is anarchy; his function is to undo what better men have done. In wind he lives and moves and has his being. When the gods are angry, he can raise it to a hurricane and lay waste whole nations in ruin and revolution. It was said long ago, a man full of words shall not prosper upon the earth. Times have changed, for in these days no one prospers so well. Can he make a speech? is the first question which the constituencies ask when a candidate is offered to their suffrages. When the Roman commonwealth developed from an aristocratic republic into a democracy, and, as now with us, the sovereignty was in the mass of the people, the oratorical faculty came to the front in the same way. The finest speaker was esteemed the fittest man to be made a consul or a prætor of, and there were schools of rhetoric where aspirants for office had to go to learn gesture and intonation before they could present themselves at the hustings. The sovereign people and their orators could do much, but they could not alter facts, or make that which was not, to be, or that which was, not to be. The orators could perorate and the people could decree, but facts remained and facts proved the strongest, and the end of that was that after a short supremacy the empire which they had brought to the edge of ruin was saved at the last extremity; the sovereign people lost their liberties, and the tongues of political orators were silenced for centuries. Illusion at last takes the form of broken heads, and the most obstinate credulity is not proof against that form of argument.

CHAPTER XXII.

Going home—Retrospect—Alternative courses—Future of the Empire—Sovereignty of the sea—The Greeks—The rights of man—Plato—The voice of the people—Imperial federation—Hereditary colonial policy—New Irelands—Effects of party government.

Once more upon the sea on our homeward way, carrying, as Emerson said, 'the bag of Æolus in the boiler of our boat,' careless whether there be wind or calm. Our old naval heroes passed and repassed upon the same waters under harder conditions. They had to struggle against tempests, to fight with enemy's cruisers, to battle for their lives with nature as with man—and they were victorious over them all. They won for Britannia the sceptre of the sea, and built up the Empire on which the sun never sets. To us, their successors, they handed down the splendid inheritance, and we in turn have invented steam ships and telegraphs, and thrown bridges over the ocean, and made our far-off possessions as easy of access as the next parish. The attractive force of the primary ought to have increased in the same ratio, but we do not find that it has, and the centrifugal and the centripetal tendencies of our satellites are year by year becoming more nicely balanced. These beautiful West Indian Islands were intended to be homes for the overflowing numbers of our own race, and the few that have gone there are being crowded out by the blacks from Jamaica and the Antilles. Our poor helots at home drag on their lives in the lanes and alleys of our choking cities, and of those who gather heart to break off on their own account and seek elsewhere for a land of promise, the large majority are weary of the flag under which they have only known suffering, and prefer America to the English colonies.

They are waking now to understand the opportunities which are slipping through their hands. Has the awakening come too late? We have ourselves mixed the cup; must we now drink it the dregs?

It is too late to enable us to make homes in the West Indies for the swarms who are thrown off by our own towns and villages. We might have done it. Englishmen would have thriven as well in Jamaica and the Antilles as the Spaniards have thriven in Cuba. But the islands are now peopled by men of another colour. The whites there are as units among hundreds, and the proportion cannot be altered. But it is not too late to redeem our own responsibilities. We brought the blacks there; we have as yet not done much for their improvement, when their notions of morality are still so elementary that more than half of their children are born out of marriage. The English planters were encouraged to settle there when it suited our convenience to maintain the islands for Imperial purposes; like the landlords in Ireland, they were our English garrison; and as with the landlords in Ireland, when we imagine that they have served their purpose and can be no longer of use to us, we calmly change the conditions of society. We disclaim obligations to help them in the confusion which we have introduced; we tell them to help themselves, and they cannot help themselves in such an element as that in which they are now struggling, unless they know that they may count on the sympathy and the support of their countrymen at home. Nothing is demanded of the English exchequer; the resources of the islands are practically boundless; there is a robust population conscious at the bottom of their native inferiority, and docile and willing to work if anyone will direct them and set them to it. There will be capital enough forthcoming, and energetic men enough and intelligence enough, if we on our part will provide one thing, the easiest of all if we really set our minds to it—an effective and authoritative government. It is not safe even for ourselves to leave a wound unattended to, though it be in the least significant part of our bodies. The West Indies are a small limb in the great body corporate of the British Empire, but there is no great and no small in the life of nations. The avoidable decay of the smallest member is an injury to the whole. Let it be once known and felt that England regards the West Indies as essentially one with herself, and the English in the islands will resume their natural position, and respect and order will come back, and those once thriving colonies will again advance with the rest on the high road of civilisation and prosperity. Let it be known that England considers only her immediate interests and will not exert herself, and the other colonies will know what they have to count upon, and the British Empire will dwindle down before long into a single insignificant island in the North Sea.

So end the reflections which I formed there from what I saw and what I heard. I have written as an outside observer unconnected with practical politics, with no motive except a loyal pride in the greatness of my own country, and a conviction, which I will not believe to be a dream, that the destinies have still in store for her a yet grander future. The units of us come and go; the British Empire, the globe itself and all that it inherits, will pass away as a vision.

ἔσσεται ἦμαρ ὅταν ποτ' ὀλώλη Ἴλιος ἱρὴ
καὶ Πρίαμος καὶ λαὸς ἐυμμελίω Πριάμοιο

.

The day will be when Ilium's towers may fall,
And large-limbed[18] Priam, and his people all.

But that day cannot be yet. Out of the now half-organic fragments may yet be formed one living Imperial power, with a new era of beneficence and usefulness to mankind. The English people are spread far and wide. The sea is their dominion, and their land is the finest portion of the globe. It is theirs now, it will be theirs for ages to come if they remain themselves unchanged and keep the heart and temper of their forefathers.

Naught shall make us rue,
If England to herself do rest but true.

The days pass, and our ship flies fast upon her way.

γλαυκὸν ὑπὲρ οἶδμα κυανόχροά τε κυμάτων
ῥόθια πολιὰ θαλάσσας

.

How perfect the description! How exactly in those eight words Euripides draws the picture of the ocean; the long grey heaving swell, the darker steel-grey on the shadowed slope of the surface waves, and the foam on their breaking crests. Our thoughts flow back as we gaze to the times long ago, when the earth belonged to other races as it now belongs to us. The ocean is the same as it was. Their eyes saw it as we see it:

Time writes no wrinkle on that azure brow.

Nor is the ocean alone the same. Human nature is still vexed with the same problems, mocked with the same hopes, wandering after the same illusions. The sea affected the Greeks as it affects us, and was equally dear to them. It was a Greek who said, 'The sea washes off all the ills of men;' the 'stainless one' as Æschylus called it—the eternally pure. On long voyages I take Greeks as my best companions. I had Plato with me on my way home from the West Indies. He lived and wrote in an age like ours, when religion had become a debatable subject on which every one had his opinion, and democracy was master of the civilised world, and the Mediterranean states were running wild after liberty, preparatory to the bursting of the bubble. Looking out on such a world Plato left thoughts behind him the very language of which is as full of application to our own larger world as if it was written yesterday. It throws light on small things as well as large, and interprets alike the condition of the islands which I had left, the condition of England, the condition of all civilised countries in this modern epoch.

The chief characteristic of this age, as it was the chief characteristic of Plato's, is the struggle for what we call the 'rights of man.' In other times the thing insisted on was that men should do what was 'right' as something due to a higher authority. Now the demand is for what is called their 'rights' as something due to themselves, and among these rights is a right to liberty; liberty meaning the utmost possible freedom of every man consistent with the freedom of others, and the abolition of every kind of authority of one man over another. It is with this view that we have introduced popular suffrage, that we give everyone a vote, or aim at giving it, as the highest political perfection.

We turn to Plato and we find: 'In a healthy community there ought to be some authority over every single man and woman. No person—not one—ought to act on his or her judgment alone even in the smallest trifle. The soldier on a campaign obeys his commander in little things as well as great. The safety of the army requires it. But it is in peace as it is in war, and there is no difference. Every person should be trained from childhood to rule and to be ruled. So only can the life of man, and the life of all creatures dependent on him, be delivered from anarchy.'

It is worth while to observe how diametrically opposite to our notions on this subject were the notions of a man of the finest intellect, with the fullest opportunities of observation, and every one of whose estimates of things was confirmed by the event. Such a discipline as he recommends never existed in any community of men except perhaps among the religious orders in the enthusiasm of their first institution, nor would a society be long tolerable in which it was tried. Communities, however, have existed where people have thought more of their obligations than of their 'rights,' more of the welfare of their country, or of the success of a cause to which they have devoted themselves, than of their personal pleasure or interest—have preferred the wise leading of superior men to their own wills and wishes. Nay, perhaps no community has ever continued long, or has made a mark in the world of serious significance, where society has not been graduated in degrees, and there have not been deeper and stronger bands of coherence than the fluctuating votes of majorities.

Times are changed we are told. We live in a new era, when public opinion is king, and no other rule is possible; public opinion, as expressed in the press and on the platform, and by the deliberately chosen representatives of the people. Every question can be discussed and argued, all sides of it can be heard, and the nation makes up its mind. The collective judgment of all is wiser than the wisest single man—securus judicat orbis.

Give the public time, and I believe this to be true; general opinion does in the long run form a right estimate of most persons and of most things. As surely its immediate impulses are almost invariably in directions which it afterwards regrets and repudiates, and therefore constitutions which have no surer basis than the popular judgment, as it shifts from year to year or parliament to parliament, are built on foundations looser than sand.

In concluding this book I have a few more words to say on the subject, so ardently canvassed, of Imperial federation. It seems so easy. You have only to form a new parliament in which the colonies shall be represented according to numbers, while each colony will retain its own for its own local purposes. Local administration is demanded everywhere; England, Scotland, Wales, Ireland, can each have theirs, and the vexed question of Home Rule can be disposed of in the reconstruction of the whole. A central parliament can then be formed in which the parts can all be represented in proportion to their number; and a cabinet can be selected out of this for the management of Imperial concerns. Nothing more is necessary; the thing will be done.

So in a hundred forms, but all on the same principle, schemes of Imperial union have fallen under my eye. I should myself judge from experience of what democratically elected parliaments are growing into, that at the first session of such a body the satellites would fly off into space, shattered perhaps themselves in the process. We have parliaments enough already, and if no better device can be found than by adding another to the number, the rash spirit of innovation has not yet gone far enough to fling our ancient constitution into the crucible on so wild a chance.

Imperial federation, as it is called, is far away, if ever it is to be realised at all. If it is to come it will come of itself, brought about by circumstances and silent impulses working continuously through many years unseen and unspoken of. It is conceivable that Great Britain and her scattered offspring, under the pressure of danger from without, or impelled by some general purpose, might agree to place themselves for a time under a single administrative head. It is conceivable that out of a combination so formed, if it led to a successful immediate result, some union of a closer kind might eventually emerge. It is not only conceivable, but it is entirely certain, that attempts made when no such occasion has arisen, by politicians ambitious of distinguishing themselves, will fail, and in failing will make the object that is aimed at more confessedly unattainable than it is now.

The present relation between the mother country and her self-governed colonies is partly that of parent and children who have grown to maturity and are taking care of themselves, partly of independent nations in friendly alliance, partly as common subjects of the same sovereign, whose authority is exercised in each by ministers of its own. Neither of these analogies is exact, for the position alters from year to year. So much the better. The relation which now exists cannot be more than provisional; let us not try to shape it artificially, after a closet-made pattern. The threads of interest and kindred must be left to spin themselves in their own way. Meanwhile we can work together heartily and with good will where we need each other's co-operation. Difficulties will rise, perhaps, from time to time, but we can meet them as they come, and we need not anticipate them. If we are to be politically one, the organic fibres which connect us are as yet too immature to bear a strain. All that we can do, and all that at present we ought to try, is to act generously whenever our assistance can be of use. The disposition of English statesmen to draw closer to the colonies is of recent growth. They cannot tell, and we cannot tell, how far it indicates a real change of attitude or is merely a passing mood. One thing, however, we ought to bear in mind, that the colonies sympathise one with another, and that wrong or neglect in any part of the Empire does not escape notice. The larger colonies desire to know what the recent professions of interest are worth, and they look keenly at our treatment of their younger brothers who are still in our power. They are practical, they attend to results, they guard jealously their own privileges, but they are not so enamoured of constitutional theory that they will patiently see their fellow-countrymen in less favoured situations swamped under the votes of the coloured races. Australians, Canadians, New Zealanders, will not be found enthusiastic for the extension of self-government in the West Indies, when they know that it means the extinction of their own white brothers who have settled there. The placing English colonists at the mercy of coloured majorities they will resent as an injury to themselves; they will not look upon it as an extension of a generous principle, but as an act of airy virtue which costs us nothing, and at the bottom is but carelessness and indifference.

We imagine that we have seen the errors of our old colonial policy, and that we are in no danger of repeating them. Yet in the West Indies we are treading over again the too familiar road. The Anglo-Irish colonists in 1705 petitioned for a union with Great Britain. A union would have involved a share in British trade; it was refused therefore, and we gave them the penal laws instead. They set up manufactures, built ships, and tried to raise a commerce of their own. We laid them under disabilities which ruined their enterprises, and when they were resentful and became troublesome we turned round to the native Irish and made a virtue of protecting them against our own people whom we had injured. When the penal laws ceased to be useful to us, we did not allow them to be executed. We played off Catholic against Protestant while we were sacrificing both to our own jealousy. Having made the government of the island impossible for those whom we had planted there to govern it, we emancipate the governed, and to conciliate them we allow them to appropriate the possessions of their late masters. And we have not conciliated the native Irish; it was impossible that we should; we have simply armed them with the only weapons which enable them to revenge their wrongs upon us.

The history of the West Indies is a precise parallel. The islands were necessary to our safety in our struggle with France and Spain. The colonists held them chiefly for us as a garrison, and we in turn gave the colonists their slaves. The white settlers ruled as in Ireland, the slaves obeyed, and all went swimmingly. Times changed at home. Slavery became unpopular; it was abolished; and, with a generosity for which we never ceased to applaud ourselves, we voted an indemnity of twenty millions to the owners. We imagined that we had acquitted our consciences, but such debts are not discharged by payments of money. We had introduced the slaves into the islands for our own advantage; in setting them free we revolutionised society. We remained still responsible for the social consequences, and we did not choose to remember it. The planters were guilty only, like the Irish landlords, of having ceased to be necessary to us. We practised our virtues vicariously at their expense: we had the praise and honour, they had the suffering. They begged that the emancipation might be gradual; our impatience to clear our reputation refused to wait. Their system of cultivation being deranged, they petitioned for protection against the competition of countries where slavery continued. The request was natural, but could not be listened to because to grant it might raise infinitesimally the cost of the British workman's breakfast. They struggled on, and even when a new rival rose in the beetroot sugar they refused to be beaten. The European powers, to save their beetroot, went on to support it with a bounty. Against the purse of foreign governments the sturdiest individuals cannot compete. Defeated in a fight which had become unfair, the planters looked, and looked in vain, to their own government for help. Finding none, they turned to their kindred in the United States; and there, at last, they found a hand held out to them. The Americans were willing, though at a loss of two millions and a half of revenue, to admit the poor West Indians to their own market. But a commercial treaty was necessary; and a treaty could not be made without the sanction of the English Government. The English Government, on some fine-drawn crotchet, refused to colonies which were weak and helpless what they would have granted without a word if demanded by Victoria or New South Wales, whose resentment they feared.

And when the West Indians, harassed, desperate, and half ruined, cried out against the enormous injustice, in the fear that their indignation might affect their allegiance and lead them to seek admission into the American Union, we extend the franchise among the blacks, on whose hostility to such a measure we know that we can rely.

There is no occasion to suspect responsible English politicians of any sinister purpose in what they have done or not done, or suspect them, indeed, of any purpose at all. They act from day to day under the pressure of each exigency as it rises, and they choose the course which is least directly inconvenient. But the result is to have created in the Antilles and Jamaica so many fresh Irelands, and I believe that British colonists the world over will feel together in these questions. They will not approve; rather they will combine to condemn the betrayal of their own fellow-countrymen. If England desires her colonies to rally round her, she must deserve their affection and deserve their respect. She will find neither one nor the other if she carelessly sacrifices her own people in any part of the world to fear or convenience. The magnetism which will bind them to her must be found in herself or nowhere.

Perhaps nowhere! Perhaps if we look to the real origin of all that has gone wrong with us, of the policy which has flung Ireland back into anarchy, which has weakened our influence abroad, which has ruined the oldest of our colonies, and has made the continuance under our flag of the great communities of our countrymen who are forming new nations in the Pacific a question of doubt and uncertainty, we shall find it in our own distractions, in the form of government which is fast developing into a civil war under the semblance of peace, where party is more than country, and a victory at the hustings over a candidate of opposite principles more glorious than a victory in the field over a foreign foe. Society in republican Rome was so much interested in the faction fights of Clodius and Milo that it could hear with apathy of the destruction of Crassus and a Roman army. The senate would have sold Cæsar to the Celtic chiefs in Gaul, and the modern English enthusiast would disintegrate the British Islands to purchase the Irish vote. Till we can rise into some nobler sphere of thought and conduct we may lay aside the vision of a confederated empire.

Oh, England, model to thy inward greatness,
Like little body with a mighty heart,
What might'st thou do that honour would thee do
Were all thy children kind and natural!

FOOTNOTES:

[18]

I believe this to be the true meaning of ἐυμμελίης. It is usually rendered, 'armed with a stout spear.'

Kelly Co.

, Printers, Gate Street, Lincoln's Inn Fields, W.C.; and Kingston-on-Thames.

Lightning Source UK Ltd.
Milton Keynes UK
UKOW052324281211

184477UK00002B/144/P